TAXES ON CAPITAL INCOME IN CANADA: ANALYSIS AND POLICY

Robin W. Boadway
Neil Bruce
Jack M. Mintz

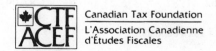

Canadian Tax Foundation
L'Association Canadienne
d'Études Fiscales

Canadian Cataloguing in Publication Data

Boadway, Robin W., 1943-
  Taxes on capital income in Canada

(Canadian tax papers; 80)
Includes index.
ISBN 0-88808-028-X

1. Capital levy – Canada. 2. Income tax – Canada.
I. Bruce, Neil, 1943- . II. Mintz, Jack M.
III. Canadian Tax Foundation. IV. Title
V. Series.

HJ4662.A3B62 1987   336.24 '0971   C87-093913-0

Foreword

The treatment of income from capital under the personal and corporate income taxes is a source of distortion in the pattern of investment in Canada. There are wide variations in effective tax rates on capital income, depending on the type of investment (machinery, buildings, or inventories), the method of finance (debt, equity, or retained earnings), and the industry in which the investment is made.

In this book, the authors provide a comprehensive examination of the taxation of capital income at both the corporate and the personal levels. They identify the various ways in which income taxes distort investment decisions, measure such distortions by means of effective tax rates, and quantify the effect of the corporate and personal income tax systems on the structure of investment, financing, and domestic savings available to businesses in Canada.

The authors also present their own program for an equitable, efficient, and less complex tax structure. In their view, a full-fledged, consumption-based personal income tax would be preferable to the present, imperfect income tax. They would also reform the corporate tax structure in the light of the two main rationales for such a tax in Canada: first, as a withholding tax, primarily on income paid to non-residents; and second, as a tax on economic rents, particularly for the resource industries.

Robin Boadway, Neil Bruce, and Jack Mintz are professors of economics at Queen's University in Kingston, Ontario. Professor Boadway is the author of *Intergovernmental Transfers in Canada* and co-author of *Canadian Tax Policy* (Second Edition), both published by the Canadian Tax Foundation.

Ingrid Cook and Frances Emery edited the manuscript and Jane Clarke and Alysa Neal verified the references and quotations. Diane Gula provided valuable assistance in checking final page proofs. Paula Pike prepared the index.

As with other foundation publications, the views expressed in this volume are those of the authors and should not be attributed to the foundation or its members.

D. J. Sherbaniuk
Director
November 1987

Contents

Tables and Illustrations

Preface

This monograph is a culmination of work that we began in 1980 when we wrote our first piece on the financing of large and small businesses in Canada for the Economic Council of Canada. Since then, we continued our research on the topic of capital income taxation. Much of our work was analytical, concentrating on the measurement of tax rates imposed on capital. Other work dealt with tax policy issues especially with regard to consumption taxation at the personal level and cash flow taxation at the business level. This particular monograph brings together the ideas that we have developed over the past several years. We focus on the derivation of the "effective" tax rate, which is now a common measure used by economists to assess the impact of taxation on savings, financing, and investment. Using the analysis that we have developed on "effective tax rates," we also discuss our ideas for reform of the personal and corporate income tax in Canada.

Over the years, we benefited from discussions we had with various individuals who commented on our work. We are especially grateful to faculty members and students at Queen's University; participants at public economics workshops at the University of Western Ontario, University of Toronto, University of British Columbia, Harvard University, Université Catholique de Louvain, and Tel Aviv University; and economists at the Department of Finance, Canada, the Taxation Group at the Economic Council of Canada, and the Bank of Canada. We also wish to thank John Greene who provided useful information with regard to Canadian tax law.

There are also several whom we wish to thank for their help in the preparation of this monograph. Dorothy MacKenzie and Sharon Sullivan assisted us in preparing the manuscript. John Groulx provided research assistance in preparation of the calculations presented in Chapter 3. Ingrid Cook, Frances Emery, Diane Gula, Jane Clarke, and Alysa Neal provided editorial assistance through the Canadian Tax Foundation. We are especially grateful to the Canadian Tax Foundation and its Director, Douglas J. Sherbaniuk, for supporting the preparation of this monograph.

The time taken in writing this monograph also required support from our families. We wish to thank Bernie Boadway, Janice Bruce, and Eleanor Mintz who had to put up with the evenings and summer time devoted to preparing this manuscript.

Robin W. Boadway
Neil Bruce
Jack M. Mintz
November 1987

1

Capital Income Taxation in Canada: Institutional Structure and an Outline of the Issues

Introduction

Capital income is taxed in a variety of ways in Canada. It is taxed at the personal level under the personal income tax by both the federal and provincial governments. It is taxed at the corporate level under the corporation income tax by both governments. Income earned in the resource industries is subject to special levies such as royalties, mining taxes, and stumpage fees at the provincial level, and a variety of taxes on oil and gas at the federal level. Although these various forms of income taxation constitute multiple taxation of the same income, some attempt is made in the tax system to integrate one tax with another by means of credits or deductions. There are also myriad other taxes that indirectly tax capital income, such as property taxes and other capital levies.

This study is restricted to the two main forms of direct taxation of capital income applying to all industries: the personal income tax (PIT) and the corporate income tax (CIT). Our aim is really twofold. The first aim is to identify the various ways in which this composite of taxes distorts decision-making on capital markets and to measure such distortions by means of marginal effective tax rates, hereafter referred to simply as *effective tax rates*. An effective tax rate is a measure of the distortion imposed by the tax system on marginal investments, whose returns are just enough to cover costs and no more. It is the difference between the gross (before-tax) rate of return on the marginal investment project of a given type and the net (after-tax) rate of return on the savings used to finance that investment. Sometimes it is measured as a proportion of a rate of return rather than as a level. By measuring effective tax rates for various types of investment goods (buildings, machinery, inventories, and so on) for various types of industries, one can discern how the tax system provides incentives to misallocate capital among uses as well as to discourage aggregate investment. The following section outlines in slightly more detail the nature of an effective tax rate and the general methodology for measuring it. The detailed theory underlying these measures is presented in more detail in Chapter 2 and the effective tax rate calculations themselves are given in Chapter 3.

The second aim of the study is to review and evaluate the various options for capital income tax reform in the light of the measured distortions. Tax reform is invariably an incremental procedure that depends not only on the

1

ideal toward which one wishes the tax system to move but also on where the system is now. One of the purposes of this introductory chapter is to discuss both of these. Following the next section on effective tax rates is a summary of the important institutional features of the personal and corporate tax systems, stressing those issues most important for discussing tax reform and for analyzing effective tax rates. The final section considers the question of the ideal tax treatment of capital income under the two kinds of taxes. It will summarize what we have learned from the substantial recent literature on capital income tax reform both in Canada and abroad.[1] These issues of tax reform are examined in more detail in chapters 4 and 5.

The Concept of an Effective Tax Rate

As mentioned, the effective tax rate on an investment activity is the difference between the before-tax rate of return on a marginal investment and the after-tax rate of return on the savings used to finance the investment. The basic idea is illustrated in Figure 1.1. The diagram depicts the market for investment of a given sort. It shows an investment demand schedule relating levels of investment I to the before-tax rate of return on investment r_g. The return r_g can be thought of as the return to the economy from the marginal investment, since it includes both the return to the owners plus the tax revenues. The savings supply schedule depicts the levels of savings S that would be forthcoming at various after-tax rates of return r_n. The rate of return r_n is the opportunity cost to savers of an additional unit of saving. Both r_g and r_n should be measured in real terms.

Because of the taxes that apply on capital income, the before-tax rate of return on the marginal project will differ from the after-tax return on savings. Figure 1.1 depicts an equilibrium on the capital market where the tax payable on the marginal investment project is given by the vertical distance t. At this equilibrium, the rates of return at the margin are r_g^e and r_n^e and the levels of investment and savings are I^e and S^e. In this particular case, the effective tax rate t is positive, so $r_g^e > r_n^e$, and investment is less than it would be in the absence of the tax distortion. As we shall see in subsequent chapters, there are cases in which the effective tax rate on the marginal investment is negative; that is, where the tax system subsidizes investment. This occurs where the tax system is so generous in the tax credits and/or exemptions and deductions that it allows, that the present value of all deductions for capital costs (including the deduction to which any tax credit would be equivalent) is more than the cost of acquiring the asset.

---

[1] This literature includes Institute for Fiscal Studies, *The Structure and Reform of Direct Taxation: Report of a Committee Chaired by Professor James E. Meade* (London: Allen & Unwin, 1978); United States, Department of the Treasury, *Blueprints for Basic Tax Reform* (Washington, D.C.: U.S. Government Printing Office, 1977); Martin Feldstein, *Capital Taxation* (Cambridge, Mass.: Harvard University Press, 1983); and Wayne R. Thirsk and John Whalley, eds., *Tax Policy Options in the 1980s*, Canadian Tax Paper no. 66 (Toronto: Canadian Tax Foundation, 1982).

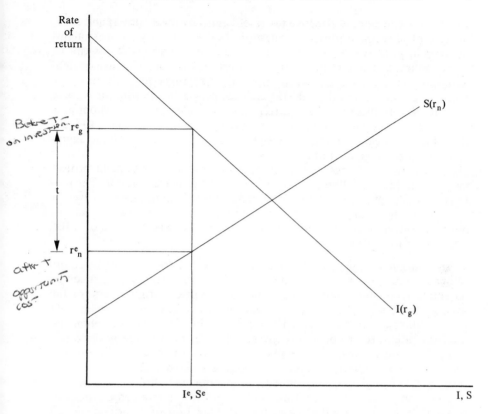

Figure 1.1   Capital Market Equilibrium with Taxes

It is important to note that the effective tax rate t refers only to the tax payable by the marginal investment project whose revenues just cover costs. If the investment demand schedule slopes downward, inframarginal projects can earn a return in excess of r_g. If so, the tax rate applicable on inframarginal projects will not necessarily be t: it will probably be more. The same applies if the savings supply curve slopes upward. This implies that if r_g is measured as an *average* of rates of return on investment (which can be done quite readily from published data on profitability), r_g^e, and hence t, are not measured properly. Instead, the average tax rate is measured.[2] For the purposes of determining the direction and magnitude of the distortion that is imposed by the tax system on capital markets, it is the marginal distortion that is relevant.

---

[2]This is what is done, for example, in Martin Feldstein, James Poterba, and Louis Dicks-Mireaux, "The Effective Tax Rate and the Pretax Rate of Return," in Feldstein, *Capital Taxation*, supra, at Chapter 2. It is also the tax concept implicit in Glenn P. Jenkins, "The Impact of Inflation on Corporate Taxes and the Cash Flows of Business" (July-August 1985), 33 *Canadian Tax Journal* 759-85.

The measurement of effective tax rates begins by measuring r_g^c and r_n^c for the type of investment project in question. In the case of r_n^c, this is straightforward in principle. Rates of return to savings in various forms can be measured on the basis of observed market prices. The rate of return on debt is simply the interest rate, which must then be converted to an after-tax return to the holders of the debt through the use of the appropriate income tax rate. Where there are many different debt-holders, each of whom may face different marginal income tax rates, and when it is impossible to identify which of them financed the marginal investment project, some aggregate rate of personal taxation must be used. A further complicating factor is that some of the savings used to finance the marginal investment project may be held in tax-sheltered form—for example, as pension funds. The preferential tax treatment of these forms of savings should be given due weight when obtaining an aggregate tax rate. Finally, the after-tax return to savings must be converted to real terms by subtracting the expected rate of inflation, which must be estimated in some way.

The marginal project may have been financed in part or wholly by equity rather than debt finance. The market rate of return to equity owners can be measured from stock market data, such as the price-earnings ratio or the average dividend yield plus capital gain earned on shares. As with debt finance, this rate must be reduced by a personal income tax rate to obtain an after-tax rate of return on equity finance. The tax rates will typically differ from those on interest income since the tax treatment of dividends and capital gains is different than for interest. As discussed in Chapter 2, the appropriate personal tax rate on equity income will differ according to whether the source of equity finance for a project is retained earnings or new equity issues. In either case, the after-tax rate of return on equity finance must be reduced by the expected inflation rate as before. The after-tax real rate of return on savings r_n will then be an appropriately weighted average of the after-tax real returns on debt and the two forms of equity finance.

The before-tax marginal rate of return on investment r_g is more difficult to measure because it is virtually impossible to identify the marginal project, and various projects can have different rates of return. We must infer the rate of return on the marginal investment project by other means. Theory tells us that the before-tax rate of return on the marginal project must be enough just to cover all costs of the project, including both capital and tax costs. The rate of return r_g is inferred from measurement of these costs. Our method involves using the neoclassical theory of investment to determine the nature of these costs. Although this theory may not provide a perfect description of reality, it is widely accepted among economists, it is consistent with rational profit-maximizing behaviour by firms, and its analytical implications have been worked out much more fully than other theories. According to neoclassical theory, investment will be carried to the point at which the marginal benefit of a dollar's worth of capital per period equals the cost of holding the dollar of capital for a period. This cost, referred to as the *user cost of capital*, consists of the cost of financing the dollar of capital (the interest and/or equity cost as the case may be) plus the loss in value of the capital due to economic depreciation, which is the physical wear and tear of capital net of the capital gain in the case of a change in the price of capital goods. All these items can be measured directly from market data or estimated. Incorporating taxes into the user cost (in the manner discussed in Chapter 2) yields the before-tax marginal product of the dollar's worth of investment. Subtracting the rate of loss in the value of capital due to economic depreciation from the user cost yields the before-tax rate of return on the marginal investment r_g.[3]

The above description applies to depreciable capital. Similar expressions can be derived for other kinds of capital, such as inventories and land. The details of such derivations are presented in Chapter 2.

This discussion of the concept of effective tax rates has ignored one rather important institutional feature of Canadian capital markets—their openness to international capital markets. The fact that Canada is a net importer of capital implies that some of the financing of the marginal project might come from foreign rather than domestic sources. Given the freedom with which financial capital can move across Canadian borders and the fact that Canada is a small actor in the financial capital markets of the world, it is reasonable to view Canada as a price-taker on world capital markets, so that changes in investment or savings behaviour in Canada do not affect interest rates or rates of return on equity. Whether Canada is, in fact, a price-taker on capital markets is ultimately an empirical question. It could be argued that the assumption is a reasonable one for large corporations with access to public capital markets, but that for small private corporations that are financed by entrepreneurs, there can be some independent determination of rates of return.

The implication of Canada facing fixed interest rates on capital markets is illustrated in Figure 1.2, which amends Figure 1.1 to account for the openness of Canadian capital markets. The availability of finance on world capital markets at a fixed price effectively separates domestic investment decisions from domestic savings decisions. Correspondingly, we can disaggregate the effective tax rate into two portions, one operating on the investment decision and another operating on the savings decision.

The effective tax rate on investment t_c is essentially due to taxes levied on the firm. These could include not only corporate taxes, but also property taxes, capital taxes, mining taxes, and so on. Since our empirical work concentrates solely on provincial and federal corporate taxes, we refer to t_c as the effective corporate tax rate. The effective tax rate on investment is

---

[3] This is a very cryptic description of the neoclassical theory, which may make it appear more restrictive than it really is. For example, adjustment costs and uncertainty can be added and the concept of a user cost and effective tax rates used here remains intact. For a fuller discussion, see R. W. Boadway, "The Theory and Measurement of Effective Tax Rates," in J. M. Mintz and D. D. Purvis, eds., *The Impact of Taxation on Business Activity* (Kingston: John Deutsch Institute for Economic Policy, Queen's University, forthcoming).

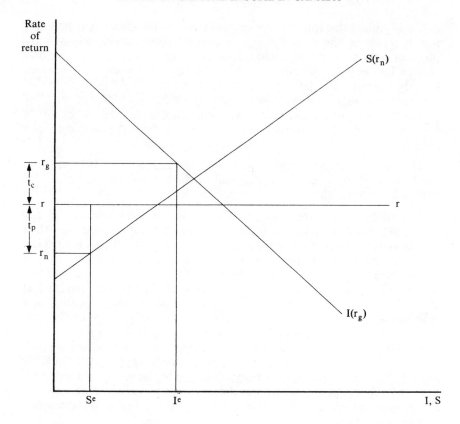

Figure 1.2   Capital Market Equilibrium in an Open Economy with Taxes

defined as the difference between the before-tax rate of return on marginal investment r_g and the cost of funds on world capital markets r. The technique for measuring r_g is as outlined above, and r is readily measurable from market data.

One further complication arises in measuring effective corporate tax rates in open economies: the question of which corporate tax system to use for foreign firms operating in Canada. Under certain arrangements of crediting foreign tax, as long as Canadian corporate tax liabilities are higher than those under the tax system of the foreign country concerned, the effective corporate tax rate is that of the Canadian tax system. If Canadian tax liabilities are lower, however, effective tax rates are generally higher than those of the Canadian tax system, since foreign corporations will be liable for taxes in their own country. Because the taxing and crediting arrangements for the subsidiaries of the corporations of many countries (especially the United States) operate only on repatriation, the full brunt of foreign taxes on subsidiaries can be lessened by reinvesting earnings in Canada (or elsewhere) and postponing repatriation. This applies only to subsidiaries and not to branch plants, whose taxes and credits are often calculated on a worldwide basis as corporate income accrues. We have not attempted to measure effective tax rates for these cases.

The effective tax rate on saving t_p is the difference between r—the opportunity cost of funds to the economy—and r_n—the after-tax rate of return to domestic saving. This adjustment primarily reflects the distortion due to personal taxation, though it also allows for any provisions that exist for integrating personal and corporate taxes. The sum of the two tax rates, $t_c + t_p$ is the overall effective tax rate t, as before.

These techniques for measuring effective tax rates can readily be extended to calculate what effective tax rates would be under differing tax structures or with changes in exogenous parameters such as inflation or interest rates and the structure of investments. For example, we can calculate how the effective tax rate would change if various tax reforms were instituted in the tax treatment of capital income at the personal or corporate levels. These sorts of exercises are undertaken in later chapters.

The Tax Treatment of Capital Income in Canada

The Corporate Income Tax

The CIT is levied on the income earned by corporations. Not all firms are incorporated. Those that are not are taxed under the PIT, even though many provisions for taxing business income of unincorporated business under the PIT are similar to those of the CIT. These will be discussed later.

All corporations carrying on business in Canada are subject to the federal CIT. In addition, corporations resident in Canada must pay Canadian tax on any income earned elsewhere. They do, however, receive a tax credit for corporate taxes paid on branch profits in other countries. Dividends from foreign affiliates paid out of business income earned in treaty countries are exempt from Canadian tax and receive no credit. Other dividends and income received are taxable but receive a credit for foreign corporate taxes and withholding taxes.

All provinces also levy a CIT on corporations carrying on business within their jurisdictions. Alberta, Ontario, and Quebec levy and collect their own CIT; the other seven provinces have tax collection agreements with the federal government under which it collects the taxes for the provinces in exchange for an undertaking by them to use the same tax base. The provinces are then free to set their own tax rates as a percentage of the base and may institute their own system of nondiscriminatory tax credits. In cases in which a corporation carries on business simultaneously in more than one province, the tax base is allocated among provinces according to an allocation rule. The rule is that the proportion of taxable income allocated to a province is the average of the proportion of the gross revenue of the firm in Canada earned in that province and the proportion of wages and salaries paid in that province. Despite the fact that Alberta, Ontario, and Quebec have CIT systems separate from the federal government, their bases are

similar to those of the other provinces, and they adhere to the same allocation rule. Therefore, our discussion of the tax base does not have to dif-
ferentiate among jurisdictions. In the empirical analysis of Chapter 3, we
need only take account of differences in tax rates across provinces.

Corporate taxes are calculated by applying the appropriate tax rate to
taxable income. Much of our discussion will be concerned with describing
exactly how taxable income is defined. In discussing taxable income, it is
useful to distinguish between active business income and non-active business (or investment) income. Active business income is earned as a result of
the spending of time, labour, and attention by the employees of the firm. A
firm is engaged in an active business if a significant part of its profits is
gained from such activities. All other income is non-active business income,
which is mainly investment income. Since the rules for defining taxable income differ in each case, it is worth considering them in turn.

Active Business Income

The taxable income of corporations engaged in active business is the difference between total revenue and allowable costs over the taxpaying year.
Each firm is free to define its own taxpaying year; it may or may not coin-
cide with the calendar year, although many firms use the calendar year.
Total revenue includes the value of all sales at the time of sale regardless of
whether payment is made at the time of sale. Thus, total revenue is included
in the tax base on an accrual basis (rather than on a cash or realization
basis). There will often be a lag between the time of sale and the receipt of
payment. This lag gives rise to *accounts receivable*, one of the types of
"assets" that the firm must finance.

From total revenue, the firm is allowed to deduct the costs incurred in the
course of earning income over the tax year. These costs are of two main
sorts—current and capital costs. As well there are certain special deductions, such as depletion allowances for the resource industries. Each of
these deductions will be discussed in turn.

Current Costs

Current costs include all expenses of a current nature incurred during the
tax year, such as wages and salaries, fuel, materials, rents, advertising and
promotion, and insurance. As with total revenues, costs are deductible on
an accrual basis at the time at which the expenses are incurred regardless of
whether payment is made at the same time. Any lag between the undertaking of an expenditure and the payment will give rise to *accounts payable*.
Accounts payable can be thought of as liabilities that are a source of finance
to the firm, since they are postponements of payment.

Capital Costs

Capital expenditures are those undertaken to acquire an asset that will be
used to produce income over a period of time. These include machinery and
equipment, nonresidential structures, land, resources, inventories, and in-

tangible assets such as goodwill and knowledge or information. The tax system treats each of these differently, but there are basically two types of expenses allowed for capital: an interest cost and an expense for the use of the asset (for example, depreciation). The actual interest paid on all interest-bearing debt of the firm is deductible from income.[4] No deduction is allowed for the imputed cost of non-interest-paying sources of finance (for example, equity). Note that the nominal interest expense on borrowed capital is deducted rather than the real expense. To compensate the lender for the loss in the real value of debt, the nominal interest rate is equal to the real interest rate plus the inflation rate. By deducting nominal rather than real interest expense, firms are, in effect, writing off a proportion of the principal as well as the real interest cost. The deductions allowed for the use of the asset vary from asset to asset, as will be discussed in the following sections.

1) Depreciable assets

Machinery and equipment and nonresidential structures are depreciable assets, which are allowed a depreciation expense or *capital cost allowance* (CCA). Each type of depreciable asset is assigned to a class and is written off at the declining balance rate of the class. The declining balance rate is based upon the original cost of the asset, although since 1981 only one-half of the ordinary CCA is deductible in the first year for new assets. The rates for each class are meant to accord roughly with the economic life of the asset. It is likely, however, that for many assets, the rate of economic depreciation does not correspond to that allowed for tax purposes. For example, certain machinery and equipment falls in Class 8 as set out in the Income Tax Regulations and is written off at 20 per cent per year. Recent estimates of the average life span of machinery and equipment in this class found it to be approximately 13 years. This corresponds approximately to an exponential depreciation rate of 15 per cent, which is three-fourths of that allowed for tax purposes.[5]

---

[4] Interest deductibility on foreign debt is limited by the "thin capitalization" provisions. According to these, a portion of the interest on outstanding debt to specified nonresidents (generally foreign shareholders) is not tax deductible if the debt outstanding is three times the book value of equity. The portion is calculated as debt owing to specified nonresidents less three times the book value of equity divided by outstanding debt owing to specified nonresidents.

[5] For the service lives of various types of capital see Statistics Canada, *Fixed Capital Flows and Stocks* (annual), catalogue no. 13-211 (various years) and Charles R. Hulten and Frank C. Wykoff, "The Measurement of Economic Depreciation," in Charles R. Hulten, ed., *Depreciation, Inflation, and the Taxation of Income from Capital* (Washington D.C.: Urban Institute Press, 1981), 81-125. The first document calculates capital stocks in Canada by using straight-line depreciation and a given service life. The exponential depreciation rate corresponding roughly to a straight-line rate for an asset of service life T is calculated as follows.

Consider the following diagram, which depicts the capital remaining at various times t as a result of $1 of capital being depreciated under straight-line and exponential depreciation:

(Continued on next page.)

When an asset is sold, recapture of depreciation applies. To calculate re-captured depreciation, the undepreciated base of the whole CCA class of assets is first reduced by the lesser of the cost and the value of the assets that are disposed of. If disposals are more than the undepreciated base, there is recapture of depreciation as long as the asset has been sold for an amount greater than its undepreciated value. The firm adds to taxable income the difference between the sale value and the undepreciated value for tax pur-poses (or subtracts it from taxable income if negative). If the asset sells for more than its original cost, the firm is subject to capital gains taxation on one-half the sale value less the original cost of the asset.

To summarize, the firm is allowed a write-off for the interest and depre-ciation costs of holding a depreciable asset. In neither case, however, is the amount allowed for tax purposes likely to reflect the true cost of using the asset. CCA rates may not be the same as actual economic depreciation rates. Also, only the cost of debt is deductible rather than the full imputed costs of finance. Interest on debt could be more or less than the true costs of finance: although equity costs are not deductible, interest is deducted in nominal rather than real terms.

When depreciation allowed for tax purposes is greater than the actual cost of depreciation incurred by the firm, the firm is implicitly receiving an interest-free loan from the government equal to the corporate tax rate times the difference between the amount written off under CCA rules and the ac-tual depreciation rate. These *deferred tax liabilities* are another source of finance for businesses; one that varies with the amount of investment of the particular sort undertaken.

The declining balance CCA rates discussed above are those normally given for depreciable assets. Since 1972, special accelerated depreciation provisions have been in effect for certain assets such as those used for man-ufacturing and processing in Canada. Machinery and equipment used in these activities can be written off using a 50 per cent straight-line method. Similar provisions exist for pollution control and energy conservation equipment. Before 1981, these assets could be fully written off in two years.

---

[5]Continued . . .

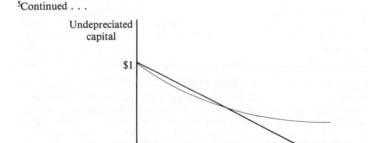

The two streams of depreciation will be approximately the same when the areas beneath the two curves are the same; that is, after integration, when $T/2 = 1/\alpha$ where α is the exponential rate of depreciation. Thus when $T = 24$ years, $\alpha = 0.083$.

With the amendments introduced in the 1981 budget, only one-half the normal CCA applies in the first year, so that the asset requires three years to be written off and follows a different write-off pattern (one-fourth, one-half, one-fourth) over the three years. Accelerated depreciation has also been available on a declining-balance basis for heavy construction equipment (50 per cent) and motion film equipment (60 per cent), and on new mine assets (as fast as the mine earns income). This rapid write-off affords a substantial tax advantage to these firms and increases deferred tax liabilities as a source of finance. The federal budget of May 1985 proposed to eliminate accelerated CCA rates.

If assets are leased rather than purchased by the firm, the lease payments are deductible from the taxable income of the company (the lessee) using the asset. The company that owns the asset (the lessor) includes lease payments in income and depreciates the asset at the prescribed CCA rate. If the lessor and lessee both face the same corporate tax rate, taxes paid will remain the same regardless of whether the asset is purchased or leased by the lessee. If tax rates differ, the company using the asset will have an incentive to lease rather than purchase it if the present value of taxes paid by the lessor is less than that paid by the lessee. This will occur, for example, if the asset is written off quickly and the lessor's corporate tax rate is higher than the lessee's. In this case, the lessor can shelter the tax write-offs, which are more than the cost of holding the asset, against other forms of taxable income. Another example is a company in a loss position that leases a capital good from a taxpaying firm rather than owning the asset, as in the case of a bank leasing a building to a manufacturer. This allows CCA write-offs to be effectively "transferred" from the loss company to the taxpaying company, since the CCA write-offs can be used more quickly by a taxable firm. The federal government has, for the most part, circumscribed this action by prohibiting lessors from claiming CCA deductions in excess of lease payments.

2) Land

Land is a nondepreciable asset and so is afforded no CCA. Only the interest costs incurred in the purchase of the land used for business purposes are deductible (as well as property taxes paid to lower levels of government). On the other hand, if land is not purchased but is rented, the rental costs are considered current costs, which may be written off as discussed above. Once again, since the full imputed interest costs are not deducted, the firm is not able to write off the full costs of owning land unless the ability to deduct the inflationary component of interest costs happens to compensate for these costs. Also, any capital gains or losses realized from the sale of land are treated as capital gains for tax purposes and taxed on a nominal basis at one-half the ordinary tax rate.

3) Resource properties

Many of the costs of acquiring resource properties are written off quickly. These include exploration and drilling costs as well as development costs in mining, which are written off at a 100 per cent rate. Development costs in oil and gas are written off at a 30 per cent CCA rate. The costs of acquiring oil and gas property rights have been depreciated at a rate of 10 per cent since 1979. Since the acquisition of resource properties and their development represents the acquisition of an asset of lasting value, their 100 per cent write-off in conjunction with the deductibility of interest payments incurred in their financing affords a substantial tax advantage to investment in the resource industries. From a viewpoint of economic efficiency, this can provide an incentive for relative over-investment in these activities. This incentive is compounded by yet another deduction for the depletion of the resource which can be obtained despite the fact that all expenses of acquiring resource properties have already been written off. The earned depletion allowance is one-third of exploration, development, new mine, and processing asset expenditures incurred by mining companies (earned depletion no longer qualifies in oil and gas). The allowance claimed in a year is limited to 25 per cent of net income, the excess carried forward indefinitely. An extra two-thirds of drilling costs in excess of $5 million on an exploratory well can also be deducted. Until recently, a petroleum incentive payment (PIP) was available to oil and gas as a replacement for earned depletion. PIP is now being phased out.

4) Inventories

Firms hold inventories whenever they purchase or produce items before they use them in their production processes or sell them. The general principle in expensing inventories is that they are deductible when used rather than when acquired (except for certain cases discussed below). The value at which the item is written off is determined using the first in, first out (FIFO) accounting method. Thus, each time an item is taken out of inventory it is expensed at the original cost of acquiring the oldest item in the inventory. Since the value of the inventory when it is used may exceed the cost allowed for tax purposes, the firm effectively pays a tax on the rise in the value of the inventory over the holding period. The holding of inventories must, of course, be financed and firms are allowed to write off any interest expenses incurred in financing the inventory. In addition, firms have been allowed to deduct from taxable income an "inventory allowance," which provided an indirect way of compensating the firm for the taxation of nominal capital gains in inflationary periods. The write-off was 3 per cent of the value of inventories held at the beginning of the tax year. The inventory allowance was eliminated in 1986. Some industries—namely, agriculture and fishing—can use cash accounting for inventories—this allows them to expense the cost of inventory when purchased. No inventory allowance was given when cash accounting was used.

5) Intangible assets

One may also view the acquisition of goodwill and knowledge as an asset. Virtually all costs of acquiring goodwill and knowledge are immediately deductible, such as research and development (R & D), advertising, and marketing expenses. In addition, interest costs incurred in financing these expenditures are tax deductible, and special tax credits and deductions are available on R & D expenditures.[6] Thus the firm is given generous tax incentives to undertake these types of capital expenditures. The only exception to the above treatment occurs when goodwill, rights, or franchises are acquired by purchase from another firm instead of being accumulated by expenditures. In this case, one-half the sale value of the intangibles (or "nothings") is taxed as income by the selling firm, while one-half may be written off by the purchasing firm at a 10 per cent declining balance rate.

Tax Rates

The above description provides an overview on how active business income is defined for tax purposes. Once taxable income has been calculated, the appropriate corporate tax rate is applied to determine the taxes payable. The basic federal corporate tax rate in Canada has been 36 per cent, which will be lowered to 33 per cent by 1989. The standard provincial tax rate is 10 per cent, but the legislated provincial rates vary from province to province (the top rate ranges from 5.5 per cent in Quebec to 17 per cent in Saskatchewan). As well, there are some special cases in which preferential tax rates are given. For one, profits earned in manufacturing and processing activities in Canada have been subject to a reduced federal tax rate of 30 per cent, which will be lowered to 26 per cent by 1989.

Also, certain Canadian-controlled private corporations (CCPCs) have effectively been taxed at a reduced federal and provincial combined rate of 25 per cent on their active business income by a *small business tax credit* of 21 percentage points. (For manufacturing and processing, the small business rate was 20 per cent.) By 1988, the small business tax rate will be 13 per cent on nonmanufacturing and 8 per cent on manufacturing firms. This lower tax rate applies to the first $200,000 of taxable active business income. Before 1982, the small business tax credit was limited to corporations whose retained earnings were less than $750,000 (total business limit less cumulative deduction account [CDA]). Firms were required to maintain a CDA, which rose as income subject to the lower rate was claimed. The CDA was reduced, however, by the amount of dividends paid out of income. Firms could thereby keep their CDA below the upper limit almost indefinitely by continually paying out dividends. This stipulation provided a strong incentive for firms to finance by debt or new issues rather than by retained earnings. After 1981, the total business limit was increased to $1 million, but dividends could no longer increase the limit. Moreover, a dividend distribution tax of 12½ per cent was imposed on dividends paid. Then in 1985, the CDA account was eliminated, and now the first $200,000 of CCPC active business income is taxed at the low rate. Formerly, if a corporation became public or became controlled by nonresidents, it lost the small business tax credit. The 1986 federal budget has eliminated the small busi-

---

[6]Current and capital R & D expenditures are eligible for an investment tax credit as outlined below.

ness distribution tax of 12½ per cent along with the reduction in the dividend tax credit, which will be discussed below.

Before 1985, some private Canadian corporations were denied the small business tax rate by the federal government. Ineligible corporations were of three main types—certain professions (doctors, lawyers, dentists, accountants, veterinarians, and chiropractors), personal service corporations deriving more than two-thirds of revenue from one entity, and management companies. These nonqualifying corporations received a tax credit of only 12⅔ rather than 21 percentage points. The effect of this provision was to remove the incentive for many of these firms to incorporate solely for the purpose of saving taxes. After 1985, these firms became eligible for the small business tax rate, since the incentive to incorporate was eliminated by changes in the law with respect to integration, which is discussed later.

As was already mentioned, both the full corporate tax rate and the small business tax rate will vary because provinces are free to set their own tax rates and need not adhere to the so-called basic one. Table 1.1 summarizes the corporate tax rates currently in effect across provinces.

Tax Credits

After having calculated taxes payable under the rates discussed above, there are several tax credits that corporations may deduct. We will discuss the

Table 1.1 Provincial Corporate Income Tax Rates, 1986 and 1987[a]

Province	Small business		Other	
	1986	1987	1986	1987
	per cent			
Newfoundland	10	10	16	16
Prince Edward Island	10	10	10	15
Nova Scotia	10	10	15	15
New Brunswick	5/9	5/9	15	15
Quebec[b]	3.15	3.22	5.77/13.63	5.90/13.94
Ontario	10	10	14.5/15.5	14.5/15.5
Manitoba	10	10	17	17
Saskatchewan	0/10	0/10	17	17
Alberta	0/5	0/5	5/11	8.01/14.01[c]
British Columbia	8	9.51[d]	16	15
Yukon	2.5/5	2.5/5	2.5/10	2.5/10
Northwest Territories	10	10	10	10

[a]For explanations of these rates, see source below. [b]Quebec introduced a 7.25 per cent surtax effective May 1, 1986; the rates shown here include the prorated surtax for the 1986 calendar year. [c]Alberta increased its corporate tax rate on manufacturing and processing income to 9 per cent and on other income to 15 per cent effective April 1, 1987; the rates shown here are for the 1987 calendar year. [d]British Columbia increased its corporate tax rate on small business income to 11 per cent effective July 1, 1987; the rate shown here is for the 1987 calendar year.

Source: *Provincial and Municipal Finances 1987* (Toronto: Canadian Tax Foundation, forthcoming).

ones mainly used, which are the investment tax credit and the credit for foreign taxes paid, and exclude lesser credits, such as that for political contributions, from consideration here.

1) Investment tax credit

Until recently, firms have been able to deduct from taxes payable a tax credit based on certain investment expenditures. The basic rate was 7 per cent and was applicable to all new investment for machinery and buildings and certain heavy construction and transport equipment in agriculture, forestry, fishing, manufacturing, and resource industries. The rate was 10 per cent for areas designated by the Department of Regional Economic Expansion (DREE) as slow growth areas, 20 per cent in the Atlantic provinces and the Gaspé region in Quebec, and 50 per cent in specially designated areas (60 per cent in Cape Breton). Scientific research and development expenditures (both current and capital) were eligible for a basic 10 per cent tax credit, while those in the Atlantic provinces and Gaspé region got 20 per cent. The February 1986 federal budget phases out these investment tax credits except for the Maritimes, the Gaspé, and certain slow growth areas. The investment tax credit will also remain available for high cost exploration and R & D expenditures.

2) Foreign tax credit

As mentioned earlier, corporations resident in Canada are subject to taxation on worldwide income. Qualifying dividends and retentions of foreign subsidiaries are exempt from tax. Taxable dividends are eligible for a foreign tax credit equal to the underlying foreign corporate and withholding taxes. In addition, resident corporations are allowed to deduct from taxes payable income taxes that have been paid to foreign governments at both higher and lower level jurisdictions.

Tax Losses and Unclaimed Tax Credits

The preceding discussion assumes that firms are earning positive taxable income, and are subject to taxes payable that are large enough to be able to claim all tax credits and deductions. In practice, of course, this need not be the case. In some years firms may make small or negative taxable income, and the tax system makes an allowance for loss offsets in these cases. Any losses in taxable income may be carried back three years or forward seven years and set against income of those years.[7] In addition to these rules, corporations can carry forward indefinitely certain unclaimed deductions instead of reporting tax losses. These include CCAs, exploration and development expenditures, and earned depletion. In addition, all the tax credits discussed above may be carried back three years and forward for seven years. The investment tax credit is also partly refundable for small business.

---

[7] Before 1983, the carryback period was one year and the carryforward was five years.

These liberal loss-offset provisions allow a firm to claim at least some losses against future income gains. If all the losses are eventually claimed, the only difference between the existing carryforward provisions and full loss offsetting is that the postponement of tax credits to future years involves the cost of forgone interest receipts.

Investment Income

In addition to producing income from real assets, firms may also hold assets that provide purely investment income—especially financial assets but also real assets for rental. This type of income is treated differently under the corporate tax system. A main consideration determining the tax treatment of investment income is the fact that the corporation holding the income-earning asset is acting more or less as an intermediary between its own capital owners (shareholders or debt issuers) and the institution issuing the asset. Many of the provisions of the tax system exist solely to prevent the double taxation of the income originally generated that passes through two or more corporations before it ultimately reaches the household. The provisions, however, differ according to whether the investment income is held by a public corporation or a private corporation. These are considered in turn.

Public Corporations

Investment income earned by a corporation may come in several forms including dividends and capital gains on shares held, interest on debt, and rental on real assets. Dividends received by public corporations from taxable Canadian and certain foreign corporations are exempt from taxation on the principle that to tax them would be to impose a corporate tax twice. At the same time, one-half of capital gains are taxed.[8] There is, therefore, an element of double taxation of capital gains, which will be discussed more fully later. Interest income is fully taxed when received by public corporations as are rental income from real assets and portfolio dividends from foreign corporations. Of course, interest payments are also fully tax deductible, so that to the extent that debt holdings of the firm are financed by debt issue, no net tax is incurred on interest. If the debt holdings are financed by equity, the costs of financing are not deductible, and the interest does not flow through tax-free. This source of tax distortion will be returned to again later in our analysis of the impact of the tax system on financing decisions of firms.

There are a number of special provisions in regard to the taxation of financial institutions that are important in relation to the financing of business. First, financial corporations such as banks, trust and loan corporations, and credit unions are permitted to deduct from taxable income a reserve for doubtful debts. Debts are the aggregate of outstanding principal

---

[8] Capital losses may be offset against capital gains within the same firm in the current year or indefinitely into the future. Also, when mutual funds pay out the capital gain to shareholders, they receive a refund of capital gain taxes paid.

and unpaid interest due on loans and mortgages excluding those mortgages issued under the National Housing Act. Financial institutions may compute a reserve equal to 1½ per cent of the first $2 billion of total amounts of qualifying securities and 1 per cent of any excess. The total deduction allowed is limited to the previous year's deduction plus one-third of the maximum amount of debts owing. Since the deduction for doubtful assets is not related to the actual riskiness of a loan, loans to less risky businesses may be subsidized where the deduction is of greater value than the actual loss incurred on the loan.

Second, the tax law recognizes certain special cases for tax treatment:

1) Pension corporations are tax exempt. When payments are made to owners, the income is taxed as employment earnings. There is, however, a gain to the holders of pensions in being able to write off contributions to plans and in delaying the payment of taxes on interest accruing over time.

2) Credit unions are considered to be private corporations for the purpose of claiming the small business tax credit, and it is calculated on a somewhat different basis than that allowed for nonfinancial corporations.[9]

3) Dividends paid by mutual funds to their shareholders are treated as capital gains income.

4) Special treatment applies to insurance firms with respect to policy reserves.

We shall discuss in Chapter 2 how the relative differences in the taxation of certain financial institutions can affect the cost of capital and the flow of funds to small and large businesses.

Private Corporations

The investment income of private corporations, unlike public corporations, is supposed to be fully integrated with that of their owners to ensure a completely tax-free flow of investment income through the corporation to the shareholder. Since small businesses fall into the category of private corporations, this ensures that the investment income of small corporations is tax-free. The integration of the investment income of private corporations is accomplished by a combination of refundable taxes and tax credits. Private corporations receiving dividends from taxable Canadian corporations are required to pay a 33⅓ per cent refundable tax. When the dividends are paid out, a tax credit exactly compensates for the refundable tax originally paid, so that the dividends flow through the firm untaxed. The refundable tax on dividends received serves the purpose of removing an incentive for shareholders to accumulate dividend income in a private corporation in order to postpone the payment of tax.

---

[9]An additional tax credit of 25 per cent is allowed on taxable income over the amount allowed for the small business income deduction. The amount of income allowed for this additional tax credit is limited by the increase in a year of the cumulative reserve. The reserve is equal to 5 per cent of the total of debts owing to members and of shares held by members.

The other sources of investment income (interest, rent, dividends from non-Canadian sources, and one-half of capital gains) are fully taxed when received by the corporation (at the rate of 46 per cent since the small business rate applies only to active business income). Full integration of interest income is almost achieved by a combination of a $1 tax credit for every $3 of dividends paid out and a dividend tax credit of 33⅓ per cent, which will be discussed later under the personal income tax.[10] The tax credit on dividends received by the firm is limited by the amount of tax that has been paid by the firm on its investment income and not yet credited. This is called the "refundable dividend tax on hand." The firm obtains a tax credit on dividends paid out only to this extent to prevent the tax credit from applying to active business income earned or to the one-half of capital gains that has gone untaxed. In this way, the investment income is all eventually integrated with the personal tax structure.

Summary

The corporate tax system seems to afford favourable treatment to both the active business income and, to a lesser extent, the investment income of small corporations. As far as active business income is concerned, small corporations eligible for the small business deduction obtain the benefit of a lower flat rate of tax. Investment income is fully integrated to ensure a tax-free flow through private corporations. For public corporations, only dividends flow through tax-free in addition to interest income on bonds that are financed out of debt.

In addition to corporate income taxes as described above, there are certain provincial capital taxes levied on corporations carrying on business in Quebec, Ontario, Manitoba, Saskatchewan, and British Columbia, and at the federal level, there is a capital tax on banks. To calculate the federal capital tax, tax rates are applied to taxable paid-up capital liabilities, which include share capital, reserves, bank loans, and long-term debt less any deductions made for certain eligible investment. Exemption levels from the tax are provided in Manitoba and British Columbia and tax rates are graduated with the amount of capital in Ontario.

The Taxation of Capital Income Under the Personal Income Tax

Capital income is taxed again when received by individuals as personal income. The personal and corporate income taxes both fall under the same Income Tax Act and similar rules apply. Residents in Canada are taxed on their worldwide income but receive a tax credit for personal income taxes

---

[10]The integration is not exact for two reasons. First, the tax credit provisions on dividend payments are designed to offset one-half the corporate tax paid under a corporate tax rate of 50 per cent. Since the corporate tax rate is only 46 per cent, more than one-half is offset by the credit. The other half is supposed to be offset by the effective dividend tax credit of 50 per cent. Because of the complicated way in which the dividend tax credit is shared by the provincial and federal governments, the correspondence is only approximate here as well. The exact mechanism for computing the dividend tax credit is discussed below.

paid to foreign governments. It is again useful to distinguish between the tax treatment of business income under the PIT and the treatment of investment income. Once again, most provinces (except Quebec) are party to the tax collection agreements with the federal government, and our discussion will be limited to the common case.

Business Income

Income earned by individuals through unincorporated businesses is subject to personal income taxation. Since the general principles for calculating taxable income (allowable costs are subtracted from total revenue) are identical to those for corporations, there is no need to repeat them here. Taxable income so calculated is then taxed according to the PIT rate structure rather than the corporate tax rate.

One interesting feature of the tax system is that there can be a tax advantage to incorporating a business instead of earning active business income as an unincorporated individual. Business income earned by an unincorporated individual is taxed at progressive personal rates; business income when earned by a corporation is first subject to the corporate income tax and then again subject to the personal income tax when paid out as dividends. Some relief for the double taxation of business income under incorporation is afforded, however, by the dividend tax credit discussed in the following section. Before the February 1986 budget, the effective dividend tax credit rate was 50 per cent. This dividend tax credit system was designed to give the shareholder full credit for the corporate taxes paid for a corporate tax rate of 33⅓ per cent. Therefore, if a firm was subject to the small business rate of 25 per cent, the effective dividend tax credit overcompensated the shareholder for corporate taxes paid.[11] There was therefore a tax advantage to taking business income through the small corporation. It was for this reason that the federal government imposed a 12½ per cent tax on dividends distributed from active business income eligible for the small business rate. The incentive was thereby removed for incorporating solely for tax purposes, although recent reductions of provincial rates on small business have introduced an advantage to incorporation. As of January 1, 1987, the effective dividend tax credit has been reduced to 33⅓ per cent, thereby fully integrating corporate and personal taxes for a firm paying a 25 per cent corporate tax rate. The 12½ per cent dividend distribution tax has also been eliminated, since it is no longer required to achieve full integration at the small business level.

---

[11]Suppose $1,000 of taxable income is earned by a small corporation. Corporate taxes of $250 are paid and, say, the remaining $750 is paid out as dividends. With a 150 per cent gross-up, $750 of dividends is grossed up to $1,125 and added to taxable income, and a tax credit equal to one-third or $375 is given. This credit exceeds the $250 originally paid in corporate taxes. Note that this overcompensation is even greater if the corporation paying the dividends has not been fully in a taxpaying position. In this case it may be paying less than 25 per cent on average on income out of which dividends are paid.

Investment Income

Individuals receive investment income in the form of dividends, interest, rent, and capital gains. Interest, rent, and dividends from non-Canadian corporations are all generally included as taxable income (subject to the exclusions discussed below). Dividends from Canadian corporations are also taxed but are subject to a dividend tax credit. Until the February 1986 budget, the dividend tax credit was meant to be applied at a rate of 50 per cent, with grossed-up dividends being added to taxable income. But because the credit had to be divided between federal and provincial governments, its calculation was not so straightforward and its amount was only approximately 50 per cent. The calculation was done as follows. Dividends were grossed up by 150 per cent and added to taxable income. A federal tax credit of $22\frac{2}{3}$ per cent of the grossed-up dividend was then applied. Since provincial taxes are calculated as a percentage of federal taxes, the credit was compounded by the provincial rate applicable. For example, if the rate was 48 per cent of the federal tax (as was the 1985 Ontario rate), the total dividend tax credit was $0.2267 + 0.48 (0.2267) = 0.336$ of grossed-up dividends. Since the gross-up of dividends was 150 per cent, the total effective credit given against dividends received was about 50 per cent in this case. If the marginal rate of personal tax on other forms of income was 50 per cent, then after the gross-up, the tax rate on a dollar of dividends received was 75 per cent. When the credit was subtracted, the effective tax rate on dividends received was 25 per cent. Given a corporate tax rate of 46 per cent, the total corporate and personal tax rate net of the credit on dividends paid out was about 60 per cent, calculated as $0.46 + (1 - 0.46)(0.25)$, where 0.46 is the tax applied at the corporate level, leaving $(1 - 0.46)$ of profits to be taxed at the 25 per cent rate when distributed as dividends. Hence, the total credit did not fully reduce the amount of the corporate tax paid in this case. If the small business tax rate applied, the total corporate and personal tax rate net of the dividend tax credit was 25 per cent plus the dividend distribution tax of $12\frac{1}{2}$ per cent of dividends paid. This was equivalent to a combined corporate and dividend distribution tax of $34\frac{3}{8}$ per cent calculated as $0.25 + (1 - 0.25)(0.125)$. Since the personal tax net of tax credits on each dollar of dividends was 16 per cent, the combined tax rate was close to 50 per cent. The amount of the credit did, of course, vary from province to province according to the marginal rate of personal tax.

As mentioned above, the effective dividend tax credit is reduced beginning January 1987. The gross-up rate on dividends received is reduced from 150 per cent to $133\frac{1}{3}$ per cent, and the federal tax credit is reduced from $22\frac{2}{3}$ per cent to $16\frac{2}{3}$ per cent. In addition, the $12\frac{1}{2}$ per cent distribution tax is eliminated. For small corporations facing a 25 per cent tax rate, these changes leave the underlying tax on pre-tax corporate income the same. For large corporations, the reduction in the effective dividend tax credit from 50 per cent of dividends received to $33\frac{1}{3}$ per cent means that dividends received from a large corporation paying taxes at a 46 per cent rate will now be less integrated.

Not all investment income is taxed in the hands of individuals. Though one-half of nominal capital gains enters the tax base, the May 1985 budget introduced a lifetime cumulative exemption of $500,000. This virtually eliminates capital gains taxation except for wealthy persons. Also, an investment deduction of up to $1,000 may be claimed for interest and grossed-up dividends from Canadian assets. Before 1985, net taxable capital gains also qualified for this investment deduction. For individuals with these types of investment income amounting to less than $1,000, the marginal tax rate is therefore zero. For those with more than $1,000 in investment income from interest or dividends, the marginal tax rate is that applicable to their other personal income. The same principle also applies to registered retirement savings plans (RRSPs), registered pension plans (RPPs), and deferred profit-sharing plans (DPSPs) and to income from them. Individuals deduct contributions to these plans from taxable income and pay tax upon the withdrawal of funds. If the marginal rate of personal tax is the same (or less) at the time of withdrawal as at the time of contribution, this income is not (or negatively) taxed. Individuals who have not contributed funds up to the permitted limit for immediate tax write-offs face a marginal personal tax rate of zero. Until the 1986 tax year, these limits were $5,500 each year if no contribution was made to pension plans, or $3,500 otherwise. These limits are to be increased gradually to $15,000 per year except for persons who have defined-benefit pension plans. Finally, capital dividends paid by private corporations are untaxed in the hands of the investor. These dividends arise from the capital gains earned by private corporations with respect to property and goodwill and from life insurance proceeds net of costs. As these forms of income are taxed in the hands of the private corporation, the exclusion of dividends avoids double taxation.

Beginning in 1987, high income earners will also be liable for an alternative minimum tax if their taxes payable under the ordinary income tax are less than those calculated under the minimum tax. A minimum tax liability is calculated as 25 per cent of income broadly defined, but in excess of $40,000. The minimum tax base is similar to the federal income tax base, except that it disallows certain fast write-offs such as those associated with movie productions, exploration and development, flow-through expenses, rental losses due to excess CCA, RRSP and pension income deductions, and the exclusion of one-half of capital gains. In addition, the dividend tax credit is not applied against the minimum tax, and actual rather than taxable (grossed-up) dividends are included in the minimum tax base. Finally, the minimum tax is credited against normal federal tax liablities, with the excess minimum tax carried forward at no rate of interest.

The Effect of Income Taxes on Financial and Investment Decisions of Canadian Firms

Firms require funds to finance lags that occur between the outlay of cash for expenditures and the receipt of payments for goods and services. That is, they need financing to cover negative cash flows. It is useful at this point to set out explicitly the sorts of expenditures that typically require financing from different sources and to discuss some of the tax implications of each.

Firms need financing for the following main categories of expenditures: real capital, inventories, accounts receivable, cash, and financial assets. In the purchase of real capital, we include depreciable capital (such as machinery and equipment and plant), nondepreciable capital (such as land), and depletable resources (such as oil and gas reserves). We could also include the acquisition of intangible assets, since the principles involved are the same. Inventories may include materials and intermediate goods purchased for use in production processes at a later date, work in progress, and final goods to be sold at a later date. All holdings of stocks of inventories require the outlay of funds for financing as well as any holding costs that may be incurred. Accounts receivable arise out of lags between the sale of products and the receipt of payment. Finally, firms may purchase financial assets such as bonds or shares that will yield a return in the future.

In each of the above cases, some financing will be required, and the amount of the expenditures actually undertaken will depend, among other things, upon the cost at which the financing can be attained. The firm will have several sources of finance potentially available to it. We shall classify these sources into five types. The first is debt issue, which generally includes all forms of interest-bearing securities of both a long-term and short-term nature. The next two categories comprise the equity finance of the firm-retained earnings and new issues. Retained earnings are profits otherwise available for dividend payout that are retained for investment in the firm. New issues are sales of shares in the market. Next, accounts payable represents trade credit obtained from other firms on the purchase of inputs. Finally, the deferment of taxes may be viewed as a form of financing in the sense that it is a postponement of tax payments.

In discussing the cost of financing firms, most of our attention will be devoted to the interaction between the tax system and the first three categories of finance encompassing debt and equity. The latter category of financing, deferred taxes, is associated directly with particular uses of the funds, specifically, certain categories of real capital expenditures. This source of financing will be incorporated into the costs associated with that particular type of investment. Accounts payable will be dealt with only briefly.

It should be stressed at the outset that it is not our intention to analyze the determinants of the financial structure of the firm. Such a study would take us much too far afield. Rather, we shall take the financial structure of various sorts of firms as given and analyze the impact of the tax structure on the cost of financing the firm, given the observed financial structure. It is undoubtedly the case that the tax system itself influences the debt-equity structure of the firm by, for example, favouring debt to equity financing or retained earnings to new share issue. Our analysis will, however, be limited to investigating the effect of taxes on firms' financing costs for given debt-equity ratios and will not incorporate induced effects on the cost of financing via changes in the debt-equity ratio.

The subsequent chapters of this study undertake to analyze theoretically and empirically the impact of the Canadian tax system on the various investment decisions of firms. As a prelude to that more detailed analysis, we will also summarize here in a rather more cursory manner the main ways in which taxes impinge upon the financing and investment decisions of firms. The corporate and personal income taxes affect both the relative costs of using funds for various types of investments and also the relative costs of financing by sources of funds. Here we shall review the impact of the tax regulations on the uses and on the sources of financing.

The Uses of Financing

The main uses of financing are for the purchase of real capital, inventories, accounts receivable, and financial assets. These are each subject to special tax regulations that have an influence on their relative costs.

Real Capital

The user cost of capital in the absence of taxes includes depreciation and interest charges less capital gains. The corporate tax system attempts to give write-offs for some of these but does so only imperfectly. If it worked perfectly, the tax would be neutral at the margin.[12] The CCA is intended to account for depreciation. On the one hand, as was suggested above, the rate at which CCA is offered is likely to diverge from the economic rate of depreciation on capital. On the other hand, since CCA is based upon historical cost, the write-off allowed in periods of inflation is less than the replacement cost, and this may entail some taxation of nominal capital gains. Overall, it is not clear whether the CCA provisions increase or decrease the user cost of capital in the presence of taxation.

Interest deductibility is allowed, but only for interest actually paid. Some of the interest costs associated with holding capital are imputed; namely, those associated with the equity financing of capital. Since only interest paid on debt is deductible but the imputed interest cost of equity finance is not, the user cost of holding capital is likely to be higher on this account in the presence of corporate taxation. In the presence of inflation, nominal interest rates may be written off, which presumably incorporate some element of the inflation in them. This is beneficial to the firm and partly compensates for the fact that only historical cost depreciation is allowed.[13] In fact, the granting of a write-off for nominal interest payments is equivalent to a partial write-off of the real principal of a security (as long as the principal is not indexed). This is simply the other side of the well-known phenomenon that if inflation is incorporated in securities via an increase in the interest rate rather than an indexing of the principal, the debtor is in fact being required to pay off part of the real principal through interest rate payments. Overall, in periods of inflation it is not clear how much, if at all, the user cost of capital is increased. We can only be certain that the lower the debt-equity ratio, the higher will be the increase in the cost of capital.

---

[12]For discussion of the circumstances in which the corporate tax is neutral, see Robin W. Boadway, Neil Bruce, and Jack M. Mintz, "Corporate Taxation in Canada: Toward an Efficient System," in Thirsk and Whalley, supra footnote 1, at 171-211.

[13]In fact, with full debt financing and the true depreciation rate as the CCA rate, the compensation would be exact and the tax would be neutral. See R. W. Boadway and N. Bruce, "Depreciation and Interest Deductions and the Effect of the Corporation Income Tax on Investment" (February 1979), 11 *Journal of Public Economics* 93-105.

In addition to the ordinary write-offs for depreciation and interest, a number of special concessions in the tax system serve (or have served) to reduce the user cost of capital. The first is the investment tax credit, which subsidizes the purchase of real capital by all firms at the same rate. Next, the accelerated 50 per cent straight-line write-off for manufacturing and processing machinery and equipment provides a substantial reduction to the user cost of capital for that use of funds. Finally, there are the immediate write-off provisions for the acquisition of intangible capital (goodwill and knowledge) and resource properties as well as the depletion allowances on the latter, which reduce the user cost associated with capital tied up in those uses.

Inventories

Inventories obtain two sorts of write-offs as well—an interest write-off on debt used to finance them, and a write-off at the time of actual use which is based on the FIFO accounting principle (except for agriculture and fishing, which can expense inventories). The interest write-off only partly covers the full imputed interest costs of holding inventories, since no write-off is allowed against equity financing. Once again, firms with low debt-equity ratios will be discriminated against. Also, the FIFO accounting method, like historical cost depreciation, requires that the firm pays a corporate tax on all capital gains whether real or nominal. In periods of inflation, this can significantly increase the cost of holding inventories. That increase can be expected to be greater the higher the tax rate of the firm. It was for this reason that the 3 per cent inventory allowance was introduced, which allowed firms to deduct each year 3 per cent of the value of inventories held. The inventory allowance was discontinued with the February 1986 budget. The effect of taxation on inventories also depends on the holding period, as will be discussed in Chapter 2.

Accounts Receivable

Under the tax system, firms must include sales as taxable income when they are billed, not when payment is made. Firms, in turn, must finance the value of such sales until payment is received. Firms are then allowed to deduct from taxable income their borrowing costs but not the opportunity cost of equity financing. Moreover, the rate of return on accounts receivable, which may be in the form of higher prices on goods sold or credit charges, is included in taxable income. For tax purposes, accounts receivable are thus treated as any financial asset held by a firm.

Financial Assets

The tax treatment of financial assets (including cash) and the income earned thereon differs for private and public corporations. For private corporations, investment income is fully integrated with the personal tax of the ultimate shareholder, so that it flows through untaxed at the corporate level. In contrast, certain types of investment income of public corporations are subject to corporate taxation, a fact that imposes some tax burden on these corporations vis-à-vis others. Consequently, the cost of capital for firms partly owned by public corporations can be somewhat higher.

There are two potential sources of additional corporate taxation on investment income flowing through public corporations. The first is associated with the return to equity held by these corporations. Only the dividends from Canadian corporations are tax-free when received by a resident corporation, not the capital gains. This taxation of capital gains imposes a double source of corporate taxation on the ultimate shareholder, since the original income yielding the dividends and capital gains was already taxed at the corporate rate. Receiving the income through a public corporate intermediary implies an additional layer of corporate taxation as opposed to receiving the equity income directly. This increases the cost of financing firms by way of equity issued to public corporations rather than to individuals.

The other source of discriminatory treatment is interest income, which is fully taxed when received by the corporation. If the debt is itself financed by debt issued by the public corporation, the interest written off on account of the latter will offset the interest paid on debt held and tax-free flow-through will occur. If, however, the public corporation uses equity financing, it obtains no write-off, and the corporate tax on the interest received represents an added layer of corporate tax that the shareholders would not have borne if they had held the debt themselves. Both of the distortions discussed in this section are avoided in private corporations by the refundable tax credit paid to the firm on the payment of dividends.

Other effects can reduce the tax imposed on corporations. For example, this can happen when tax rates differ between corporations. A manufacturing corporation could issue preferred shares (dividends paid are tax-free) to a nonmanufacturing corporation that finances the transaction by selling a bond to the household. Since the nonmanufacturing company's tax rate is greater than the manufacturing one, from the point of view of the owners of firms it is better for the manufacturing company to transfer interest deductions to the nonmanufacturing businesses.

The Sources of Financing

The main sources of financing for the firm are debt, retained earnings, and new issues. The interaction of the corporate and personal tax systems influences the relative costs of financing by these three sources. The most important tax consideration here is the interest deductibility of debt at the corporate level. Since the costs of equity finance are not deductible, the cost of debt in relation to equity finance is reduced. Firms that have higher debt-to-equity ratios will face relatively lower costs of finance.

Personal tax treatment of the various sources of capital income will also influence the relative costs of debt to equity finance. Interest payments are subject to full personal taxation after the initial $1,000 deduction. In contrast, dividend and capital gains income is taxed preferentially. Dividends from Canadian corporations enjoy the benefit of the dividend tax credit while only one-half of capital gains is taxed.[14] This preferential treatment of equity income in the hands of shareholders partially offsets the preferential treatment given to debt finance at the corporate level, as mentioned earlier.

The dividend tax credit was designed to make the effective tax rate on dividends roughly equivalent to that on capital gains. Although the credit has the intended effect of reducing the incentive for individuals to take equity income in the form of capital gains rather than dividends, it also removes the tax advantage of financing investment by retained earnings rather than new issues. This will be elaborated further in Chapter 2.

Finally, as discussed above, firms obtaining equity finance from public corporations may face a higher cost of capital because of the double taxation of capital gains.

It is clear from the previous discussion that the tax system imposes myriad distortions on the investment decisions of firms. The purpose of the next two chapters is to investigate empirically how large these distortions really are. The fact that the existing system appears to be distortionary leads us to the normative issues of what the tax treatment of capital income might ideally look like. The final section in this chapter reviews the economic literature on the design of ideal personal and corporate tax systems from the point of view of the treatment of capital income. This will serve as a useful benchmark against which to consider the question of reform of the existing tax system in chapters 4 and 5. Indeed, many of the summary arguments presented in the following section are elaborated much more fully in those chapters.

Designing an Ideal Tax System

Criteria for Tax Reform

The various criteria that economists use when judging a tax system can be conveniently summarized under three headings—efficiency, equity, and administrative simplicity. These are the criteria we have in mind in designing an ideal tax system. It is important to note, however, that there can be no unique ideal system. The criteria above are normally in conflict, and a value judgment is involved in trading off one goal against the other. There are often ambiguities involved in applying any one criterion. For example, what is equitable depends upon the ethical views of the observer. We shall partially circumvent these difficulties by concentrating upon the choice of a tax *base* rather than a rate structure. This will allow us to avoid the important question of how progressive the rate structure should be—a question that is largely, though not entirely, separate from the choice of base. We shall also restrict ourselves to those aspects of the tax base that are relevant to the treatment of capital income, thus avoiding such issues as indirect taxation, research and development, gifts, the family, and so on. The design issues in-

---

[14] With the May 1985 budget, the taxation of capital gains at the personal level has been virtually eliminated except for those earning large capital gains over their lifetimes.

troduced here will be developed in considerably more detail in chapters 4 and 5.

Efficiency

A more efficient tax system is one that interferes less with the allocation of resources by the market, or to use the economist's jargon, distorts the economy less. Taxes distort the economy by introducing a difference, or wedge, between the amount demanders must pay and the amount suppliers must receive to engage in a market transaction. Loosely speaking, the larger is the size of the tax wedge, and the more responsive are supplies and demands to market prices (that is, the more elastic they are), the greater will be the economic cost of a given tax distortion. The economic cost of a distortion, referred to as the *deadweight loss*, is a measure of the net loss to all participants in the economy from not allowing market transactions to the point at which the benefit of the trade to the marginal demander just equals the cost to the marginal supplier. That is, it is a measure of the extent to which gains from market trading are not being fully exploited.

In an economy in which markets work competitively and efficiently, the tax system imposes economic costs or deadweight losses by impeding the use of market prices as a signal for resources to be reallocated from one use to another. The most efficient tax system in such an economy is one that is neutral: market decisions made by individuals and firms would not be distorted since price signals would not be affected by taxes. A neutral tax would have no deadweight loss associated with it.

In economies in which markets are not competitive or that fail to allocate resources properly, however, the deadweight loss of the tax system has to be judged relative to the allocation of revenues achieved by the distorted price system. A tax that purposely distorts market signals may be appropriate. Such a case may exist for research and development (R & D) expenditures, which are often judged to be inefficient because each firm does not appropriate fully the social return on R & D that accrues to the whole economy. In this case, a tax subsidy that lowers the cost of R & D would be appropriate, and there would be a gain in economic efficiency. It still remains an issue, however, as to whether tax policy or some other public policy (such as regulation, direct expenditures, or grants) is a better instrument for achieving certain social goals. The use of tax policy for such social objectives may achieve desired ends but at the cost of creating a more complex tax system. It is our view that regulatory or direct expenditure policies are better to use than tax policy to achieve other social policy objectives so that the aim of the tax system can be focussed on achieving simplicity, equity, and efficiency in the absence of market failures.

The measurement of these deadweight losses is reasonably straightforward, in principle, when one is dealing with the distortion in a single market. But, when several markets are simultaneously distorted because of taxes and other market failures, the measurement of deadweight loss becomes complicated. There is a voluminous literature dealing with this topic, and from that literature it is clear that the science of measuring dead-weight losses is far from perfect.[15] Consequently, much of what we say about the efficiency effects of a tax system will be based on educated guesses.

The situation is even more complex when one is looking at capital market distortions, because such distortions are inherently dynamic in nature. Although it is possible to devise measures of deadweight loss from taxes in dynamic settings, such measures are all the more difficult to apply in prac-tice because of the added conceptual difficulties of having time as a compo-nent of the analysis. The temporal element requires one to stipulate some-thing about the future as well as the present, and any projection involves the difficult notion of uncertainty.

Equity

The equity of a tax system concerns the way in which the system treats households in different circumstances. As a matter of economic theory, equity and efficiency are inseparable and can be dealt with jointly using the abstract concept of a *social welfare function*. This is a device for aggregat-ing the welfare of all households in the economy into a single welfare measure by using some evaluative weighting scheme (such as utilitarianism, which simply sums utilities, somehow measured). Such a procedure ob-viously requires one to make strong a priori value judgments about how to measure individual welfare (in utility) and how to compare and aggregate the welfare of different households. Public finance economists have con-ventionally avoided this general procedure in practice and instead have dealt separately with the equity of the tax system, further breaking down the equity question into two separate components—*horizontal equity* and *verti-cal equity*. This was the procedure followed, for example, in the Carter Report.[16]

A tax system is said to be horizontally equitable if two persons in like cir-cumstances before the tax are also in like circumstances after the tax is im-posed. To know when two persons are in like circumstances, it is necessary conceptually to have some index for measuring the welfare level of a house-hold—an index whose level can be compared across households.

The concept of vertical equity involves the treatment of persons at var-ious levels of welfare. The application of the criterion of vertical equity re-quires not only that one have an index for measuring individual welfare, but also that one have a value system for indicating how much improvements in the index for one household are worth in terms of improvements for another. That is, one must be able to compare changes in the index across households as well as levels.

---

[15]This literature is surveyed in Robin W. Boadway and Neil Bruce, *Welfare Economics* (Oxford: Basil Blackwell, 1984), chapters 7 and 8.

[16]Canada, *Report of the Royal Commission on Taxation* (Ottawa: Queen's Printer, 1966).

The choice of the appropriate index will itself involve a value judgment as will the weights attached to changes in the index across households. As we shall see below when investigating the personal income tax, the choice of an index for measuring well-being is at the heart of the choice of tax base on equity grounds.

Administrative Simplicity

A final, and important, criterion for judging the tax system is the ease with which the tax system can be administered. This includes not only the compliance costs imposed on the taxpayer and the taxpayer's ability to understand the the system, but also the costs imposed on the government in collecting taxes and enforcing the regulations.

These criteria will now be used to evaluate alternative ways of treating capital income in the tax system. The reader is reminded that we are dealing here with the *design* of an ideal tax system as opposed to the *reform* of the existing one. The issue we are considering is the following. If we had a choice as to what kind of a tax system we could be living under now, what would that tax system look like? This is a somewhat different question than how would we like to change the existing system. Changes in the existing system will inevitably involve transitional problems that must be taken into account. For example, some groups will obtain windfall gains and others windfall losses, and these short-run gains and losses must be set against the long-run gains to be had from reforming a tax system to make it more nearly ideal.

Personal Income Taxation

The broad issue of concern for us in the design of a PIT system is the treatment of capital income in the tax base. It turns out that the fundamental debate in the tax reform literature for the past decade has been concerned with just that issue. The central dispute has been over the ideal base for personal taxation—consumption or income. It turns out that the difference between these two bases is simply capital income. The ideal consumption base is the same as the ideal income base with capital income, or its present value equivalent, excluded. Thus, our discussion here will concentrate upon setting out the cases for and against the use of income, comprehensively defined, as a tax base and the use of consumption or its equivalent.

Comprehensive Income Taxation

The concept of comprehensive income as an appropriate base for taxation is associated historically with the names Haig and Simons and has figured prominently in the public finance literature as illustrated by the classic textbook by Musgrave and in the policy literature.[17] It formed the conceptual

---

[17]Richard A. Musgrave, *The Theory of Public Finance* (New York: McGraw-Hill, 1959); see, for example, Richard Goode, "The Economic Definition of Income," in Joseph A. Pechman, ed., *Comprehensive Income Taxation* (Washington, D.C.: The Brookings Institution, 1977), 7-20.

basis for the recommendations of the U.K. Royal Commission on the Taxation of Profits and Income[18] and the Carter Report. Comprehensive income is defined to include current consumption plus changes in the wealth of the taxpayer. Consumption ideally includes all imputed forms of consumption currently enjoyed including the services of leisure and household production and the services currently obtained from durable consumer goods such as housing. Changes in wealth include all changes in the value of wealth held by the taxpayer whether accumulated through savings or accrued by capital gains. Comprehensive income thus defined is intended to represent an index of a taxpayer's well-being or ability to pay and is therefore thought, by its proponents, to be an equitable base for taxation.

Comprehesive income is not, however, a perfect tax. It has a number of drawbacks from the point of view of all three criteria outlined above. We begin with administrative simplicity, since some of the difficulties in administering the ideal tax also have efficiency and equity implications.

Administrative Simplicity

The difficulties involved in measuring all the components of comprehensive income are such that the base is, in practice, virtually impossible to implement. Comprehensive income as defined above to include consumption and net accruals to wealth cannot be measured as such. Instead, it has to be measured indirectly by measuring all sources of accrued income that are used to finance the consumption and wealth increases. Both imputed income and income passing through the market must be measured, and there are several problems with measuring income. Since all capital income must be measured as it accrues, capital gains should be included when the change in value of an asset occurs rather than when it is realized. This requires evaluating all forms of wealth held each tax year. Furthermore, such accrued capital gains have to be purged of their purely inflationary component by indexing to the rate of inflation and subtracting the inflationary gain from the nominal gain. Imputed forms of income would have to be included in the tax base—for example, the imputed rent on owner-occupied housing and other consumer durables. Negative forms of capital income (for example, interest payments) would have to be deducted from the base, again in real terms rather than nominal terms. Imputed forms of consumption such as the value of leisure and the value of household services would have to be included in the base. Human capital should also be depreciated and financing costs associated with it made deductible so that only the imputed return is taxable. Receipts of gifts and bequests could be deductible if they were not viewed as acts of consumption. Finally, one would presumably want to average the tax base over time, since comprehensive income tends to fluctuate from one year to the next, at least for some taxpayers.

---

[18] See United Kingdom, *Royal Commission on the Taxation of Profits and Income*, Second Report, Cmd. 9105 (London: HMSO, 1954).

The difficulties involved in including all of these items in the tax base implies that any actual tax base will deviate from comprehensive income. Pertinent to our purposes is the fact that not all forms of capital income will be treated symmetrically. Because of the difficulties of measuring imputed rent, owner-occupied housing and other durables will be favoured. The same applies to human capital investment. In addition, the inability to tax capital gains on accrual means that this form of capital income will be favoured unless the inability to index capital gains for inflation just happens to compensate.

Efficiency

Even a perfectly administered comprehensive income tax system would distort the operation of the market economy. Since part of the tax base is the return to holding assets (capital income in all its forms), the tax imposes a distortion on capital markets. From the point of view of the household, the tax on future consumption is heavier than the tax on present consumption, since the "price" of converting present consumption into future consumption is the rate of return on savings. The comprehensive income tax is said to impose a double tax on savings. The income tax will also impose a distortion on labour markets, since leisure is untaxed while wage payments are taxed. Furthermore, high wage jobs will be discriminated against relative to low wage jobs with the same skill in cases where the high wage compensates for a differential in job attractiveness, while the nonpecuniary benefit goes untaxed. The inability to index the tax system fully for inflation will imply that inflation itself will introduce further distortions into capital markets. The income tax system will also generally discriminate against marketable forms of income and favour imputed forms (for example, household services) that go untaxed.

Equity

The main equity argument against comprehensive income taxation is the equity argument in favour of the alternative approach, that is, consumption taxation. The concern is that under the comprehensive income tax future consumption is taxed more heavily than current consumption. We return to this below. In addition, actual income tax systems are virtually certain to violate horizontal equity norms. For one thing, in the absence of a perfect general averaging system, taxpayers with fluctuating incomes will be discriminated against, even though on average they are otherwise equally well off. For another, those taxpayers who obtain relatively larger proportions of their comprehensive income in an imputed form will be favoured compared with others on the same level of welfare. Imputed income can take the form of leisure or household production, imputed rent on consumer durables, the return to holding cash balances, and the rate of return on investment in human capital. The consumption tax base avoids all of these imputation problems except for the case of leisure or household production.

Personal Consumption Taxation

As the name implies, a personal consumption tax (PCT) has as its base the consumption of the taxpayer over the tax year. It therefore differs from the income base by excluding accretions of net wealth, or saving. The fact that it excludes wealth accumulation from the base need not imply, in itself, that the tax is in some sense less progressive than an income tax. One can apply whatever rate structure one wishes to this narrower base and achieve whatever degree of progressivity one desires. Of course, the progressivity will be defined in terms of consumption if that is decided to be the appropriate base, rather than income. Note also that a PCT differs from an indirect tax on consumption expenditures. The latter does not distinguish among taxpayers, and so is incapable of being made progressive with respect to the consumption of households except indirectly by the exemption of specific types of expenditures or multiple tax rates or both.

The fundamental argument for using consumption as a base rather than comprehensive income is based on equity considerations. The equity argument is also the most contentious, since it is based ultimately upon a value judgment with which reasonable persons can disagree. Therefore, we begin with a discussion of the equity effects of consumption taxation followed by considerations of administrative simplicity and efficiency.

Equity

The equity case for using consumption rather than income as the tax base consists mainly of the argument that a person's welfare depends upon the amount consumed rather than the amount of income earned. To use Kaldor's phrase, the tax base should be determined by what one "takes out of the social pot" rather than what one "contributes to the social pot."[19] Looking at it in another way, advocates of consumption taxation argue that the index for taxation ought to be some monetary measure of how well off one is. Aggregate consumption each year represents a proper index or "money metric" of utility that gives the correct weight to consumption in the present and future. It is therefore based on welfare economics theory. Income, on the other hand, discriminates against those who take their consumption in the future rather than the present. Savings are said to be "double-taxed." The income base is more appealing to those who wish the base to reflect potential ability to pay.

One problem with the consumption base is that not all consumption is taken in taxable form. Some is imputed, such as leisure and household services. A similar problem arises with respect to the comprehensive income base of which true consumption is also a component. In principle, either measured income or measured consumption could be a better approximation, or proxy, of true consumption. If future consumption is highly correlated with leisure and household services, income would be a better proxy,

---

[19]Kaldor was one of the early and most influential proponents of consumption as a base for personal taxation. See Nicholas Kaldor, *An Expenditure Tax* (London: Allen & Unwin, 1955).

while if ordinary measured consumption is better correlated with these imputed forms, the consumption base would be.

Administrative Simplicity

Whatever one thinks of the equity arguments for a personal consumption tax, the administrative simplicity arguments clearly favour the PCT over the PIT. It is true that the two share similar problems in defining certain imputed forms of consumption, such as the difficulty of taxing leisure and household production, but because of its treatment of capital income, a consumption base avoids the need to index capital income for inflation and the need to measure accrued capital gains, the imputed rent of consumer durables, the rate of return on human capital investment, and the accrued capital income from unincorporated business. In addition, the need for supplementary averaging of the tax base is much less in the case of a PCT than for a PIT. To see why, it is useful to outline how a PCT would operate.

If one wanted literally to define the tax base to be current consumption, the tax base would have to measure both the current purchases of nondurable consumer goods and the imputed consumption services obtained from consumer durables. Fortunately, there is another way. Since the present value of future consumer services equals the original purchase price of a durable, instead of taxing consumption services one can define the tax base to be consumption expenditures on a cash flow basis. This still seems to be a difficult task, since it could require the taxpayer (and the government) to keep track of all consumer expenditures. This too can be avoided, however, by recognizing that consumer expenditures equal income less saving, all defined on a cash flow basis. Thus, to arrive at one feasible consumption tax base, one could include all income on a cash flow basis and allow the consumer to deduct current savings (or add current dissavings). The deductibility of savings would be equivalent to a system of unlimited RRSP contributions and withdrawals. The consumer would have to "register" or "designate" and keep track of all savings and withdrawals from savings. The income concept that enters into the tax base is cash flow income, which avoids both the requirement to include accrued capital gains and the need to index capital income for inflation. (The tax brackets and exemption levels would still have to be indexed, however, to avoid "bracket creep.")

Although this definition of consumer expenditures as a base is feasible and reasonably straightforward, there are three difficulties with it. First, over a person's lifetime it would give rise to a very uneven tax base, since consumer expenditures on durables are very lumpy. Larger tax liabilities would occur at a stage in life when a taxpayer is least able to pay taxes—when consumer durables are being accumulated. Second, it would be cumbersome for a taxpayer to designate and keep track of all savings including small bank savings, and so on. Third, since dissavings would be taxable, the dissaving of consumer durables as their value is run down through use would be difficult to account for.

There is a solution to these problems as well. It comes from recognizing that the present value of the future capital income (net of economic rents) from a dollar's worth of savings is simply one dollar. Thus, instead of allowing savings to be deducted from income, the tax base would be equivalent in present value terms if the income from the savings were tax exempt. The consumption tax base could therefore be either cash flow income less savings or cash flow income net of capital income.

Combining both these ways of taxing asset accumulation would do away with the difficulties mentioned earlier. An ideal PCT would observe the following principles. All assets would be treated in one of the following ways: either (1) the savings to acquire assets would be "designated" and tax deductible and the running down of assets would be taxable, or (2) the assets would be neither deductible when accumulated nor taxable when they (and their income) were spent. The second choice is sometimes referred to as the "prepaid" method of taxing consumption. All assets that yield a return in an imputed form, including housing, would have to be treated on a prepaid basis (as is currently done). In this way, their imputed income would automatically be tax exempt. For similar reasons, unincorporated income would have to be treated on a designated (cash flow) basis. Since it is difficult to distinguish capital income from labour income in unincorporated business, it is not feasible to treat it on a prepaid basis and to exempt capital income only. Otherwise, the taxpayer would have the choice between treating each asset accumulated on a designated or on a prepaid basis. This would allow the taxpayer to arrange his affairs so as to achieve any lifetime profile of tax base desired—that is, to self-average.

The tax base thus described has a number of advantages over an income base, as already mentioned. Since incomes are always measured on a cash or realization basis, there is no need to tax capital gains on accrual. Nor is there any need to index capital income. Imputed capital income including imputed rent need not be measured at all; it can be excluded from the tax base if the assets giving rise to it are treated on a prepaid basis. Finally, averaging is less of a problem than under the PIT.

Efficiency

On efficiency grounds, the main difference between the PIT and the PCT is that the latter avoids the distortion on capital markets. That is, present consumption is not favoured relative to future consumption. This does not necessarily imply that the consumption tax will be more efficient (that is, have lower deadweight loss). Because the consumption tax base is smaller, tax rates must be higher to collect the same tax revenue. Hence the magnitude of remaining distortions is larger and the size of the distortion on labour markets will be larger. More generally, the removal of one distortion in an economy consisting of several distorted markets will not guarantee an improvement in efficiency. Thus, the efficiency case for a PCT is uncertain.

The Present Personal Tax System

Although the existing system of personal taxation is referred to as an income tax system, its base falls far short of comprehensive income. In fact, several of its provisions move the system in the direction of a consumption tax system, so much so that it could be argued that it is closer to a PCT than to a PIT.

If we focus our attention on the treatment of capital income and assets, we see that even when capital income does enter the tax base, it does not do so according to the requirements of a truly comprehensive income tax. Capital gains are taxed upon realization rather than on accrual. Also, capital income is not indexed for inflation to remove purely inflationary components. Furthermore, there are several provisions that are equivalent to treating capital income on a consumption tax basis—either by exempting capital income altogether (or disallowing interest costs) or by deducting saving and including dissaving. Housing and other durables are treated on a prepaid basis, since their imputed rent is tax-free. Returns to human capital investment are treated basically on a cash flow basis, since education costs are deductible and lifetime labour earnings are taxable. Some capital income goes tax-free by virtue of the $1,000 deduction on interest and dividends. Until 1985, capital gains themselves were only one-half taxed, and those realized on one's principal residence are exempt altogether. With the budget of May 1985, all capital gains were made exempt up to a lifetime maximum that will eventually reach $500,000. Savings that are taxed on a designated basis include registered retirement savings plans, registered pension plans, and deferred profit-sharing plans. Pension benefits are more favourably treated still, since the first $1,000 is exempt each year.

All in all, the availability of these various ways of sheltering savings or capital income implies that the personal tax system is not too different from a PCT except perhaps at high income levels. The only assets treated on a PIT basis are unincorporated business assets and those items of capital income that are taxable. It would be a reasonably simple matter to move the tax system all the way to a PCT, whereas it would be nearly impossible to make it a proper comprehensive income tax system. At the same time, it would be necessary to change the rate structure if one wanted the change to be distributionally neutral. One may even wish to reconsider whether bequests ought not to be taxed in their own right, though that is an issue that also arises under the PIT.

Corporate Income Taxation

Although corporations are legal entities, they are ultimately owned by individuals. Since the income paid out by corporations is taxed at the personal level, it is often argued that corporate income taxation constitutes double taxation of capital income. This was the view of the Carter Report, which argued that in an ideal world there should be no separate taxation of corporations. Recent economic literature has reconsidered this view by asking explicitly, what is the economic rationale for taxing corporations?

There are a number of reasons why an ideal tax system would include a CIT. The two most prominent ones, to which we shall devote our attention below, are that the CIT is potentially a fully efficient source of tax if the base is designed to be equivalent to economic rent, and that the CIT serves as a useful withholding device to prevent the postponement or outright avoidance of tax at the personal level. There are a number of other reasons sometimes cited that are, in our view, of somewhat lesser importance. One is simply that it is a good source of revenue relatively easily administered. Another is that it is a device whereby the government becomes a silent partner in all corporations and thereby helps them to spread their risks. According to this view, the tax is basically a tax on the equity income of the corporation. The loss-offsetting provisions of the Act mean that the government, as tax collector, is like a shareholder with no voting rights. It shares in the costs of investment (by tax deductions) and shares in the losses as well as the gains in income. In so doing, it effectively reduces the variability of the income earned by other shareholders and reduces the risk faced by the firm. A final argument for the CIT is that the existence of the tax provides the government with a policy instrument that it can use periodically to influence the allocation of investment across industries as well as in the aggregate. It does this by changing its system of credits and deductions, in line with its industrial policy goals or fiscal policy goals.

Our discussion will focus entirely on the rent collecting and withholding functions of the CIT. These seem to be the most fundamental reasons for the existence of the tax.

The CIT as a Tax on Pure Rents

Pure profits or rents exist whenever a firm is earning more revenues than are required to cover the full economic costs of generating the revenues. There are various reasons why rents exist in a market economy. Natural resource ownership will result in rents if the costs of production of the resource vary with the deposit found. The market price will be set by the most costly resource in production and owners of inframarginal resources will earn rents. Similarly other special advantages such as location, brand names, inventions, and the like can lead to rents. Another source of rents is the existence of monopoly power.

The taxation of economic rents provides an ideal source of taxation from an efficiency point of view. Since rents are a return over and above economic costs, a proportionate reduction in rents does not affect the investment and operating decisions of firms. Put differently, a tax on rents does not affect the marginal decisions of firms, since no rents accrue at the margin. Thus, if economic rents could be established as a tax base and a tax applied thereon, the tax would be fully efficient, or *neutral*. Such a tax is especially appropriate if the ownership of rents rests with the government. If the ownership of rent-generating property is deemed to be purely private, the tax may not be equitable either horizontally or vertically, since rents may not be allocated in a pattern corresponding to the way in which one would like to levy taxes. Furthermore, the burden of the introduction of such a tax would fall disproportionately upon members of the existing generation who hold rent-yielding property, since the value of this property would fall by the expected present value of all future tax payments. To the extent that future rents were anticipated, all of the tax on them would be capitalized. Nonetheless, if supplemented by other taxes better suited to fulfil equity objectives, a tax with economic rent as its base can be a useful component of a tax system.

If such a tax were feasible, it would be natural to design the CIT to correspond with economic rents. One possible route would be simply to define the tax base to be economic rent. All revenues would have to be included on an accrual basis, and all true economic costs would have to be deducted, again as they accrued. The economic costs would include all current costs, the replacement costs of using inventories, true economic depreciation (net of real capital gains) evaluated at replacement costs, and the full imputed real costs of finance (both debt and equity).

Such a tax base would be virtually impossible to administer. Many of the cost items are difficult to measure since there is no market price to which they correspond. Such things as the real cost of equity finance, the true rate of depreciation, and the replacement value of inventories used make a tax base that literally corresponds with economic rent administratively infeasible.

Fortunately, there is a tax base that is equivalent to economic rents in present value terms and that is straightforward to implement—namely, the *cash flow* of the firm. The cash flow of a firm engaged in productive activities (as opposed to financial intermediation) is defined as the revenues of the firm on a cash basis less all current and capital expenses net of disposals on a cash basis. No deductions are allowed for interest, depreciation, or depletion. It can readily be shown that the present value of this tax base is the same as the present value of economic rents. Thus, the tax will be neutral as regards the investment and production decisions of the firm.

For firms earning financial income, two alternatives are available. First, purely financial transactions can simply be ignored and only cash flows arising on production of goods and services taxed. This would be appropriate if it were deemed that financial intermediation gave rise to no significant rents. Alternatively, to capture rents arising from financial intermediation, the tax base could include investment income to the firm on a cash flow basis but allow the deduction of the purchase of financial assets.

A tax base thus defined, though it is very simple to administer, has one property that policy-makers will be concerned about. Relative to a tax on economic rents, the cash flow tax will yield revenues later in time. Indeed, for the new or growing firm, tax liabilities will be negative while investment is taking place and positive when the benefits are reaped. To be truly neutral, the government must make good on these negative tax liabilities, preferably by a system of full loss offsetting or refundability. For example, the government can pay the firm outright for any negative taxes owing. In addition to ensuring that the decisions of firms (including the incentive to take risk) are unaffected by the tax, this provides the firms with a source of external finance at a time when their cash flows most need financing. This may be particularly important for small firms with limited access to external sources of funds.

Of course, the government must find the financing to make the CIT fully refundable. From an economic point of view, this is a perfectly legitimate role for government debt. The refunding of negative tax liabilities is equivalent to the government's making a loan to the firm, which will be repaid with interest when tax liabilities become positive later on.

There may be political reasons why the government feels unable to provide the financing to make the CIT fully refundable. In this case, the cash flow tax could be amended so that it is nearly neutral and so that the government need never refund negative tax liabilities. There are two ways to achieve this. First, the government simply can keep an account of the tax credits owing a corporation and allow it to earn interest each year. The appropriate interest rate is the nominal risk-free cost of finance facing the firm. This cost of finance may be difficult to measure accurately, since it may not correspond with any observed rate of return on the market. Instead, the government may choose to use a nominal market interest rate, and that is why we say that the tax is only nearly neutral. If the firm is wound up and a credit is owing to it, then the credit should be paid to maintain tax neutrality.

The second method accomplishes the same thing but essentially has the firm keep track of its tax credits and liabilities. Instead of allowing the firm to write off all its expenditures as they occur, it limits the deductions the firm may write off by the revenues it receives. All unused deductions are then cumulated and held over to the following tax year. These cumulated unused deductions are compounded at the nominal rate of interest, and the resulting account is gradually written off as revenues allow. A still more general approach is to allow the firm to write off some proportion of its cumulated past expenditures each year, but instead of allowing the fund to compound at the rate of interest, allow as an additional write-off the nominal interest rate multiplied by the sum of past expenditures less past write-offs. It can be shown that if this procedure is followed, the tax system will be neutral regardless of what proportion of unused deductions is written off each year. [20] The proportion can be set arbitrarily and can vary from year to year provided the appropriate interest is given either by compounding the unused deductions or as a current deduction. The simplicity of these schemes means that neutral corporate taxation is feasible.

It should be noted again that although this type of tax is fully efficient and easy to administer, there may be some equity objections to it. The tax will be incident upon persons who own rent-generating property. The income from this property will be subject to "double taxation," once at the

---

[20]This method was analyzed in Robin W. Boadway and Neil Bruce, "A General Proposition on the Design of a Neutral Business Tax" (July 1984), 24 *Journal of Public Economics* 231-39.

corporate level and again at the personal level. It is important that no measure be taken to undo this double taxation, since rents should accrue to the government. In particular, the CIT on rents should not be integrated with the PIT. To give persons credit for taxes paid on their behalf by the corporation would imply that the PIT is the only tax payable on capital income. Because the PIT is incapable of differentiating rents from other types of capital income, the ability to tax rents would be lost.

By similar reasoning, unincorporated businesses, which pay their taxes at the personal level, could not be subject to a separate tax on their rents. This may not be too great a problem if the rents in the economy tend to accrue mainly to larger businesses. Difficulty may arise, however, if firms have an incentive to remain unincorporated to avoid being liable for the rent tax.

The CIT as a Withholding Tax

The use of the CIT as a neutral tax on rents has dominated the work of academic economists on the subject. Policy-makers and practitioners, however, have tended to view the tax as a withholding device. Indeed, the Carter Report argued that this was the only rationale for the CIT, since an equitable tax system should ideally tax only persons. Thus, any effects the CIT might otherwise have on its own should be undone by a system of complete integration with the PIT.

To justify a role for the CIT as a withholding device, it must be the case that the PIT is not properly taxing all capital income generated by the corporation. This can occur when the existence of corporations allows owners to postpone tax liabilities or to avoid them altogether. There are two circumstances in which an argument can be made for withholding. First, it is desired to tax persons on a comprehensive income basis but if capital gains are taxed on realization rather than accrual (or if they are preferentially taxed), there will be an incentive for shareholders to postpone tax liabilities by retaining earnings within the corporation and postponing realization of the capital gains that result. Taxing the income at source in the corporation and giving full credit to the shareholder for corporate taxes paid when income is removed from the corporation will avoid this problem. Of course, if the personal tax were based upon consumption rather than comprehensive income, withholding tax against capital income generated at the corporate level would be unnecessary, since this income would be effectively untaxed at the personal level anyway.

The second argument for withholding results from the fact that many corporations have foreign shareholders. Since these shareholders are not subject to Canadian personal taxation, capital income earned by them in Canada would otherwise go untaxed, except for the explicit nonresident withholding taxes that exist. The decision to withhold taxes on foreigners by way of the CIT is seldom taken without consulting other countries. Other countries have their own corporate tax systems, and the important question is whether these tax systems allow credits for taxes paid by foreign corporations in Canada. The question of whether both countries used income or consumption as their tax base is also relevant. If all countries adopted consumption taxation, they might agree that the use of the CIT for withholding was unnecessary.

Assuming that withholding is a legitimate objective for the CIT, let us consider the design of the tax base that will accomplish it. Ideally, the tax should apply to all capital income generated at source. This is equivalent to value added less wage payments, or total revenues less current costs including wages less true depreciation at replacement cost. Such a tax base will withhold tax against all forms of capital income including both income to equity owners and interest income. When the income reaches the hands of domestic asset owners, there will have to be a mechanism whereby credit is given to persons for corporate taxes paid on their behalf. This can be accomplished by grossing up the capital income by the corporate taxes paid and giving a tax credit for the same taxes once personal tax liabilities have been credited.

This ideal withholding tax is difficult to implement because of the need to measure true depreciation. It is also apparently difficult to implement fully on political grounds, since in virtually all tax systems, interest payments are also deductible from the corporate tax base. Consequently, no withholding is done against interest income generated at source. This is no particular problem in regard to domestic taxpayers, since interest income can readily be taxed at the personal level, but it does imply that no tax is withheld at the corporate level against interest income accruing to foreigners. If the interest income is earned by a foreigner who can credit Canadian corporate taxes against foreign tax liabilities, then there is a loss in tax revenue to Canada and a gain to foreign treasuries. Only foreign corporations, not individuals, can credit Canadian corporate taxes. If Canada were to disallow deductions of interest, however, foreign corporations would be unable to fully credit Canadian taxes, since Canada's tax base would be too wide.

It should be noted that the ideal withholding tax (with or without interest deductibility) differs from the ideal tax on economic rents. The withholding tax includes the full amount of capital income in its base (or all of equity income if interest is deductible), while the rent tax only includes that portion that is due to economic rents. As well, the withholding tax is fully credited at the personal level, while the rent tax is not. That does not mean that both cannot be incorporated into the same CIT system. It is possible to design a system under which part of the revenue is collected as part of a rent tax and part as a withholding tax.[21]

Even a CIT that withheld against all equity income might be too broadly based. If domestic personal taxation is on a consumption basis, there is no need to withhold on corporate retained earnings. Also, if foreign tax credits

---

[21]This is discussed further in Robin W. Boadway, Neil Bruce, and Jack Mintz, "The Role and Design of the Corporate Income Tax" (1984), Vol. 86, no. 2 *The Scandinavian Journal of Economics* 286-99.

operate mainly on the repatriation of earnings (as is the case for U.S. subsidiary firms), then there is no need to withhold tax on corporate retentions. In these circumstances, a case can be made for basing the CIT on equity income less retentions, or, equivalently, on dividends. This alternative CIT is considered more fully in Chapter 5.

The Existing CIT System

The CIT as it is presently constituted achieves neither the withholding nor the rent-taxing objectives. Instead, it contains elements of both. It is probably reasonable to suggest that the tax is viewed by policy-makers more as a withholding tax than a tax on rents, and that fact is reflected in its design. It is roughly a tax on equity income of the corporation but, as such, has several shortcomings. Integration is less than full for the large taxpaying firms since the effective dividend credit rate is based on a corporation's paying corporate taxes at a 25 per cent rate. The deduction for depreciation is unlikely to approximate true depreciation; the rates are higher than true depreciation and the base is historical cost rather than replacement cost. Inventories are also costed using historical (FIFO) costs rather than replacement costs, and interest is deducted in nominal rather than real terms. The consequence is a tax base that withholds only approximately against equity income and that is imperfectly integrated and is therefore distortionary. Exactly how distortionary it is will be discovered in Chapter 3.

Despite all the emphasis in the economics literature, the use of the CIT as a rent collector is basically abrogated, even in those industries in which rents are likely to be considerable—that is, the resource industries. Indeed, in the resource industries, the tax system, if anything, appears to be overly generous in its deductions. Even though taxes are collected from these industries, the structure of the taxes used (for example, royalties and mining taxes) is often far removed from a tax on pure rents. From an economic point of view, one of the potentially useful tax reforms that could be undertaken would be to use a proper rent tax (possibly of the cash flow sort) to collect rents efficiently from the resource industries. There is no reason such a tax cannot exist side by side with a CIT devoted to withholding. We will return to these issues in the final chapter.

2

The Theory of Effective Tax Rates

Introduction

The main device that we use in evaluating the incentive effects of capital taxation on the investment decisions by firms is the *effective tax rate* as outlined in Chapter 1. The effective tax as defined here[1] is the difference between the *required gross (of tax) real return* on an investment r_g and the *net (of tax) real return* to the ultimate saver r_n. The effective tax can be expressed as a rate in proportion to the required gross of tax real return or the net of tax return to the saver. The required gross real return is the rate of return that an investment must earn per period before taxes at all levels in order to be just profitable to the firm (that is, in order to just cover all economic costs). The net real return is the return to the ultimate saver after taxes at all levels have been paid and adjustments have been made for the loss in purchasing power of the funds saved as a result of inflation.

In measuring effective tax rates, careful attention must be paid to the openness of Canadian capital markets. Much of the earlier work in effective tax rates examined the impact of both corporate and personal taxes on capital investment and savings in an economy closed to international capital markets. The underlying assumption of this analysis was that firms, owned by domestic savers, would issue financial instruments (bonds and equity) so that the after-tax risk-adjusted rate of return on these assets was the same. An increase in either corporate or personal taxes on capital would reduce both savings and investment depending on the sensitivity of corporate investment and household savings decisions to changes in rates of return on assets.

In an open economy, such as that of Canada, it is reasonable to assume that world interest rates are affected neither by Canadian investment and savings levels nor by Canadian capital taxes. That is, market interest rates in Canada are determined by world capital markets. In this case we can separate the effective tax rate into two components: (1) the effect of taxes that are applied at the personal level and that affect saving behaviour in Canada, and (2) the effect of taxes that are applied at the level of the firm and that affect business investment decisions. The first component is

---

[1] This is the definition commonly used in the literature. See, for example, Robin Boadway, Neil Bruce, and Jack Mintz, "Taxation, Inflation and the Effective Marginal Tax Rate on Capital in Canada" (February 1984), 17 *Canadian Journal of Economics* 62-79; Mervyn A. King and Don Fullerton, eds., *The Taxation of Income from Capital: A Comparative Study of the U.S., U.K., Sweden, and West Germany* (Chicago: the University Press, 1984).

assumed to be uniform across industries and types of physical capital (although varying by financial instrument). The second varies by industry and type of physical capital, thereby "distorting" investment decisions relative to those that would be made in the absence of taxation.

There remains some controversy as to how "open" capital markets are in Canada. Bond interest rates are clearly set in international markets, but it has been argued that the cost of equity funds is determined by Canadian savings behaviour. There is evidence, however, that for publicly traded securities, the cost of equity funds is determined by international capital markets. For example, many Canadian shares are listed on both the Toronto and New York stock exchanges—the value of these shares is largely determined by international traders. Even for those shares that are not interlisted between exchanges, foreigners are not prevented from conducting transactions in Canadian markets. Private corporations, however, tend to be marginally financed by Canadians, so that personal taxation could have some effect on their cost of equity funds. Our theory and empirical work can handle both an open and a partially open capital market assumption.

The purpose of this chapter is to derive the expressions for the effective tax rates, which will then be evaluated for different firms of various sizes and types and different types of capital in the next chapter. To this end, we use the "neoclassical" theory of the firm. This theory is based on the assumption that the managers of the firm maximize the present value of the firm's payments to its owners. In the next section, we provide an intuitive derivation of the expressions we use in our evaluations. Our theoretical discussion is based on the tax system that was in existence before the 1985-1986 changes, since that is the tax system used in our empirical work. Thus, we include in our discussion the inventory allowance and the investment tax credit, which were eliminated or phased out by the February 1986 budget.

The Required Return on Investments in Physical Capital, r_g

Consider a firm that generates active business income by producing a commodity or service by using current inputs such as labour, intermediate goods, raw materials, and the services of physical capital such as plant and equipment, buildings, land, and inventories.[2] Although the firm may also hold financial assets that provide a direct stream of returns, for now our focus is on physical capital. We will discuss financial assets later in the chapter.

Investment activities by the firm involve the acquisition of physical capital to augment or replace its existing capital stock. Under the assumption that managers seek to maximize the present value of the income that the firm pays to shareholders, discounted by the shareholders' discount rate, any investment will be undertaken if it increases the market value of the firm's equity. This occurs if the incremental unit of capital, when added

---

[2]The firm may also use proprietory capital such as productive know-how, reputation, and organizational know-how. These "soft" forms of capital are ignored for our purposes.

to the firm's productive capacity, provides a stream of real returns that is sufficient to cover all of the costs associated with the investment. Specifically, the present value of the real returns to the investment when discounted at the appropriate interest rate must be no less than the present value of the economic costs.[3] Of course, tax factors that affect these returns and costs must be considered. Under the additional assumption that a firm's financial policy is determined independently of the firm's capital decision, it can be shown that a firm maximizing the present value of income accruing to both debt and equity owners (discounted by a weighted average of the bond and equity owners' discount rate) will be equivalent to a firm maximizing the value of its equity.[4] This relationship between equity and firm-value maximization will be used below in our discussion of alternative rates.

The costs associated with an investment can be expressed on a per period basis. This is sometimes referred to as the *user cost* or *implicit rental cost* of using a dollar of capital for one period. This user cost consists of two parts. The first is the *real cost of finance*, which results from the payments the firm must make on funds raised to purchase the physical asset. The second is the *capital consumption cost*, which results from the loss in the value of the capital asset due to depreciation, obsolescence, and changes in the prices of capital goods. We derive the cost of finance first, in the following section.

The Real Cost of Finance Through Debt and Equity

To purchase a physical capital asset, the firm can raise the necessary funds from three sources. It can (1) issue bonds or take out loans (both of which we will refer to as debt finance), (2) issue new equity shares, or (3) use the firm's retained earnings instead of paying them out as dividends. The last two methods are alternative ways of financing through equity. In order to borrow a dollar through issuing debt, the firm must make interest payments at the market rate i per dollar borrowed. The after-tax nominal cost of a dollar of debt finance is $i(1 - u)$, where u is the corporate tax rate, since interest payments on debt are deductible in calculating taxable corporate in-

---

[3] Economic costs may be defined as wages and accrued current costs, replacement cost of depreciation, the real cost of financing, and corporate taxes payable. These costs will differ from accounting income to the extent that (1) accounting depreciation is based on historical costs and is at the incorrect rate, (2) some assets are expensed rather than being depreciated (research and development, advertising, etc.), (3) borrowing costs (without any adjustment for inflation) are deductible but equity costs are not, and (4) no valuation for the cost of risk is included in accounting costs.

[4] This equivalence is demonstrated in A. J. Auerbach, "Wealth Maximization and the Cost of Capital" (August 1979), 93 *Quarterly Journal of Economics* 433-46.

come.[5] The *real* after-tax cost for one period of finance through corporate debt, denoted r_b, is given by

$$r_b = i(1 - u) - \pi \qquad (2.1)$$

where π is the general inflation rate. The inflation rate is subtracted from the after-tax nominal interest rate to take into account the reduction in the real (or constant dollar) value of the corporate debt over the period because of inflation.

The firm that raises financial funds through new equity, either by issuing new shares or retaining dividends, must pay out a certain nominal yield in dividends or capital gains on the new equity in order for households (or other institutions) to hold it. We denote this nominal yield as ρ per dollar of equity and assume it to be the same for retained earnings and new equity finance. The real yield on equity is denoted r_e and is given by

$$r_e = \rho - \pi. \qquad (2.2)$$

In general, r_e and r_b may vary, because of risk, transaction costs, and the differential tax treatment of interest, capital gains, and dividends.

The Overall Cost of Finance

As discussed above, the firm can finance its investments through debt or equity; consequently the one-period real costs per dollar of funds from the respective sources, denoted r_b and r_e, may differ. To obtain an overall cost of finance to the firm, which is denoted r_f, we take a weighted average of r_b and r_e, where the weights are equal to the fraction of an extra dollar of finance obtained from each source. Specifically, we use

$$\begin{aligned} r_f &= \beta r_b + (1 - \beta) r_e \\ &= \beta i(1 - u) + (1 - \beta)\rho - \pi \end{aligned} \qquad (2.3)$$

where β is the fraction of an extra dollar of finance raised through debt. We assume debt and equity financing decisions are independent of the use to which financing is put. That is, the same ratio of debt to equity applies to all types of investment.

Even though this expression can be calculated from observed data, it is necessary to justify its use. For example, because one would expect a profit-maximizing firm to use only the least-cost source of finance, the procedure of using a weighted average of the costs of two different sources appears inappropriate. In fact, the weighted average is the correct marginal cost of finance under some special, but for our purposes not unreasonable, circumstances.

---

[5] In this section we assume that the firm always has sufficient taxable income against which to deduct interest and other costs. The problem of "imperfect loss offset" that occurs when this is not true and the tax system does not refund negative taxes owing is dealt with below, in the section entitled "Some Complications."

The main idea is that r_b and r_e represent the average (per dollar cost) of a dollar of debt and equity but not the *marginal* cost of an extra dollar from the respective sources. The marginal or incremental cost of funds from each source takes into account the effect of an extra dollar of debt or equity on the returns the firm must pay on its liabilities as a result of changes in the firm's financial structure—specifically, its debt-equity ratio.

Following one strand in the financial literature,[6] we assume that a firm's debt-equity ratio is important to the holder of the firm's securities. A higher debt-equity ratio raises the probability of bankruptcy by the firm, because of the accompanying fixed interest obligations. Such obligations mean that a possible interruption in revenues or an increase in operating costs could force the firm into liquidating its assets or winding up on unfavourable terms. This could result in the firm's declaring bankruptcy with its associated costs. Bankruptcy costs entail direct costs (the cost of hiring lawyers, trustees) and indirect costs (loss in sales due to the threat of bankruptcy). Therefore, creditors are willing to lend to a firm with a higher debt-equity ratio only at a higher interest rate, which compensates them for their increased exposure to the bankruptcy costs. The marginal cost of raising a dollar through debt thus exceeds r_b, because an extra dollar of debt raises the debt-equity ratio and the interest rate that the firm must pay on its existing debt.[7] Correspondingly, the marginal cost of raising a dollar of equity is less than r_e, since an increment in equity lowers the debt-equity ratio and the interest rate the firm must pay on its outstanding debt.

The foregoing analysis explains why the firm will diversify its financial structure even when r_b and r_e are different. Furthermore, in special circumstances the marginal cost of funds to the firm will be exactly equal to the weighted average of r_b and r_e. Specifically, we assume that the optimal way of financing an extra dollar of investment is the same regardless of the amount to be financed. This means that the firm's optimal financial structure is determined separately from the firm's optimal level of investment.

The firm's optimal financial structure will be the one that minimizes the real cost per dollar of finance by the firm. Suppose, as seems likely, that r_b is considerably less than r_e when the firm's debt-equity ratio is very low. Then the cost per dollar of finance can be reduced by adding debt and reducing equity. As the debt-equity ratio rises, so does the interest rate on the firm's debt, but this is initially more than offset by corporate tax savings arising from issuing debt, since interest is deductible from corporate taxable income. The firm continues to issue debt until the marginal increase in bankruptcy cost via higher interest costs equals the corporate tax savings of

6This procedure can be justified using the "static trade-off" theory of finance, where the tax advantage of issuing debt is offset by the increased bankruptcy and agency cost of issuing debt. See S. C. Myers, *Capital Structure Puzzle*, National Bureau of Economic Research Discussion Paper no. 1393 (Cambridge, Mass.: the Bureau, 1984). For an elaboration of various theories see Jan Bartholdy, Gordon Fisher, and Jack Mintz, *Taxation and the Financial Policy of Firms: Theory and Empirical Applications to Canada*, Discussion Paper no. 324 (Ottawa: Economic Council of Canada, 1987).

7We assume, for simplicity of exposition, that all debt is short-term and is rolled over at the existing interest rate.

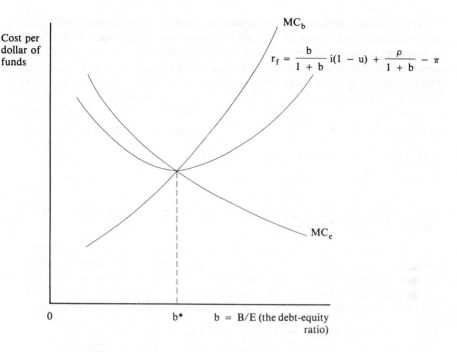

Figure 2.1   **Marginal and Average Costs of Finance**

issuing debt. Increasing the leverage of the firm beyond this point would increase the cost of finance to the firm.

The relationship between marginal and average finance costs is illustrated in Figure 2.1. In this figure, the marginal cost of debt (MC_b) is the extra financial costs incurred when the firm's debt is increased by \$1 and the firm's equity is held constant. MC_b is shown as increasing as the debt-equity ratio of the firm (b) is increased, because an extra unit of debt, other things being equal, raises the debt-equity ratio of the firm and, correspondingly, the interest rate the firm faces on its debt. The marginal cost of equity (MC_e) is the extra financial costs incurred when the firm's equity is increased by \$1 and the firm's debt is held constant. The marginal cost of equity declines as the debt-equity ratio increases, because an extra unit of equity, other things being equal, lowers the debt-equity ratio and the interest rate the firm faces on its debt. Note that the "marginal cost" of funds from each source incorporates the effect of the change in the debt-equity ratio on the firm's borrowing rate, so that it does not equal r_b or r_e.[8]

---

[8]Formally, let $C = (r_b \cdot B) + (r_c \cdot E)$. Then $MC_b = \frac{\partial C}{\partial B} = r_b + b \cdot \frac{\partial r_b}{\partial b} > r_b$ is increasing in b. Also, $MC_e = -b^2 \frac{\partial r_b}{\partial b} + r_e < r_e$ is decreasing in b if $\frac{\partial^2 r_b}{\partial^2 b}$ is small. Finally, setting $MC_b = MC_e$ we get $r_e - r_b = b(1 + b)\frac{\partial r_b}{\partial b}$, which is exactly the condition for $\partial r_f / \partial b = 0$. Thus, with the second order condition met, r_f is minimized.

The weighted average cost of finance to the firm (r_f) is shown on the diagram as initially declining as b increases, reaching a minimum at the point where the marginal cost of debt is just equal to the marginal cost of equity, and then rising. At this point, r_f is also equal to MC_b and MC_e. This defines the optimal debt-equity ratio b*. The firm is indifferent between debt and equity as long as it finances its investments so as to maintain this desired debt-equity ratio.[9] The fraction of debt issued on an extra dollar of finance (β) is given by $\beta = \dfrac{B}{E + B}$. Dividing the numerator and denominator by E we obtain the relationship between β and the debt-equity ratio b. It is

$$\beta = \frac{B/E}{1 + B/E} = \frac{b^*}{1 + b^*} \tag{2.4}$$

assuming that the firm maintains its optimal debt-equity ratio b* when financing marginal investments.

The cost of finance variable (r_f) given by equation 2.3 is very important in our analysis. In addition to being a major component of the user cost of capital, it is also the "real interest rate" to the firm. That is, r_f represents the rate at which all receipts to and outlays by the firm occurring at different times are made comparable through discounting and compounding.

Costs Resulting from the Depreciation of Investment Goods

For a physical asset that does not wear out or change in real value in any way, the real cost of finance is the user cost, as given in equation 2.3. Assets such as plant, equipment, and buildings "depreciate" as they wear out and/or become obsolete. Also, they may increase or decrease in real (constant dollar) value because of relative price changes—that is, changes in the prices of investment goods may change at a rate different from the overall inflation rate. Tax deductions are allowed for the costs of depreciation, but these deductions are usually quite different from the actual change in the real value of the asset ("true economic depreciation") for reasons discussed in Chapter 1. Also, firms are permitted a tax credit for qualifying investment expenditures. Our purpose in this section is to analyze how these factors can be incorporated into the required return on capital.[10]

First, we ignore the investment tax credit and the capital cost allowance (CCA). We assume that the capital wears out physically at a constant declining-balance rate δ.[11] That is, the productivity of a unit of capital declines by the amount δ in each period. Also, let q be the relative price of investment goods (that is, the price index of investment goods divided by a general price index) at a point of time, and let Δq be the change in the relative price of investment goods at a point in time. We can then add

---

[9]We have assumed a unique optimal debt-equity ratio. In fact, the marginal cost curves and the weighted average could flatten out, giving an optimal debt-equity range.

[10]The February 1986 budget phases out the investment tax credit concept for certain special cases. See Chapter 1 for details.

[11]The simplifying assumption of declining-balance depreciation does not seriously limit the applicability of our analysis, since any depreciation schedule can be duplicated by a declining-balance schedule where the depreciation rate varies over time.

($\delta - \Delta q/q$) to r_f to get the one-period real cost of holding one dollar in physical capital. It is equal to r_f (the real cost of finance to the firm) plus δ (the physical rate of depreciation) less $\Delta q/q$ (the rate of change in the real value of the capital). Note that if $\Delta q/q$ is positive, the cost of holding the capital is reduced because of the real capital gains accruing on the capital, whereas if $\Delta q/q$ is negative, the cost of holding the capital is increased.

Now it is necessary to take into account the investment tax credit and CCA. To begin with, if the purchase of capital qualifies for the investment tax credit, a dollar spent on capital will actually cost the firm only $(1-\phi)$, where ϕ is the investment tax credit rate. (For example, the 7 per cent investment tax credit rate means $\phi = 0.07$). Second, the purchase of a dollar of capital by the firm makes possible a stream of future CCA deductions. These will be accounted for in our calculations by deducting from the investment expenditure of one dollar an amount equal to the present value (to the firm) of these future tax deductions. We assume for simplicity that a tax depreciation schedule with a constant declining-balance rate of depreciation equal to d is permitted for tax purposes. That is, in each tax period the firm can deduct from its taxable income a fraction d of the undepreciated value of its capital.

In the first period, therefore, the purchase of a dollar of capital gives rise to a tax deduction of d times the corporate tax rate u, or ud. Future tax deductions decline in real value for three reasons. First, the undepreciated value of the asset declines over time at rate d. Second, the tax authorities permit only the historical (purchase) dollar value of an asset to be depreciated for tax purposes. If the general price level in the economy is rising at rate π, then the real value of the permitted depreciation deduction is expected to decline at the rate π. Finally, real flows occurring in the future are worth less to the firm because of discounting. The rate for discounting real flows received by or paid out by the firm is r_f, the real cost of finance to the firm. (It could be argued that to the extent that future tax savings from CCA deductions are risk-free, a risk-free discount rate should be used for discounting them, rather than r_f, which may include a risk premium.)

We can use the well-known perpetuity formula for finding the present value of the future tax deductions for capital cost, which we denote Z. It is,

$$Z = \frac{ud}{r_f + \pi + d}. \tag{2.5}$$

This expression is strictly correct only if the tax rate u, the real cost of finance to the firm r_f, the expected inflation rate π, and the allowed depreciation rate d are anticipated to be constant over the future.[12]

---

[12]Technically, the real discounted value of the tax deduction for depreciation that the firm can claim t periods in the future on a dollar of capital purchased now is

$$ud \times e^{-(r_f + \pi + d)t}$$

Thus, the present value of the entire stream of future tax deductions on a dollar of capital purchased now is found by summing (integrating) the stream or

(Continued on next page.)

The Required Return on Depreciable Capital

Canadian tax law allows only the firm's investment expenditures net of the investment tax credit to be added to the yet undepreciated stock of capital of the firm. Thus the effective price of a dollar of capital to the firm is $(1 - \phi)(1 - Z)$, where ϕ is the investment tax credit and Z is given by equation 2.5. For example, if $\phi = 0.07$ (an investment tax credit of 7 per cent) and $Z = 0.25$, a dollar of capital would have an effective price to the firm of $(1 - 0.07)(1 - 0.25) \approx 0.70$ dollars after the investment tax credit and present value of depreciation deductions are taken into account.

The cost of holding a (constant) dollar of capital for one period is equal to the effective price of a dollar of capital to the firm $[(1 - \phi) \times (1 - Z)]$ times $(r_f + \delta - \Delta q/q)$. For the marginal investment, this cost is equal to the marginal net revenues (revenues less wages and other current costs) generated by capital. These revenues are taxed at the corporate tax rate u. If we define R_g as the marginal return to capital gross of corporate taxes and all capital costs, then $R_g(1 - u)$ is the marginal return to capital after corporate taxes on net revenues. For the marginal investment, $R_g(1 - u)$ would be equal to cost of capital, which is $(r_f + \delta - \Delta q/q)(1 - \phi)(1 - Z)$. If we divide both terms by $(1 - u)$, we derive an expression where the gross of tax real return to capital is set equal to the *user cost of capital*:

$$R_g = (r_f + \delta - \Delta q/q)(\frac{1 - \phi}{1 - u})(1 - \frac{ud}{r_f + \pi + d}). \qquad (2.6)$$

The right-hand side of equation 2.6 is the gross real rate of return the investment must earn in order to be just profitable to the firm and is denoted as the user cost of capital. Part of R_g is used to maintain the real value of the capital stock in the firm, part of it goes to the revenue authorities, and the rest goes to the saver. We subtract $(\delta - \Delta q/q)$ from R_g to obtain the real rate of return before taxes that must be earned by a profitable investment after enough has been subtracted to maintain the real value of the capital stock. We call this amount the *required gross of tax rate of return* and denote it r_g, thus

$$r_g = R_g - \delta + \Delta q/q. \qquad (2.6.1)$$

The return r_g is partly paid out to the tax authorities in corporate taxes, and the remainder is paid out to the holders of the firm's securities—who in turn pay part of such receipts to the government in personal taxes. It is the real rate of return to the economy from a marginal investment. Note that for nondepreciable assets (for example, land), the physical rate of depreciation, investment tax credit, and capital cost allowance are all zero, so $r_g = (r_f - \Delta q/q)/(1 - u)$.

---

[12]Continued . . .

$$Z = \int_{t = 0}^{\infty} ud \times e^{-(r_f + \pi + d)t}\, dt$$

If u, d, r_f, and π are constant over time, mathematical integration yields the expression in equation 2.5.

The required real return can be calculated given the interest rate on corporate debt (i), the nominal return on equity (ρ), the inflation rate (π), the rate of change in the relative price of capital goods ($\Delta q/q$), the proportional investment financed by new debt (β) and new equity ($1 - \beta$), the investment tax credit rate (ϕ), the corporate tax rate (u), the physical depreciation rate (δ), and the CCA rate (d). This value will vary from industry to industry and across types of capital. We are particularly interested in how the tax parameters (u, ϕ, and d) influence the average value of r_g and the extent to which they cause r_g to vary across industries and types of capital. Thus r_g provides a summary measure of how the tax system distorts the level and type of investments that firms undertake. We use r_g in calculating the effective tax rate on depreciable capital.

The Required Return on Inventory Capital

Firms generally hold stocks of raw materials, real property, and final goods in order to facilitate production and exchange. Also, since production takes time, value-added is tied up as work-in-progress. This type of inventory capital does not depreciate, but its holding cost differs from the cost of finance to the firm (r_f) because of the way inventory must be costed for tax purposes.[13] As discussed in Chapter 1, firms in Canada generally must use first in, first out (FIFO) accounting methods for costing inventory. Also, a tax deduction equal to some fraction of the beginning of the year value of the inventory stock was allowed before 1987. Let us now examine how these factors determine the required return on an extra dollar of inventory capital.

To simplify matters, we assume that the physical stock of inventory remains constant over time and turns over at a constant rate. We also assume that the average holding time of a unit of inventory under the FIFO rule is equal to the period for which taxes are collected.[14] We know that, in the absence of the FIFO rules and the inventory allowance, the real holding cost of a dollar of inventory would be ($r_f - \Delta q/q$) where r_f is the real cost of finance to the firm and $\Delta q/q$ is the rate of change in the relative price of goods in inventory (that is, real capital gains).

Under the FIFO accounting rules, an extra unit of inventory imposes an additional cost of $u\gamma$ per period where γ is the rate of change in the money price of the goods in inventory (that is, $\gamma = \pi + \Delta q/q$). Over the holding period, the price of the goods in inventory has risen at the rate γ. Goods taken out of inventory are thus sold for a price that is $(1 + \gamma)$ times greater than the price at which they were put into inventory. Because the latter is the

---

[13]Also, there may be direct holding costs for inventory in the form of storage costs or waste. We ignore these costs since we cannot evaluate them.

[14]Elsewhere, we determine a general expression for the required return on inventory when the holding period of inventory exceeds the taxation period. See R. W. Boadway, N. Bruce, and J. Mintz, "Corporate Taxation and the Cost of Holding Inventories" (May 1982), 15 *Canadian Journal of Economics* 278-93. In fact, our estimates of the inventory holding period indicate that it is approximately one-quarter of a year, so we use the expression discussed in the text.

cost allowed under FIFO, a capital gain of γ is added to corporate income and is subject to tax. The inflation-induced component of γ is, of course, spurious in the sense that the real value of the goods in inventory is unchanged.

The inventory tax deduction (used from 1977 to 1986) allows some fraction v (where v = 0.03 or 3 per cent in Canada) of the FIFO value of the inventory stock to be deducted from taxable income, yielding a tax saving of uv. Thus the holding cost of a unit of inventory is $r_f - \Delta q/q + u(\gamma - v)$. The holding of a unit of inventory earns a return to the firm by increasing revenues and/or reducing current costs. The former is taxable while the latter is deductible, so we gross up this holding cost by dividing it by (1 − u) as we did with depreciable capital. This gives us the required return gross of corporate taxes that the marginal inventory investment must earn to be just profitable. Thus, the gross return on inventory capital (before 1987) is given by

$$r_g = \frac{r_f - \Delta q/q + u(\gamma - v)}{1 - u}.$$

(2.7)

This expression can then be evaluated along with the expressions for r_g for other types of capital.

Some Complications

Imperfect Loss Offsets

In this study, we assume that losses and gains are treated symmetrically by the tax system (that is, no distinction is drawn between positive and negative tax liability situations). Such symmetry would be valid only if there were full loss offsetting—that is, if negative taxes could effectively be fully realized by the taxpayer either through refundability in the current period, marketable tax losses, or unlimited carryback and carryforward with interest cost.

The Canadian tax system at both the personal and corporate levels falls short of this full loss-offset ideal. Carryback is limited, and the carryforward of losses and unused deductions is not with interest. Refundability of tax losses is generally not available. As a result, negative tax liabilities have a lower value to the firm than the amount recorded, and tax savings from deductions to firms in a tax loss position are less valuable.

The above discussion suggests that our expressions for the required return on capital in the section on "The Required Return on Depreciable Capital" understate this variable. But this is the case only because we are considering the cost deduction side of the problem alone. Revenues on marginal investments made by firms that are in a nontaxable position during some time periods go partly untaxed as well. For example, if a firm is never in a taxable position, the required rate of return on the marginal investment is independent of the corporate tax rate, because neither revenues nor costs are affected.

More generally, firms that are in a nontaxable position part of the time will find the value of their deductions reduced because of the absence of full loss-offset. During loss periods, firms can defer their deductions through loss carryforwards or by not taking the CCA. This reduces the value of their deductions (because future deductions are discounted), say by proportion f, which we assume to be the same for all types of deductions and credits. At the same time, any marginal revenues generated during these loss periods bear no tax. Suppose this effectively reduces the tax applying to revenues in some proportion that we call g. The required real rate of return gross of corporate taxes and depreciation is now given by

$$(r_g)' = (r_f' + \delta - \Delta q/q)(\frac{1 - \phi(1 - f)}{1 - u(1 - g)})(1 - \frac{ud(1 - f)}{r_f' + \pi + d}) \qquad (2.6')$$

where the real cost of interest contained in r_f' is equal to

$$r_b' = i[1 - u(1 - f)] - \pi. \qquad (2.1')$$

Clearly the net effect on the required rate of return depends on the relative sizes of f and g.

Mintz included imperfect loss offsetting in effective tax rate calculations for Canada.[15] He computed the present value of losses written off for various industries. Applying these measures to effective tax rates, he found that effective tax rates were higher for corporations that were sometimes not taxable, when compared with taxpaying firms. If firms had large banks of losses and expected not to pay taxes for several years, then effective tax rates were lower on highly taxed assets and higher on assets with fast write-offs for loss firms than they were for taxable firms.

The Cost of Risk

We developed our expressions for the required return on capital and the effective tax rate in the context of a risk-free environment. When investments pay returns that are uncertain, there is a cost associated with the risk of the investment. If households in the economy are averse to risk, they will value the uncertain stream of returns to an investment at less than its actuarial value. Accordingly, a risky investment requires a higher expected return to compensate investors for the cost of risk.

For our purposes, the primary concern is the degree to which the cost of risk is affected by corporate and personal taxes. We are interested in the degree to which the effective tax rates calculated for an environment of certainty apply equally in the case of uncertainty.

The effect of taxes on the cost of risk depends on the amount of loss offsetting permitted by the tax system. It has been shown in a relatively general context that full loss offsetting is equivalent to allowing a deduction for the

---

[15] Jack M. Mintz, *An Empirical Estimate of Imperfect Loss Offsetting and Effective Tax Rates,* Discussion Paper no. 634 (Kingston, Ontario: Institute for Economic Research, Queen's University, 1985).

cost of risk,[16] since the government shares both gains and losses on income owing to investors. A tax with a full loss offset reduces variability in investor income in proportion to the tax rate. It is as if the government allows a deduction for the cost of risk.

Although the government shares the *income* risk faced by an investor, it fails to share the *capital* risk associated with fluctuations in the prices of capital goods. Capital cost allowances are based on the original price of assets and not replacement costs. Because CCA rates do not vary with the prices of capital goods, firms facing reductions (increases) in these prices are not rewarded with higher (lower) CCA deductions under tax law. Thus the government does not share *capital* risk.[17]

The Net Real Return to Domestic Savers

In this section, we will calculate the real return to domestic savers after all taxes, both corporate and personal, have been paid. Under our assumption that the gross of personal tax interest rate on bonds and the nominal return on equity is given by world capital markets, the net of personal tax returns will vary on debt, new issues, and retained dividends. We will consider each in turn.

The Net Real Return by Source of Finance

Under Canada's tax system, nominal interest accruing directly to individuals is taxed beyond the $1,000 investment income deduction unless such funds flow through special tax sheltering assets such as registered pension or retirement savings plans. We assume that the marginal dollar of saving from middle and upper income individuals does not go into such funds, because the typical individual has savings in excess of the limits imposed on these contributions and earns nominal interest, dividends, and until 1984, capital gains in excess of the $1,000 deduction. Thus, the real return to the saver that is relevant for the savings decision is the return net of personal taxes. The net of tax real return to the saver from corporate bonds is denoted r_b^N and is given by

$$r_b^N = i(1 - m) - \pi \tag{2.8}$$

where i is the interest rate on corporate bonds, m is the personal tax rate on interest receipts, and π is the inflation rate. The inflation rate is subtracted from the after-tax nominal interest rate $i(1 - m)$ to account for the loss to the saver in the purchasing power of the principal tied up in the bond over the holding period.

---

[16] J. M. Mintz, "Neutral Corporate Taxation, Risk-taking and Optimal Profit Taxation" (June 1982), 48 *Recherches Economiques de Louvain* 107-32.

[17] Jeremy I. Bulow and Lawrence H. Summers, "The Taxation of Risky Assets" (February 1984), 92 *Journal of Political Economy* 20-39.

The after-tax real return to the saver on holdings of equity is complicated by the fact that the return to equity is taxed differently depending on whether it accrues in the form of dividends or capital gains. In order to derive the appropriate expressions for the after-tax real return on a share r_e^N, we make use of the following identity:

$$r_e^N = (1 - \theta) \frac{D}{V} + (1 - c) \frac{\Delta V}{V} - \pi. \tag{2.9}$$

In this expression, D is dividends per share accruing over one period, V is the price of the share, ΔV is the change in the price of the share over the period, π is the inflation rate, θ is the personal tax rate on dividend income, and c is the effective personal tax rate on capital gains income *as it accrues*. This equation states that the after-tax real return on a share r_e^N is equal to the after-tax dividends per dollar $(1 - \theta)D/V$ plus after-tax capital gains per dollar $(1 - c) \Delta V/V$ minus the inflation rate π, which represents the loss in purchasing power per dollar held in shares. Note that the tax rates in this expression are not the statutory rates but must be adjusted for the dividend tax credit in the case of θ and for the tax deferral allowed by the taxation of capital gains upon realization in the case of c. The details of how θ and c are determined are found in the Appendix to Chapter 3.

The actual net real return on equity depends on how income is distributed to the shareholder. Suppose, for example, that all dividends are retained (D = 0) and the entire nominal before-tax yield on the share (ρ) is distributed as capital gains. Then, setting $\Delta V/V = \rho$ in expression 2.9, we obtain $r_e^N = (1 - c) \rho - \pi$. Alternatively, if capital gains on the share accrue at the inflation rate and the entire before-tax real yield on the share $(\rho - \pi)$ is distributed as dividends, we would set $D/V = \rho - \pi$ and $\Delta V/V = \pi$ to get $r_e^N = (1 - \theta)(\rho - \pi) + (1 - c)\pi - \pi$, or $r_e^N = (1 - \theta)\rho - (1 + c - \theta)\pi$. Note that the net return to equity would be the same in the two cases only if dividends and capital gains were taxed at the same rate ($\theta = c$).

We assume that the before-tax real return to the share (that is, over and above the inflation rate) is partly distributed as dividends and partly distributed as real capital gains (that is, $\Delta V/V$ exceeds π), since some earnings are retained and reinvested. Let $\Delta V/V = g + \pi$, where g is the real capital gain rate. Then

$$\rho = \frac{D}{V} + g + \pi, \quad \text{or} \quad \frac{D}{V} + g = \rho - \pi.$$

We assume that $g = a(\rho - \pi)$, where a is the proportion of equity financed by retained earnings. Subsequently, this fraction of the real before-tax yield $(\rho - \pi)$ is distributed as real capital gains. So we set $\Delta V/V = g + \pi = a(\rho - \pi) + \pi$. Because the remaining real return is distributed as dividends, D/V is set equal to $(1 - a)(\rho - \pi)$. Substituting these expressions for $\Delta V/V$ and D/V in 2.9, we obtain (after rearrangement),

$$r_e^N = [1 - \theta + a(\theta - c)]\rho - [1 - (1 - a)(\theta - c)]\pi. \tag{2.10}$$

This expression can be evaluated for given values of the proportion of dividends retained (a), the personal tax rates (θ and c), the nominal yield per dollar on equity (ρ), and the inflation rate (π).

The net real return to savers r_n is a weighted average of r_b^N and r_e^N. Specifically,

$$r_n = \beta r_b^N + (1 - \beta)r_e^N, \tag{2.11}$$

where β is the fraction of an extra dollar saved in the form of corporate debt. β for the household can differ from β as calculated for the firm in the section, "The Overall Cost of Finance," because of international capital flows. For example, if Canadian firms issue financial instruments to both Canadians and foreigners and if the portfolios of Canadian and foreign asset holders differ, the proportion of wealth held by Canadian savers in the form of corporate debt will differ from the proportion of investment financed by corporations through debt.

Financial Intermediation

In our analysis of the net real return to savers, we have assumed that individuals directly hold the debt and equity instruments issued by firms. In fact, the equity and debt issues of nonfinancial firms are sometimes owned by other firms that act as financial intermediaries between the producing firms and the ultimate holders of their liabilities. If funds flowed tax-free through such financial corporations, we could effectively ignore this complication in our analysis except in calculating the savers' debt-equity ratio, which takes into account this financial intermediation. The Canadian tax system does allow free flow-through of interest and, to a large extent, intercorporate dividends on financial assets held by Canadian corporations. Capital gains on equity are taxed, however, albeit at a preferential one-half rate and only upon realization. Nevertheless, the existence of this tax does impose an extra tax on the return to equity if it flows through any levels of financial intermediation. In the analysis below, we assume that the intermediary is owned by Canadian households only, so that taxes imposed on the intermediary will be fully reflected in lower returns paid to the saver.

The nominal return on equity before personal taxes at the household level but after taxes paid by the final intermediary is denoted ρ^f and is given by

$$\rho^f = \frac{D}{V} + (1 - c^f)\frac{\Delta V}{V},$$

where c^f is the accrued capital gains tax paid by the financial firm. Again assuming that the real return on equity is paid out as fraction a of real capital gains and $(1 - a)$ dividends we obtain (after rearrangement)

$$\rho^f = (1 - c^f a)\rho - c^f(1 - a)\pi.$$

If c^f were equal to zero, ρ^f would be equal to ρ. The presence of a positive tax on capital gains reduces ρ^f below ρ by an amount that depends on the fraction a and on the inflation rate π.

Clearly, in the absence of some posited benefits to financial intermediation, shares would not be held by intermediaries but would be directly held by households. Of course, when the specialized advantages in portfolio management that a financial intermediary is likely to possess are introduced, equity shares are held by financial firms and subject to this extra level of taxation. The tax itself can be thought of as a tax on the financial intermediation of equity.

When these intermediaries are owned by foreigners, the capital gains tax increases the cost of funds to the firm. In particular, the cost of equity funds will be $\rho/1 - c^f a$ if ρ is the cost of obtaining equity finance on the international market. If financial intermediaries are marginally financed from abroad, the return paid to Canadian savers will not be affected by taxes imposed on intermediaries.

The Total Effective Tax Rate on Investment and Saving

The total effective tax rate on an investment is equal to the required gross of tax real return on the investment less the net of tax real return to the saver. For example, the effective tax rate on depreciable capital in a particular industry is equal to r_g—from equation 2.6—less $(\delta - \Delta q/q)$ as derived from data drawn from the industry in question, less r_n—from equation 2.11. This effective tax rate, which in some cases could be negative (that is, an effective subsidy), incorporates all of the relevant corporate and personal tax factors that impinge on the income created by the marginal investment before it is finally distributed to the Canadian saver.

The effective tax rate on an investment is given by

$$t = r_g - r_n. \tag{2.12}$$

The value of t captures all of the taxes, corporate and personal, that form a wedge between what the investment earns, net of depreciation, less what is paid out to domestic savers. The effective tax rate on inventory investment is found by using the expression given by equation 2.7 for r_g. The total effective tax rate depends on all of the separate tax rates c, m, u, and θ as well as other tax parameters such as ϕ and d, the financial parameters of the firms and households, and the market rates of return on debt and equity. The effective tax rate is increasing in the separate tax rates and decreasing in ϕ and d.

Note that the inflation rate is also an important determinant of the effective tax rate because capital income is not indexed for its inflation-induced components in Canada. In particular, (1) nominal interest and capital gains are taxed at the personal level (capital gains are also taxed in the hands of firms), (2) nominal rather than real interest is deductible to firms, (3) depreciation deductions are based on the historic nominal values of the assets, and (4) inventory is costed on a FIFO basis. In general, the effective tax rate may be increasing or decreasing in π, although it is likely to be increasing in π when other parameters are held constant.

It should be stressed in closing this section that this effective tax rate is operative only for the *marginal* (that is, just profitable) investment. This tax rate is the appropriate one to consider when determining how the tax system influences investment and savings decisions, but it should be remembered that our marginal effective tax rate may differ substantially from tax rates calculated on the basis of *average* taxes paid. Also, as defined, the effective tax rate is in percentage points of return. It could be expressed on an ad valorem or proportional basis by dividing t by r_g or r_n. In Chapter 3, the ad valorem tax rate is expressed as a percentage of the gross of tax real return—that is, $(r_g - r_n)/r_g$.

Effective Tax Rates in an Open Economy Context

In a closed economy where all funds invested must come from domestic savers, the investment and savings decisions in the economy are interdependent through the workings of the capital markets. Thus the total effective tax rate as calculated in the previous section is the most useful summary measure available. If the economy is small and open to unobstructed capital movements between the economy and the rest of the world, however, the nominal rates of return on assets can be taken as given (that is, as determined in the rest of the world) for the economy in question. In other words, the interest rate on corporate debt (i) and the yield on equity (ρ) that the domestic firm must pay are unaffected by the amount of investment and saving carried out in the country and are also unaffected by changes in domestic tax rates providing those taxes are fully creditable abroad.[18] As a result, changes in Canadian tax rates do not affect i and ρ.

The main implication of the open capital market is that the investment decisions of Canadian firms are affected only by the provisions of the corporate tax system, while the savings decisions of the households are influenced only by the personal tax system. That is, the total effective tax rate t can be divided into two parts:

1) *The effective corporate tax rate* (t_c). This affects the investment decisions of the firms.

2) *The effective personal tax rate* (t_p). This affects the savings decisions of the households.

To do this, we define the real market return on funds, which is denoted r and given by

$$r = \beta i + (1 - \beta)\rho - \pi. \tag{2.13}$$

The real market cost of funds is a weighted average of the domestic interest rate on corporate bonds i and the yield on equity less the inflation rate. It should be distinguished from the cost of finance to the firm r_f, which is based on a weighted average of the after-tax interest rate i(1 − u) and ρ. As stated above, i and ρ can be thought of as determined in world markets for

---

[18]Specifically, the taxes in question must be creditable, as are the ones we consider, and domestic taxes paid must be less than what is owed in the home country after averaging with tax payments in other countries. We assume that these conditions are met.

a small and open economy. Because of anticipated exchange rate changes, however, i and ρ need not equal rates abroad exactly. Under perfect capital mobility, i and ρ would be equal to the respective foreign rates as given by an "interest arbitrage" expression that accounted for the anticipated exchange rate changes and any taxes on such exchange rate capital gains or losses.

We now define the effective corporate tax on investment (say, depreciable capital) by

$$t_c = r_g - r$$

and the effective personal tax on saving as

$$t_p = r - r_n.$$

Clearly, $t_c + t_p = t$; however, when these taxes are expressed as *rates* (by dividing t_c by r_g and t_p by r) they do not sum to the total tax rate. Note from expression 2.6 that r_g and hence t_c depend only on corporate tax parameters, while t_p depends only on personal tax parameters. This reflects the bifurcation of investment and savings decisions afforded by the externally determined market cost of funds. In the next chapter, t_c is evaluated by size of firm, industry, and type of capital in Canada, and t_p is also evaluated. The higher t_c is, the greater the disincentive to invest in that particular sector. The higher t_p is, the greater the disincentive to save.

Conclusions

In this chapter we have derived the expressions that will be used in the next chapter to calculate the effective marginal tax rates on capital in the Canadian economy. We have explained the basis for these effective rates in terms of the returns before and after taxes to the marginal investment that is just profitable after taxes.

We conclude this chapter with a summary of the important expressions derived to this point. This list can be used as a reference for the discussion in Chapter 3 where effective tax rates are calculated.

1) Real cost of finance,

$$r_f = \beta i(1 - u) + (1 - \beta)\rho - \pi \tag{2.3}$$

2) User cost of depreciable capital,

$$R_g = (r_f + \delta - \Delta q/q)(\frac{1 - \phi}{1 - u})(1 - \frac{ud}{r_f + \pi + d}) \tag{2.6}$$

3) Required gross of tax rate of return on depreciable capital,

$$r_g = R_g - (\delta - \Delta q/q) \tag{2.6.1}$$

4) Required gross of tax rate of return on inventory capital,

$$r_g = \frac{r_f - \Delta q/q + u(\gamma - v)}{1 - u} \tag{2.7}$$

where

$\beta = \dfrac{b}{1 + b}$ and b is the debt-equity ratio.

d is the exponential equivalent to the depreciation rate allowed for the capital cost deduction.

δ is the true rate of physical depreciation.

Δ denotes "change in."

γ is the rate of change in the money price of goods in inventory.

i is the market interest rate.

q is the relative price of capital goods.

π is the rate of general price inflation.

R_g is the required real return on depreciable capital gross of corporate taxes and economic depreciation.

r_g is R_g net of economic depreciation.

r_f is the real cost of finance to the firm.

ρ is the nominal return on equities before personal taxes.

u is the statutory marginal corporate tax rate.

v is the inventory allowance.

ϕ is the investment tax credit.

3

The Economic Impact of
Capital Income Taxes in Canada

Much of the discussion regarding the economic impact of corporate and personal income taxes on capital income centres on their effect on aggregate investment, savings, and economic growth. Less considered is the impact of capital income taxes on the production structure, financial structure, and organization of businesses, although the impact of the tax system on these business decisions can be at least as important as the effects on investment and savings. Taxes affect not only the aggregate demand for productive investment but also the production techniques and organization of firms that produce goods and services for the economy. Without taxes, we can assume that firms will maximize profits by choosing the most efficient means of production and that household savings will be used to finance the most productive investments. Taxation can distort these market decisions, since businesses and households may be induced to invest in assets with inferior before-tax rates of return in order to maximize their after-tax returns. The more taxes differ across assets, methods of finance, and organizational structure, the greater the influence of the tax system on business and household decisions. In this sense, taxes can impose substantial allocative costs on the economy by distorting prices that act as signals to businesses and households when choosing the most profitable opportunities.

The purpose of this chapter is to quantify the cumulative effect that taxes have on the structure of capital used in production and, where appropriate, the method of finance and the organization of business. The discussion in Chapter 2 suggested that the marginal or effective tax rate is the appropriate measure of the distorting effect of taxes. The effective tax rate is the amount of taxes paid as a percentage of income (before the deduction of interest) generated by the marginal investment—that is, the investment whose returns are just sufficient to cover the economic cost of investment. The effective tax rate allows one to quantify in a single statistic the effect of the various tax rates, deductions, and credits that influence the decision to invest in particular assets. It also permits one to distinguish the effect of taxes on the method of finance used to acquire capital (debt, retained earnings, and new equity issues) as well as to analyze the impact of taxes on aggregate investment and savings available to businesses.

To assess how taxes influence business decisions and household savings, we present several calculations of effective tax rates. The first set of tax rates is estimated for a historical series (1963-1981) of tax rates on various types of productive capital: buildings, machinery, land, and inventories. These calculations are based on data aggregated across all industries and sizes of firms. The purpose of this set of calculations is to see how tax dis-

61

tortions affecting investment, savings, and the production structure of business changed as the tax system and the economic environment evolved over time. We will be able to determine how taxes or economic factors, such as inflation and the level of interest rates affected the incentives to invest and save in Canada.

The second set of calculations is directed at how taxes influence the investment and financing of large businesses in relation to small businesses in Canada. The data are based on the latest period for which data were available (1977-1981), which predates some important reforms in small business taxation adopted in the federal budgets after 1981. Unfortunately, no data in the post-1981 period are yet available to determine how certain measures such as the 12.5 per cent dividend distribution tax (repealed in 1986) and the $500,000 capital gains exemption affect the dividend and financing policies of small businesses. Nonetheless, some useful results emerge using pre-1982 data.

The final set of calculations is an attempt to measure the impact of corporate taxes on sectoral investment under the current corporate tax law. Assuming businesses earn the same net of corporate tax rate of return to capital, we can show how the various provisions of the Income Tax Act influence the distribution of investment across sectors and assets. We also demonstrate the impact of the tax system across large and small firms in each sector.

All these calculations provide an assessment of the impact of taxes on various types of business investment and household savings decisions. There are, however, some important assumptions that are made in estimating effective tax rates, and these assumptions play an important role in evaluating the impact of taxation on investment and savings. Before analyzing the effect of taxation on capital decisions, we will review, in the following section, the most important assumptions used in our assessment. After that we will present the effective tax rates on capital income over time, across different-sized firms, and across various industries, before concluding this chapter.

Underlying Assumptions
for Effective Tax Rate Estimates

The estimates of the effective tax rates are based on several assumptions, some of which were explicitly mentioned in Chapter 2. The effective tax rate was defined in Chapter 2, but it is helpful to review the concept here. The effective tax is defined as the difference between the gross of tax required rate of return to capital (r_g) less the net of tax rate of return earned by savers. For depreciable capital, the gross of tax return is equal to the user cost of capital less economic depreciation on assets (that is, an amount allowed for the loss of value from physical wear-and-tear of assets less real capital gains) adjusted for taxes. Notationally, the gross of tax rate of return is, as shown in Chapter 2,

$$r_g = (r_f + \delta - \Delta q/q) \frac{(1 - \phi)}{(1 - u)} (1 - uZ) - \delta - \Delta q/q$$

where $r_f = \beta i(1 - u) + \rho - \pi$
β = debt-asset ratio
i = nominal bond interest rate
π = inflation
ρ = nominal cost of equity
δ = rate of physical wear-and-tear on asset
u = corporate tax rate
ϕ = investment tax credit rate
Z = present value of capital cost allowance
q = the relative price of investment goods.

A corresponding expression exists for inventory capital and nondepreciable capital as shown in Chapter 2.

The net of tax rate of return is

$$r_n = \beta i(1 - m) + (1 - \beta)\{a\, \rho(1 - c) + (1 - a)\rho(1 - \theta)$$
$$- \pi [1 - (1 - a)c]\}$$

where m = personal tax rate on nominal interest
c = shareholder's capital gains tax on accruals
a = proportion of equity financed by retained earnings
θ = dividend tax rate.

The total effective corporate and personal tax is $t = r_g - r_n$. If we define r as the real rate of return to savers gross of personal taxes (and also net of corporate taxes), then $r = \beta i + (1 - \beta)\rho - \pi$. The effective corporate tax is the difference between the gross and the net corporate marginal rate of return to capital: $t_c = r_g - r$. The effective personal tax is the difference between the gross and the net of personal tax rate of return paid to savers: $t_p = r - r_n$.

The tax rate is defined as the tax divided by the gross of tax rate of return to capital. In this chapter, we calculate three tax rates:

1) Effective corporate and personal tax rate: $t^r = \dfrac{t}{r_g} = \dfrac{r_g - r_n}{r_g}$,

2) Effective corporate tax rate: $t_c^r = \dfrac{t_c}{r_g} = \dfrac{r_g - r}{r_g}$,

3) Effective personal tax rate: $t_p^r = \dfrac{t_p}{r} = \dfrac{r - r_n}{r}$.

The following are the most important assumptions used to evaluate effective tax rates on capital. The complete methodology is provided in an appendix at the end of the chapter.

The Scope of Effective Tax Rate Calculations

As mentioned previously, the cost of capital and effective tax rates are calculated for four types of productive capital used by businesses: buildings, machinery, land, and inventories. Some industries are excluded from our calculations. Resource industries require further work to take into account taxes and royalties in the mining and oil and gas industries.[1] Financial intermediaries require special data beyond what we currently have available. Certain assets are also excluded, for example, depletable assets (mainly held by resource industries) and financial assets such as cash, deposits, accounts receivable, and corporate equity investments.

Tax Losses

The effective tax rate calculations are made for fully taxpaying firms in the sense that these businesses are able to use all deductions and credits when available to them. Were businesses unable to use deductions and tax credits, then tax rates would be increased on assets that contribute to tax losses and reduced on assets that generate taxable income that helps use up losses on other assets.[2] It is unclear whether accounting for tax losses in our calculations would increase or reduce the dispersion of effective tax rates. It could reduce it to the extent that assets that are most highly favoured by the tax system are also the most likely not to be able to take full advantage of the tax incentives available (for example, manufacturing machinery). On the other hand, the inability to take advantage of tax incentives will vary across firms within an industry according to their cash flow position. Thus, effective tax rates would exhibit more dispersion across firms within an industry as a result of their inability to obtain full credit for tax losses.

Uncertainty and Expectations

The calculation of effective tax rates is based on earnings and taxes payable that are expected at the time that a business decides to invest in assets. We assume that businesses predict inflation by determining the process under which prices change over time (see the appendix at the end of this chapter for more details). Current values of the tax rates, deductions, and credits are taken as expected ones. The interest paid on corporate bonds and the opportunity cost of equity are estimated from current yields on newly issued securities. Firms are assumed to act on the basis of these returns continuing into the future. The cost of equity for the time series data is estimated by using the earnings-price ratio on the Toronto Stock Exchange (earnings ad-

---

[1] We have developed a methodology for computing effective tax rates in resource firms and have applied it to the case of mining in Ontario and Quebec. See Robin Boadway, Neil Bruce, Ken McKenzie, and Jack Mintz, "Marginal Effective Tax Rates for Capital in the Canadian Mining Industry" (February 1987), 20 *Canadian Journal of Economics* 1-16.

[2] The impact of losses on the incentive to invest has been estimated by Jack M. Mintz, *An Empirical Estimate of Imperfect Loss Offsetting and Effective Tax Rates*, Discussion Paper no. 634 (Kingston, Ontario: Institute for Economic Research, Queen's University, 1985). See also Alan J. Auerbach and James M. Poterba, "Tax Loss Carryforwards and Corporate Tax Incentives," in Martin S. Feldstein, ed., *Effect of Taxation on Capital Accumulation* (Chicago: University of Chicago Press, forthcoming); and S. Majd and S. Myers, *Tax Asymmetries and Corporate Income Tax Reform*, National Bureau of Economic Research, Discussion Paper no. 1924 (Cambridge, Mass.: NBER, 1986).

justed for inflation-accounting procedures). The estimates of the cost of equity for the firm size and industry data are based on the analysis of securities returns using the so-called capital asset pricing model.[3]

Financial Ratios

In estimating effective tax rates, two financing ratios are required: (1) the ratio of debt financing to asset expenditures, and (2) the ratio of retained earnings to total equity financing (retained earnings plus new equity issues). For the time series and industry calculations, we use changes in the book value of adjusted liabilities and shareholders' equity to calculate the financial ratios. The calculation of tax rates for different sized businesses is based on the year-end book data (1977). The reliance on book data distorts financial ratios for several reasons, the most important of which is the revaluation of equity and debt in times of rising prices. Equity is undervalued to the extent that asset values are measured by using the original cost rather than replacement cost value of the asset. Long-term debt is overvalued (undervalued) if interest rates unexpectedly increase (decrease).

Financial Market Behaviour

A most important assumption underlying the analysis of tax policy concerns financial market behaviour. In our set of calculations, we assume that corporations take the cost of debt and equity financing to be determined by international markets. International investors are assumed to hold Canadian dollar assets such that the net of personal tax rate of return on Canadian assets is the same as that of other international assets. As discussed in Chapter 2, this is the "arbitrage assumption" we think is most appropriate for a small, open economy like that of Canada. If Canadian withholding taxes are fully credited against foreign tax liabilities, then foreign investment will be effectively taxed by capital gains, dividend, and interest income taxes levied by countries where the investors reside. This implies, first, that we can treat the gross of personal tax or net of corporate tax rate of return on equity and debt as exogenous, since these are determined by international markets. In our calculations, we measure from the data the interest rate payable on newly issued bonds and the rate of return to equity financing as determined by Canadian stock markets. We then adjust these rates of return to measure the gross of corporate tax and net of personal tax rates of return to capital as a basis for the measure of effective tax rates. A second implication of our assumption about financial markets is that personal tax changes in Canada that affect the amount of domestic savings have no impact on domestic investment, since the interest rate, gross of the Canadian personal taxes, is unaffected by domestic savings. Similarly, cor-

---

[3]The capital asset pricing model (CAPM) is used to estimate the risk premium by comparing the capital gain and dividend yield earned on shares with that of a risk-free asset (such as a treasury bill). For a discussion of the model, see R. Brealey and S. C. Myers, *Principles of Corporate Finance*, 2nd ed. (New York: McGraw Hill, 1984).

porate tax rate changes that affect investment undertaken by Canadian businesses have no impact on savings, since the net of personal tax rate of return paid to savers is unaffected.

These conclusions contrast sharply with "closed" economy analysis. Without international mobility of capital, individual investors in Canada will trade assets until any differences in after-tax rates of return on bonds and equity are eliminated. Investment and savings decisions are correlated (since domestic savings equals domestic investment in equilibrium), so that both the corporate and personal tax rates will affect savings and investment simultaneously. Below, we will report combined and separate corporate and personal tax rates. The combined tax rate is an indicator of the total corporate and personal tax paid on capital and can be interpreted as showing how taxes influence savings and investment in a closed economy. The separation of corporate and personal tax rates provides a better indication of how taxes influence investment and savings in an open economy. In our view, the international mobility of financial capital is an appropriate assumption, especially for large publicly traded corporations that are owned by both domestic and foreign investors. Small Canadian-controlled private corporations may be viewed differently. The equity of these corporations may be marginally owned by a Canadian investor so that the combined corporate and personal tax rate on the income might influence both the amount of investment and savings made available to the small business.

Domestic Ownership of Business Capital

Domestic owners are assumed to own equity and bonds in the same proportion as Canadian business finances its capital. Thus, if one-half of business capital is financed by debt, Canadian households hold one-half of their business investment portfolio in bonds issued by corporations (including indirect ownership through intermediaries). This also implies that foreign investors hold the same proportion of Canadian business assets in bonds and equity as do domestic investors. Evidence on foreign-controlled corporations suggests that foreigners hold more equity in comparison with debt. However, we are examining only Canadian-controlled firms (owned partly by foreigners), and we have no data to separate foreign from domestic ownership of Canadian-controlled corporations.

We also assume that savings invested in tax-sheltering devices such as pension plans, registered retirement savings plans (RRSPs), and assets that qualify for the $1,000 investment income deduction do not affect the marginal savings decisions of households unless all the savings are untaxed. Savings of lower income households, which tend to shelter all their savings, are treated as untaxed. Savings of upper income households, which cannot shelter all their savings from tax because of limits imposed by tax law, are assumed to be taxed at their marginal tax rates.

Other Capital Taxes

The effective tax rate calculations do not include other taxes imposed on business investment besides the corporate and personal income tax. These other taxes include the provincial capital levies, municipal property and business taxes, and the proportion of taxes such as the manufacturers' and retail sales tax that is levied on capital goods purchased by the firm.

Risk-Sharing Role of Taxes

The calculation of effective tax rates excludes the possible risk-sharing role of taxes that can be of benefit to the investor. The corporate and capital gains taxes do not simply reduce the return earned by investments. They also reduce risk or the variability of income faced by the investor, since the government shares both the profits and the losses faced by investors. In the absence of taxes, one could argue that the risk premiums on equity would be higher. We have not taken this possibility into account in our calculations. The presence of this risk-sharing effect depends, however, on two factors. First, not all losses are shared by the government, since tax losses are not fully refundable in a present-value sense—losses may be written off eventually, but the losses are not carried forward at a rate of interest. Without loss offsets in the tax system, the government imposes a tax on risky investments. Second, the risk faced by the investors ultimately depends on how the government spends its tax revenue—if the tax revenue is returned to individuals as a transfer, then the variability in the transfer income may offset any reduction in risk arising from the taxation of income. In this case, the riskiness of investment is unchanged.

Capital Goods Prices

We assume all prices on capital goods rise with the rate of inflation. This is equivalent to assuming that there are no real capital gains or losses on the holding of physical assets. (That is, $\Delta q/q = 0$ in equations 2.6 and 2.7.) In some previous work, we considered the impact of real capital gains on the measure of effective tax rates.[4] Building prices that were observed to rise faster than the rate of inflation contributed to a lower tax rate on building assets. The converse was true for machinery whose prices rose less quickly than the general rate of inflation. Data restrict us from including real capital gains and losses here since they are unavailable by industry and firm size and for inventory goods. Some caution must therefore be used in interpreting the results provided below. Unfortunately, given the absence of data, we are not even in a position to say in which direction the results will be biased as a result of omitting real capital gains.

Calculations

On the basis of all these assumptions, we calculate the marginal rate of return to capital (that is, the user cost of capital—equations 2.6 and 2.7—net of depreciation), the net of tax rate of return to savers—equations 2.8 and 2.10—and the marginal or effective tax rate. The effective tax rate is

---

[4]See Robin Boadway, Neil Bruce, and Jack Mintz, "Taxation, Inflation, and the Effective Marginal Tax Rate on Capital in Canada" (February 1984), 17 *Canadian Journal of Economics* 62-79.

the difference between the gross of tax rate of return on capital and the net of tax rate of return to savings divided by the gross of tax rate of return to capital. The effective *corporate* tax rate measures the difference between the gross and the net of corporate tax rate of return on investment, divided by the *gross of corporate tax rate of return* to capital. The effective *personal* tax rate is the difference between the net of corporate tax return on capital (gross of personal taxes) and the net of personal tax return to capital divided by the *net of corporate tax rate of return to capital.* Effective corporate and personal tax rates do not add up to arrive at a combined tax rate, since the base used differs in the measure of each separate tax rate. However, the personal tax as a percentage of the rate of return to capital, gross of both corporate and personal taxes, can be easily calculated by subtracting the corporate tax rate from the combined corporate and personal tax rate presented in many of the tables set out later in this chapter.

Taxation and the Cost of Capital Since 1963

Our first set of calculations is a comparison of the effective tax rates on capital over the periods 1963-1971 and 1972-1981. These rates are aggregated over the entire economy but are calculated for each type of capital good. There are several important differences between these two periods. The first is that the income tax reform of 1972 brought in several changes in the tax law. For the first time, capital gains were to be taxed. The corporate tax was lowered from 50 to 46 per cent, the dividend tax credit was revised, and the top marginal personal tax rate was lowered. However, 1972 was not the only year in which important tax changes were adopted. Throughout the entire period between 1963 and 1981, various amendments to the Income Tax Act affected capital income taxation. These included the fast write-offs for manufacturing machinery and buildings available from 1963 to 1966, the reduction of the manufacturing corporate tax rate by up to 6 percentage points since 1973, the fast write-off for manufacturing and construction equipment since 1972, the inventory allowance since 1977, the investment tax credit for qualified building and machinery expenditures since 1978, and the increase in the dividend tax credit in 1978. One can also add to this list several personal tax changes that allowed individuals to shelter parts of their capital income from taxation: the $1,000 investment income deduction beginning in 1974, the 1972 increase in limits for contributions made to RRSPs, and the creation of the registered home ownership plan in 1974. These vehicles for tax-assisted savings had less impact on the taxation of marginal savings, since most of the savings available for marginal investments came from high income households who were unable fully to shelter savings from taxation. These savings vehicles were also enhanced or instituted during times of higher inflation (which led to higher nominal interest receipts); consequently, any reduction in tax rates on marginal savings by tax-sheltering devices was offset by the tax on higher capital income induced by inflation.

A second important difference between the 1963-1971 period and the 1972-1981 period is the substantial change in the economic environment.

The 1960s period is now recognized as one of strong economic growth and low inflation. Real interest rates (the difference between the nominal interest rate and expected rate of inflation) matched historical experience. The economic experience of the 1970s, however, sharply contrasted with that of the 1960s. Economic growth—especially after 1973—was lower, inflation was much higher, and monetary policy was more permissive until the late 1970s, with the result that real interest rates were low.

Table 3.1 provides average values of tax parameters, interest rates, inflation rates, and other relevant statistics used for effective tax rate calculations. These data are aggregate numbers for all corporations and households, averaged over each of the subperiods. The most important changes have been the increase in expected inflation (2.8 to 8.3 per cent); the fall in real interest rates, unadjusted for personal taxes (2.8 to 1.8 per cent); and, in general, reductions in corporate and personal tax rates except for the capital gains tax rate.

Table 3.1   Estimated Data Used for Effective Tax Rate Calculations Averaged for the Periods 1963-1971 and 1972-1981 (in percentages)

	1963-1971	1972-1981
Tax parameters		
Statutory corporate tax rate		
Manufacturing	47	40
Nonmanufacturing	47	45
Dividend tax rate net of credits	19	14
Capital gains tax rate[a]		
Realized basis	0	21
Accrual basis	0	11
Tax rate on bond and bank interest	30	30
Investment tax credit	0	3[b]
Inventory allowance	0	3[b]
Other parameters		
Expected inflation rate	2.8	8.3
Nominal interest rate on corporate bonds	7.1	10.8
Risk premium on equity[c]	2.5	4.4
Treasury bill interest rate	5.6	10.1
Debt-asset ratio	49	52
Ratio of retained earnings to equity finance	73	72
Physical rate of depreciation		
Buildings	4.1	4.1
Machinery	14.7	14.7

[a]Capital gains tax rate on a realized basis is the average marginal tax rate on capital gains arising from the sale of shares. The capital gains tax rate on an accrual basis is the rate of tax that would be paid if an individual had to pay taxes each year on the increase in the market value of shares. [b]These are the effective rates used for the period 1978-1981. [c]The risk premium on equity is measured by taking the difference between the earnings-price ratio (adjusting measured earnings for inflation) plus the inflation rate less the interest earned on treasury bills with adjustments made for taxes.

Source: See the appendix to this chapter.

Given these changes in tax law and economic statistics over time, we are able to deduce the incentive effect of taxes on investment, savings, and the structure of capital by measuring the cost of capital and effective tax rate as outlined in Chapter 2. Table 3.2 provides the average estimates of the rates of return to capital and the corporate and personal effective tax rates. From this table, we see the incentive effects that taxes in the past two decades have imposed on business and household investment decisions.

Aggregate Corporate Investment

As discussed in the introduction, only the corporate tax influences aggregate investment in a small, open economy such as Canada, because the cost of funds is determined by world financial markets and is independent of Canadian savings decisions. As shown in Table 3.2, the effective corporate tax rate fell from an average of 29.8 per cent in the 1963-1971 period to 23.4 per cent in the 1972-1981 period. The marginal rate of return to capital, gross of corporate taxes and net of depreciation, also fell from 6.9 to 6.3 per cent in these two periods while the net of corporate tax rate of return remained virtually unchanged. Thus the reduction in the cost of capital has been wholly due to a lessening of the corporate tax burden on capital in Canada.

Why has the effective corporate tax rate fallen in aggregate or, at least, remained the same? A view taken by others[5] is that the effective corporate tax rate increased over the 1970s because of the lack of indexation for inflation in the corporate tax base. As we have discussed in detail elsewhere,[6] the impact of inflation on the effective corporate tax rate is ambiguous. While inflation erodes the value of capital cost allowances and the inventory deduction based on the original cost of the assets, the deductibility of nominal interest on borrowed funds is generous during times of inflation since interest in part compensates lenders for the loss in purchasing power of their capital, which is eroded by inflation. We have concluded that inflation has had little impact on the corporate tax rate in the *aggregate*, even though inflation has had an important impact on the structure of production. We will return to this point later.

The reduction in the aggregate effective corporate tax rate has resulted from other developments: (1) the lowering of the statutory corporate tax rate; (2) fast write-offs for equipment, especially in manufacturing (Class 29); (3) the inventory allowance; and (4) the investment tax credit. Each of the tax changes has contributed to a lower corporate tax rate on capital.

Savings Made Available to Businesses

In assessing the impact of taxation on savings, we compare the personal tax on savings across the two periods 1963-1971 and 1972-1981. Table 3.2 illus-

[5]For example, see Glenn P. Jenkins, "The Impact of Inflation on Corporate Taxes and the Cash Flows of Business" (July-August), 33 *Canadian Tax Journal* 759-85.

[6]Supra footnote 4.

Table 3.2 The Cost of Capital, Effective Tax Rates, and Net of Tax Return to Savers, Averaged for the 1963-1971 and 1972-1981 Periods (in percentages)

	1963-1971					1972-1981				
	Buildings	Machinery	Land	Inventories	Average	Buildings	Machinery	Land	Inventories	Average
Rate of return to capital[a]										
Gross of all taxes	6.4	6.4	6.0	8.5	6.9	5.5	5.4	4.1	9.1	6.3
Net of corporate tax	4.8	4.8	4.8	4.8	4.8	4.8	4.8	4.8	4.8	4.8
Net of all taxes	3.6	3.6	3.6	3.6	3.6	2.2	2.2	2.2	2.2	2.2
Effective tax rates[b]										
Corporate and personal	43.3	43.0	40.0	57.4	47.2	58.9	58.1	45.6	75.2	64.0
Corporate only	24.6	24.1	19.9	43.3	29.8	12.5	11.0	-15.7	47.2	23.4
Personal only	24.8	24.8	24.8	24.8	24.8	52.9	52.9	52.9	52.9	52.9

[a]Rate of return to capital is equal to the user cost net of depreciation (see equations (2.6) and (2.7) for the user cost). [b]Corporate and personal tax rates do not necessarily add to the combined tax rate. The corporate tax rate is equal to $(r_g - r)/r_g$ and the personal tax rate is equal to $(r - r_n)/r$ where r_g = rate of return to capital gross of all taxes, r_n = rate of return (return to savers), net of all taxes, and r = net corporate tax rate of return to capital. The rates of return are equal to

Depreciable capital: $r_g^D = (r_f + \delta)(1 - \phi)(1 - uZ)/(1 - u) - \delta$

Inventory capital: $r_g^I = [r_f + u(\pi - v)]/(1 - u)$

Cost of finance: $r_f = \beta i(1 - u) + (1 - \beta)\rho - \pi$

Net of corporate tax return: $r = \beta i + (1 - \beta)\rho - \pi$

Net of personal tax return: $r_n = \beta[i(1 - m) - \pi] + (1 - \beta)\{a[\rho(1 - c) - \pi] + (1 - a)[\rho(1 - \theta) - \pi(1 - c)]\}$

where:

ϕ = investment tax credit
β = debt-asset financing ratio
a = retained earnings as a fraction of total equity finance
π = rate of inflation
δ = economic depreciation of capital
v = inventory allowance

i = nominal interest rate (gross of personal tax)
ρ = nominal cost of equity finance (gross of personal tax)
u = corporate tax rate
c = capital gains tax rate
θ = dividend tax rate
m = personal tax rate on interest
Z = present value of capital cost allowances

trates that the effective personal tax rate rose substantially from 24.8 per cent in the earlier period to 52.9 per cent in the later period. The net of tax rate of return fell from 3.6 per cent to 2.2 per cent and the gross of personal tax rate of return to savings remained the same at 4.8 per cent across both periods.

The substantial increase in the effective personal tax rates from the earlier to later periods was not due to any significant personal tax changes. The tax on interest income was, on average, unchanged. The statutory tax rate on equity income, unadjusted for inflation (the weighted average of dividends and capital gains taxes) rose from 5 per cent in 1963-1971 when there was no capital gains tax, to approximately 12 per cent in the 1972-1981 period. Overall, the statutory tax rate on business capital income increased 3 percentage points.

The main reason for the near doubling of the personal tax rate on capital has been lack of indexation for inflation in the personal tax base. An example explains this result. Suppose inflation is 5 per cent and the interest rate on a bond is 10 per cent. As noted earlier, part of the interest compensates the lender for inflation that erodes the real value of his wealth. With no personal taxes, the real rate of interest, which is the return to savings after adjusting for inflation, is 5 per cent (10 per cent interest less 5 per cent inflation). If the tax on the bond interest is 30 per cent, then after-tax rate of return on the bond, without adjusting for inflation, is 7 per cent. The real return is 2 per cent (7 per cent after-tax interest less 5 per cent inflation). The effective tax rate is the total tax paid (3 per cent) on the gross of tax *real* rate of interest (5 per cent) and this is equal to 60 per cent. If there were no inflation, the tax rate would be only 30 per cent, so that in this example, a 5 per cent inflation rate *doubled* the effective personal tax rate on interest income.

The impact of this very substantial increase in the personal tax rate on capital income has been to reduce the supply of savings available from Canadian households to businesses in Canada. Given international mobility of capital, a reduction in domestic savings would be expected to induce a flow of capital from abroad to finance business investment in Canada. The high personal tax on Canadian savings, however, leaves business investment unaffected as it induces a flow of foreign funds into Canada, thereby reducing Canadian ownership of capital.

During the 1970s, the saving rate in Canada actually increased instead of falling, as would be suggested by these effective personal tax rate measures. This fact raises two issues. First, our measure of effective tax rates on marginal savings may be too high, since it is difficult to account fully for all the possible ways that individuals can shelter their savings from tax. In earlier work, we used a lower statutory tax rate on interest and capital gains but still calculated effective personal tax rates that were higher in the 1970s compared with rates in the 1960s. A second issue is what factors, including taxes, affect savings behaviour. Some studies suggest that the climate of uncertainty in the 1970s induced individuals to save more.

Personal taxes on savings have affected the Canadian economy in other ways as well. The high tax rates on bond and equity business assets may have induced investors to seek other types of investments that allow households to shelter capital income from taxation. The most important of these investments has been equity ownership of a principal residence—in other words, home ownership—which is exempt from tax. A typical household will have an incentive to purchase housing with as much equity as possible and retire the mortgage as quickly as possible. Because ownership of housing and other tax-shelter vehicles is not a perfect substitute for other types of assets, a household may not fully shelter all its savings from tax. If all savings are not fully sheltered from tax, the high personal tax on savings can lead to individuals substituting current consumption for savings, thus reducing the aggregate savings rate in the economy.[7]

The Structure of Business Capital

The tax on business capital has affected not only aggregate investments and savings made available to businesses but also the structure of business capital investment: buildings, machinery, inventories, and land. Table 3.2 illustrates that during the 1963-1981 period inventories were the most highly taxed asset and land the least taxed asset. Building and machinery assets were equally taxed, although the aggregate numbers mask considerable differences among the different types of machinery and building assets.

In comparing the two subperiods, it is easily seen that there was a much wider divergence among tax rates in the post-1972 period compared with the pre-1972 period. Before 1972, the difference in corporate tax rates across the highest and lowest taxed assets was 23.4 per cent; after 1972 this difference was 62.9 per cent. There are a number of reasons for the increase in the spread of effective tax rates. The most important reason was inflation, which (1) increased substantially the tax on inventories that are valued according to first in, first out principles of accounting, and (2) reduced the tax on land, because of the deductibility of interest, unadjusted for inflation, from corporate taxable income. Another reason for the greater dispersion in tax rates was the substantial revision of corporate tax law after 1972, which generally favoured buildings and machinery relative to inventories. These amendments included the investment tax credit and accelerated capital cost allowances applying to construction and manufacturing machinery under Classes 22 and 29 respectively.

The numbers reported in Table 3.2 are averages of year-by-year calculations of effective tax rates during the whole of the period 1963-1981. In Table 3.3, we report year-by-year calculations of effective tax rates. These

---

[7]Some evidence that saving is quite responsive to changes in the after-tax rate of return is found in C. Beach, R. W. Boadway, N. Bruce, and G. Ansong, *Taxation and Savings: Some Life-Cycle Estimates for Canada*, Discussion Paper no. 622 (Kingston, Ontario: Institute for Economic Research, Queen's University, 1985).

tax rates vary considerably over the years, since interest rates, tax parameters, and inflation rates vary across years. As seen in Table 3.3, the effect
of the tax system on the structure of capital held by businesses remains
qualitatively the same—inventories have been the most highly taxed and
land the least taxed form of capital.

The most important lesson to be drawn from Table 3.3 is the sensitivity
of effective tax rates to the tax law, interest rates, and inflation. A comparison of the tax rate on buildings relative to machinery makes the point clear.
As seen in Table 3.3, buildings were not always taxed more heavily than
machinery. During the years 1967-1970, 1974, and 1979-1981, the tax rate
on buildings was less than that on machinery. In the 1967-1970 period, the
capital cost allowance for machinery was not so generous—our calculation
of economic depreciation rates suggests that machinery depreciates at about
a 15 per cent rate (declining balance), while the capital cost allowance was
approximately 20 per cent. Yet, the same values for buildings were about 4
and 5 per cent, which did not give buildings any particular advantage compared with machinery. The 1974 and 1979-1981 years are even more difficult to explain—machinery in manufacturing (about 40 per cent of total
machinery investment) enjoyed a 50 per cent straight-line write-off. One
would thus expect the tax rate on machinery to be lower relative to buildings, which enjoyed no similar write-off. Assets with fast write-offs do not,
however, always face lower tax rates.

This striking conclusion, which appears to be counterintuitive, can be explained by a close examination of the relationship of inflation and corporate taxation. As discussed earlier, one cannot conclude that inflation raises
the effective corporate tax rate on assets. We have found that in periods of
high inflation, the cost of funds, adjusted for inflation, has been reduced
for businesses in Canada—the nominal cost of funds, net of the corporate
tax, in the 1979-1981 period, for example, was low relative to high inflation
in these years. Moreover, we have also found that the effective corporate
tax rate on capital may fall with higher inflation, since the deductibility of
interest on borrowed funds may more than offset the erosion by inflation
of the value of capital cost allowances. It is thus ambiguous as to whether
inflation increases or reduces the effective corporate tax rate.

It is often alleged that inflation has increased the tax on buildings relative
to machinery. Yet the data suggest otherwise: in the 1979-1981 period when
inflation averaged 10 per cent, the effective tax rate on buildings was lower
than that on machinery even though machinery was written off more
quickly for tax purposes. Why has this happened? The effective corporate
tax rate and its sensitivity to inflation are also affected by the service life, or
durability, of capital. This occurs for two reasons. First, less durable assets,
such as machinery, are written off more quickly compared with nondurable
assets. The greater the CCA rate, the lower the impact of inflation in reducing the present value of CCA write-offs. This is the standard argument made
in the literature suggesting that inflation is less harmful (or more beneficial)
to machinery than it is to buildings when the tax system is not indexed.

Table 3.3 Effective Marginal Tax Rates by Type of Capital for the Period 1963-1981

	Corporate and personal					Corporate					Personal
	Land	Buildings	Machinery	Inventories	Average	Land	Buildings	Machinery	Inventories	Average	All capital
1963	40.7	36.1	32.3	50.7	38.6	27.1	21.6	16.9	39.4	24.6	18.6
1964	42.0	39.5	36.8	55.4	43.0	28.2	25.1	21.7	44.7	29.4	19.3
1965	36.4	36.5	34.4	55.3	41.3	13.5	13.6	10.7	39.2	20.1	26.5
1966	35.6	37.0	35.7	57.1	42.7	10.6	12.5	10.7	40.5	20.5	28.0
1967	36.9	46.0	48.1	54.2	50.8	12.2	24.8	27.8	43.3	31.5	28.2
1968	41.0	46.8	48.1	58.6	50.8	21.4	29.1	30.9	44.8	34.4	24.9
1969	41.9	49.2	51.3	62.0	53.9	29.8	30.8	33.6	48.2	37.2	26.6
1970	41.8	47.1	48.2	58.5	50.8	23.5	30.4	32.0	45.4	35.4	23.9
1971	38.9	44.1	39.5	56.7	45.3	16.5	23.6	17.3	40.9	25.3	26.8
1972	44.2	52.6	46.8	65.4	53.5	10.6	24.1	14.8	44.5	25.6	37.6
1973	44.7	59.7	58.3	75.1	64.0	-8.9	20.6	17.9	50.9	29.9	49.3
1974	27.9	62.4	64.7	82.3	70.9	-112.5	-10.8	-3.9	47.8	14.4	66.1
1975	47.3	59.2	59.0	75.9	64.7	-3.1	20.1	19.8	52.8	31.0	48.9
1976	48.5	57.5	55.9	72.7	61.6	3.8	20.6	17.6	48.9	28.2	46.5
1977	51.2	59.5	56.6	70.4	61.2	4.2	20.6	14.9	41.9	23.9	49.0
1978	43.9	58.7	56.9	72.3	61.9	-19.6	11.9	8.1	41.0	18.9	53.1
1979	51.1	64.3	64.5	79.3	69.5	-19.9	12.6	12.9	44.2	25.1	54.2
1980	46.9	60.1	60.9	77.9	66.7	-23.4	7.3	9.1	48.7	22.6	57.0
1981	35.6	57.1	60.6	80.2	67.6	-77.9	-18.3	-8.7	45.4	10.5	69.8
Average											
63-71	40.0	43.3	43.0	57.4	47.2	19.9	24.6	24.1	43.3	29.8	24.8
72-81	45.6	58.9	58.1	75.2	64.0	-15.7	12.5	11.0	47.4	23.4	52.9

Note: See Table 3.2 for explanations of tax rates and the method of calculation.

Durability also influences the effective corporate tax rate in another way. When write-offs are not adequate relative to the economic cost of holding an asset, assets with shorter lives are, in fact, taxed more than more durable assets. The converse is true when assets are treated generously under the tax system. The reason why durability affects the total tax collected can be explained as follows. The more often that an asset has to be replaced, the more often that a firm will be assessed tax liabilities. When write-offs are inadequate, a firm that has to turn over capital more often will be penalized more often. Consider, for example, two assets earning the same return net of depreciation but gross of corporate taxes. The cost of owning each asset is $100 but one is replaced every five years and the other every 50 years. The capital cost allowance for the less durable asset is worth only $50 in terms of present value, so that the business facing a 50 per cent corporate tax rate will be paying $25 extra in taxes every five years. For 50 years, the total tax will be $250 (ignoring discounting). However, if capital is replaced once every 50 years and if we assume that the present value of capital cost allowances is also $50, the tax liability will be only $25 for 50 years. Thus longer-lived assets can be taxed less. On the other hand, if write-offs are generous, such as the investment tax credit, then less durable capital will benefit more compared with more durable capital.

Inflation thus has an ambiguous effect on the tax cost of holding durable assets in comparison with nondurable assets. Although inflation has less impact in reducing the value of capital cost allowances on assets that are written off more quickly for tax purposes, these assets, which are replaced more often, can be taxed more heavily when the value of CCA relative to economic depreciation is inadequate in times of inflation. In our calculations, we have found that inflation reduces the tax rate on buildings relative to machinery when we assumed that rate of economic depreciation was 4 per cent and 5 per cent respectively. If we reduced the rate of economic depreciation on machinery to 8 per cent, we found that inflation reduced the effective tax rate on machinery relative to buildings. It should, of course, be remembered that our estimates of the economic rate of depreciation are imperfect and are based on observed service lives. The magnitude of these effects would change if different estimates for rates of economic depreciation were used. Much more research is needed in this area.

Taxes have other effects on business and houshold decisions including the financing of business, the portfolio allocation of household savings across equity and bond assets issued by businesses, and the organization of businesses. These effects will be considered later in our examination of the impact of taxes on businesses of different sizes.

The Effect of Tax Rates on Different Sized Businesses

The Canadian tax system explicitly favours small Canadian-controlled private corporations by reducing the statutory corporate tax rate levied on these businesses. The federal tax allows a small business to reduce the federal tax rate by 21 percentage points, and almost all provinces have lower corporate tax rates for small businesses. A lower tax rate, however, can be a mixed blessing. While the lower rate reduces the tax collected on the net revenues (gross of capital costs), it also makes fast write-offs such as accelerated depreciation allowances less valuable to a business. When the corporate tax system effectively subsidizes investment in a particular asset, a higher statutory tax rate could increase the value of the tax incentive to the firm and lower rather than raise the effective tax rate.

In this section, we measure the extent to which taxes tend to favour small compared with larger firms. For this purpose, we use 1977 data collected by the Economic Council of Canada which provides us with a breakdown of book assets and liabilities of businesses of six different asset sizes. Corporations in the two smallest asset sizes ($0 - 1/4 million and $1/4 - 1 million) are generally eligible for the small business tax rate at the federal level (see Table 3.4). Since no data are available providing a breakdown of the ownership of equity invested in corporations of different sizes, we assume that the owners of large and small corporations earn the same amount of taxable income and face similar personal tax rates on equity and bonds.

The evaluation of effective tax rates is based on 1981 tax law, using the 1977 characteristics of firms. As mentioned in the introduction to this chapter, several changes in the tax law were made after 1981 that particularly affected small businesses. These changes include (1) the 12.5 per cent tax on distributed profits (repealed in 1986); (2) the elimination of the cumulative deduction account; (3) the $500,000 capital gains exemption;

Table 3.4 Firm Characteristics by Asset Size Category

	Asset size ($ million)					
	0-1/4	1/4-1	1-5	5-10	10-25	25+
	per cent					
Capital structure						
Buildings	13	14	13	15	14	17
Machinery	39	32	30	30	32	46
Land	6	8	6	5	5	4
Inventories	42	46	50	50	49	33
Portion of investment						
in manufacturing	20	24	27	27	30	31
Financing, per cent of assets						
Debt	82	67	68	67	64	56
Retained earnings	11	26	24	25	26	26
New equity	7	8	8	8	10	18
Other						
Portion of income claiming						
small business deduction	93	78	26	3	0	0
Corporate tax rate	26	29	41	46	47	47
Dividend tax rate	24	22	17	14	14	14
Capital gains tax rate	12	12	12	12	12	12
Tax on bond interest	30	30	30	30	30	30
Interest rate on debt	13	13	13	13	13	13
Gross of personal tax						
cost of equity finance	32	24	24	24	23	21
Expected inflation	10	10	10	10	10	10

Source: See the appendix to this chapter.

and (4) tax holidays in Saskatchewan, Ontario (now restricted), and New Brunswick for small businesses. The first change listed above affects new equity financing. The second item has little impact on marginal investment decisions, since large Canadian-controlled private corporations are likely to pay taxes at the full rate on marginal projects while small firms face a lower tax rate. The third and fourth items reduce tax rates, although the capital gains exemption is limited to $500,000, which may not affect marginal savings invested in small businesses. In our calculations, we include only the 1985 12.5 per cent dividend distribution tax and the 1985 dividend tax credit.

Table 3.4 presents the characteristics of businesses of different size with respect to capital structure, financing, and other relevant statistics. The primary differences among the different-sized businesses are as follows:

1) The largest-sized businesses invest less in inventories and more in machinery. This reflects the sectoral distribution of businesses, since inventory-holding businesses (such as those in retail and wholesale trade) are more important in the smaller-sized classes, while depreciable-capital-intensive industries (such as manufacturing) are more important in the larger-sized firm categories.

2) Small businesses tend to rely much more on debt financing compared with large businesses, while the largest firms rely much more on new equity issues compared with small firms.

3) The pre-personal tax cost of equity finance is much higher for small firms than it is for large firms. This reflects a much higher degree of debt finance used by small firms, which contributes to a higher risk premium on their equity. We constructed the cost of equity so that small firms would have the same cost of equity finance as large firms if the debt-asset ratios were identical. (See the appendix at the end of this chapter for details.)

4) The corporate tax rate is lower for small firms because of the small business deduction. The dividend tax rate is higher for small firms as a result of the 12.5 per cent dividend distribution tax.

Using the data presented in Table 3.4, we calculated combined and separate corporate and personal tax rates for each type of firm. These tax rates are sensitive to the values used for inflation and interest rates that are based on 1979-1981 averages. However, the conclusions from our analysis are, in large part, qualitatively similar regardless of the rate of interest used relative to inflation.

In Tables 3.5 and 3.6, we report combined, and separate, personal and corporate effective tax rates for each of the six asset-size categories of corporations and by each capital type. As shown in these tables, two observations regarding the differential taxation of small and large businesses are immediate.

1) The tax system does not necessarily discriminate in favour of small business. The combined effective tax rate on aggregate capital is virtually the same across different-sized firms, even though smaller firms, especially

Table 3.5   Effective Corporate and Personal Tax Rates[a] by Size of Business

Asset size, $ million	Land	Buildings[b]	Machinery[b]	Inventories	Aggregate
			per cent		
0 -1/4	51.8	55.2	56.1	71.5	64.0
1/4- 1	48.3	52.0	52.5	69.4	61.9
1 - 5	40.3	51.4	54.4	75.0	67.2
5 -10	36.4	51.3	55.6	76.7	68.8
10 -25	38.9	52.6	57.8	77.0	69.4
25+	45.5	55.4	59.3	79.0	66.9

[a]See Table 3.2 for an explanation of the calculation of effective tax rates. [b]The higher tax on machinery relative to buildings reflects the very high rate of inflation assumed for these calculations. With a lower rate of inflation (5 per cent), machinery would be taxed less relative to buildings, as shown in Tables 3.2 and 3.3.

**Table 3.6   Separate Effective Corporate and Personal
Tax Rates by Size of Business**

Asset size, $ million	Effective corporate tax rate[a]				Aggregate corporate tax rate	Effective personal tax rate
	Land	Buildings	Machinery	Inventories		
			per cent			
Actual						
0 -1/4	−20.4	−11.7	−9.6	28.8	10.0	63.0
1/4- 1	−1.1	6.1	7.1	40.2	25.4	55.2
1 - 5	−18.0	3.9	9.8	50.5	35.1	55.5
5 -10	−21.6	6.8	14.9	55.3	40.2	54.0
10 -25	−13.1	12.2	21.7	57.4	43.3	52.7
25+	5.9	22.9	29.6	60.3	42.8	50.0
Same debt-asset ratio and risk[b]						
0 -1/4	10.4	14.0	14.4	41.1	27.9	52.5
1/4- 1	11.6	16.5	16.8	45.0	32.4	50.6
1 - 5	9.2	21.2	24.0	55.9	43.6	49.9
5 -10	7.7	23.6	28.0	60.1	47.9	49.4
10 -25	7.0	25.9	30.5	60.8	48.7	49.5
25+	5.9	22.9	29.6	60.3	42.8	49.7

[a]See Table 3.2 for an explanation of the calculation of effective tax rates. [b]Some variation in effective corporate tax rates across assets arises not only from the lower corporate tax rate calculated for small firms with assets of less than $5 million but also due to differences in the proportion of manufacturing investment which tends to be higher for the larger-sized business categories.

in the first two classes, face a lower corporate tax rate. There are factors other than the tax rate that influence effective tax rate calculations—small firms rely much more on debt finance relative to large firms and small firms tend to use more inventories (which are highly taxed) relative to other types of productive assets. In Table 3.6, we see that, after we correct for financing, small businesses face a higher effective corporate tax rate and slightly lower personal tax rate. Thus, the reliance on debt finance lowers effective corporate taxes on small firms relative to large firms because interest is deductible from the corporate tax. At the same time, with increased leverage, the effective personal tax rate on the rate of return to savings increases, since bond interest is more highly taxed than dividend or capital gain income at the individual level.

2) The lower statutory corporate tax rate on small businesses has ambiguous effects on effective corporate tax rates; in some cases, a higher statutory corporate tax rate can reduce rather than increase the effective corporate tax rate. This will arise when the present value of deductions for tax purposes is more than the cost of acquiring assets. Deductions such as those associated with fast CCA write-offs and with interest, unadjusted for inflation, can be so generous that businesses facing a higher statutory corporate tax rate are better off than those facing lower tax rates. As shown in Table 3.6, the effective corporate tax on land, for example, falls rather than increases with higher corporate tax rates once financing differences among firms are eliminated. This is due to the deductibility of nominal interest under the corporate tax, which is more beneficial to businesses facing higher corporate tax rates. For other assets, depreciation deductions are not so generous, except for certain equipment such as that used by manufacturing (Class 29). In these cases, the total value of deductions is less than the economic cost of investing in the assets, so that a higher statutory corporate tax rate increases the effective corporate tax rate.

The disparity in effective tax rates across different-sized businesses and types of capital has important implications for economic incentives. We will review these economic effects in the following sections.

Investment

In the absence of taxes, all firms would earn the same rate of return to capital. Once taxes are taken into account, small firms earn a lower gross of tax rate of return for all types of capital except for land, as illustrated in Table 3.7 below. In large part, this reflects the lower statutory corporate tax rate levied on Canadian-controlled private corporations, which are prominent in the two smallest asset-size categories. It also reflects the differences in financing among firms. In the presence of the deductibility of nominal interest from the corporate income tax, more highly leveraged firms benefit more from the tax subsidy associated with debt financing. Table 3.5 illustrates that the smaller firms are considerably more debt-financed than the larger firms. In Table 3.7, we show the differences in the rate of return to capital if it were assumed that all firms, regardless of size, were financed by some amount of debt. Once differences in the debt-asset ratio (with adjustments made to risk) are removed, we see that the gross of tax rate of return to capital faced by small business is substantially higher relative to that of large firms.

Savings

In the absence of taxes, all firms would pay the same risk-adjusted rate of return on capital. As shown in Table 3.6, capital income paid from small

Table 3.7 The Rates of Return to Capital (Net of Depreciation) Faced by Small and Large Business, 1979-1981[a]

Asset size, $ million	Gross of Tax Rate of Return				
	Land	Buildings	Machinery	Inventories	Average
	per cent				
Actual					
0 -1/4	5.0	5.4	5.5	8.5	6.7
1/4- 1	5.8	6.3	6.3	9.8	7.9
1 - 5	4.9	6.0	6.4	11.7	8.9
5 -10	4.8	6.3	6.9	13.2	9.9
10 -25	5.2	6.8	7.6	13.9	10.5
25 + ...	6.3	7.7	8.5	15.0	10.4
Same debt-equity ratio and risk					
0 -1/4	6.6	6.9	7.0	10.1	8.3
1/4- 1	6.6	7.0	7.0	10.6	8.6
1 - 5	6.4	7.4	7.7	13.2	10.3
5 -10	6.3	7.7	8.1	14.7	11.2
10 -25	6.3	7.7	8.5	15.0	11.5
25 + ...	6.3	7.7	8.5	15.0	10.4

Asset size, $ million	Net of Corporate and Personal Tax Rate of Return to Capital	
	Actual	Same debt-equity ratio and risk
	per cent	
0 -1/4	2.4	3.2
1/4- 1	3.0	3.4
1 - 5	2.9	3.4
5 -10	3.1	3.5
10 -25	3.2	3.5
25 + ...	3.4	3.5

[a]See Table 3.2 for an explanation of the calculation of rates of return to capital, net of depreciation, but gross of taxes.

businesses to their owners is taxed more highly at the personal level. Thus, small business owners earn a lower net of tax return on savings compared with owners of large firms (see Table 3.7). The lower return earned by small business owners reflects the greater reliance by small firms on debt finance, which we estimate is taxed at a rate of 30 per cent compared with equity, which is taxed at a combined dividend and capital gains tax rate of 17 per cent, including the dividend distribution tax. In Table 3.7, we provide an estimate of net of tax return to capital, which is corrected for differences in financing among firms. Much of the difference in the net of tax return to capital is eliminated by assuming the same level of debt financing for all firms.

The lower net of tax return to savings for the smaller businesses can have important implications for their ability to invest in capital. Even in an open economy, where businesses can be financed by both Canadian and foreign investors, the smallest corporations are normally equity-financed only by Canadian entrepreneurs. In part this arises because of the difficulty small businesses have in issuing equity to minority owners. But it also partly reflects the need for small businesses to be Canadian controlled to maintain the small business tax credit at the corporate level. Thus, personal taxes as well as corporate taxes are important in determining the level of equity ownership in small firms and, indirectly, investment undertaken by these small firms. If the net of tax return to savings invested in the small business is too low, owners of the firm would be better off investing in larger businesses or other types of capital (such as housing) that offer higher net of tax rates of returns to equity. Consequently, personal taxes can influence not only the amount of savings invested in small firms but also their level of investment if we take the view that small businesses cannot acquire equity financing from international markets.

The Structure of Production

The data presented in Table 3.5 indicate that small firms invest more in inventories and less in machinery and, to a lesser extent, buildings than do large firms. This pattern of capital investment across different-sized businesses is due in part to the composition of industry. Trade firms that tend to invest in inventories are relatively important in the small asset-size categories, while manufacturing and utilities that use more machinery dominate the larger-size categories (see Table 3.8 in the next section). This pattern of the structure of investment may also reflect the differential effects of taxes on the cost of holding assets. As shown in Table 3.7, the gross of tax rate of return to capital is higher for inventories compared with other assets for all different-sized firms, but the difference between inventory rate of return to capital and that of other types of capital is less for the smaller-sized firms compared with the larger-sized firms. Inventories held by small firms are not as highly taxed for two reasons. First, the use of FIFO accounting for the evaluation of inventories penalizes a business by taxing inflationary profits on inventories. The higher the statutory corporate tax rate, the more that taxes impinge on the cost of holding inventories. Second, small firms are more highly debt-financed. Like other assets, inventories will be taxed less in times of inflation, when a business can take advantage of the tax subsidy associated with the deductibility of nominal interest costs.

Financing of Small and Large Businesses

The tax system can also influence the financing made available from Canadian households to corporations. Table 3.7 shows that the cost of capital is higher for firms when the debt-equity ratio is lowered to that of the largest-sized firms (risk is also adjusted). For small business owners, the income from new equity issues is estimated to be taxed at the combined statutory corporate and dividend tax rate of 44 per cent (resulting from the 26 per cent corporate tax rate and 14 per cent dividend tax rate), retained earnings at the rate of 35 per cent (resulting from the 26 per cent corporate tax rate and 11 per cent capital gains tax rate), and debt at the rate of 30 per cent (see Table 3.4 for these tax rates). For owners of the largest-sized firms, the tax rates are estimated to be 54 per cent, 53 per cent, and 30 per cent respectively, under the assumption that all firms are financed by investors of the same income class. These tax rates suggest that Canadian households prefer to own debt rather than equity issued by firms regardless of size, although the difference in taxes on equity and debt is less for the smallest asset-size categories.

Would a business prefer to be debt-financed? This question is difficult to answer once we take into account the availability of foreign savings to finance business. Studies in the United States[8] suggest that the level of personal tax rates on capital income is similar to that in Canada except for the tax on dividends, which is far higher in the United States, where no dividend tax credit is available. If we assume Canadian-controlled corporate equity is marginally financed by U.S. investors, the combined statutory corporate (Canadian) and personal (U.S.) tax rate on Canadian investments will then be 68 per cent on new equity, 52 per cent on retained earnings, and 30 per cent on debt. This suggests an even stronger tax deterrent exists against new equity financing for large taxpaying corporations that acquire financing from abroad.

All this discussion is further complicated by the availability of business financing from intermediaries such as banks and life insurance companies. We cannot provide a detailed analysis of the importance of taxation in influencing financial intermediation. These issues will be left for future research.

Industry Comparisons of Effective Corporate Tax Rates

Our final set of calculations is a comparison of effective corporate tax rates by industry and type of capital, on the basis of 1984 corporate tax law. The assumption used in this set of calculations is that all corporations, regardless of industry, pay the same gross of personal tax rate of return to savers. That is, the interest cost of debt and equity finance, as well as the financing ratios, are the same across industries. We also assume that the personal tax on domestic ownership of business capital is the same across all firms, since we do not have information to assume otherwise. For this reason, we present effective corporate tax rates only. Under these assumptions, the pattern of effective corporate tax rates reflects differences in costs of capital due to the tax system and the structure of investment rather than differences in financial structure and risk. It would be of interest to allow for such differences in calculating effective corporate tax rates, but none of the results discussed below would be affected in an important way if financial ratios and risk premiums varied across industries. The important differences among industries are with respect to the tax system, the type of capital, and size of firms in each industry. Table 3.8 provides a list of these data. As

---

[8]See Martin Feldstein, "Inflation, Tax Rules and Investment: Some Econometric Evidence" (1982), 50 *Econometrica* 825-62.

Table 3.8   Estimated Data Used for Effective Tax Rate Calculations by Industry
(in percentages)

	Agriculture, fishing, and forestry	Manufacturing	Construction	Utilities	Wholesale trade	Retail trade	Services
Tax parameters							
Statutory corporate rate	23.0	40.0	27.0	46.0	36.0	30.0	28.0
Proportion of industry claiming small business deduction	87.0	12.0	72.0	10.0	41.0	61.0	67.0
Investment tax credit	4.4	5.1	2.4	0.7	2.8	0.3	0.7
Inventory allowance	—[a]	2.8	0.4	1.2	2.7	2.9	2.0
Capital cost allowance[b]							
Buildings	10.0	5.5	6.5	5.5	6.5	7.5	6.0
Machinery	26.0	51.0	37.0	12.0[c]	36.0	26.0	28.0
Other data							
Capital investment weights[d]							
Buildings	0.12	0.12	0.19	0.12	0.09	0.16	0.27
Machinery	0.53	0.53	0.54	0.83	0.29	0.45	0.62
Land	0.19	0.01	0.07	0.01	0.04	0.05	0.10
Inventories	0.15	0.34	0.20	0.04	0.58	0.33	0.02
Physical depreciation[b]							
Buildings	4.0	4.5	4.0	4.0	4.0	4.0	4.0
Machinery	14.0	14.5	17.0	10.5[c]	20.5	22.0	22.2

[a] Agriculture, fishing, and tree farmers use cash accounting for inventory purposes. The proportion of inventories in this sector is underestimated to the degree that the inventories are not reported as an asset. [b] These are approximate numbers. A straight-line rate of 50 per cent was converted to an equivalent declining balance rate of 67 per cent for the numbers reported in this table. For the calculation of effective tax rates reported later, the value of capital cost allowances was calculated on a straight-line basis for each asset. [c] Class 2 assets held by utilities are treated as machinery rather than buildings, since no data allows us to separate these assets. [d] Weights based on gross-investment flows in Statistics Canada, *Corporation Financial Statistics* (annual), Catalogue no. 61-207 (1979–1981) and data published by the Department of Finance, "The Theory and Empirical Methodology Underlying the Measure of Marginal Tax Rates," December 1985 background paper for Canada, Department of Finance, Budget Papers, The Corporate Income Tax System: A Direction for Change, May 1985.

shown in this table, statutory corporate tax rates varied in 1984 from 23 per cent for agriculture, fishing, and forestry—which are primarily small businesses—to 46 per cent for utilities—which are mainly large firms. Manufacturing businesses faced a relatively high statutory tax rate even though those firms benefited from a special reduction of up to six percentage points in their statutory corporate rate. The reason is that most investment is undertaken by large firms that cannot be taxed at a lower small business rate.

As of 1985, investment tax credits also vary by industry. The credit can be claimed on qualifying depreciable capital used for agriculture, fishing, forestry, manufacturing, processing, and resource industries. However, a large portion of machinery and building investments is not eligible for the investment tax credits, such as automobiles and trucks in Class 10 and many machinery assets in Class 8. Even though the statutory investment tax credit rate is 7 per cent (10 per cent in slower growth areas, 20 per cent in the Atlantic provinces, and 50 per cent in special designated regions), the average value of the credit is limited by the eligibility of the investments. (The substantial amendments to the investment tax credit in 1986 include a phasing out of the general 7 per cent rate by 1989.)

The inventory allowance of 3 per cent is available to all industries. Certain types of inventories such as real property inventory are not, however, eligible for the inventory allowance. As a result, the inventory allowance claimed as a percentage of the opening year balance of inventories is much lower for construction and utilities. Since agriculture, fishing, and forestry generally use cash accounting for inventories, inventories in these industries are expensed when acquired. (This allowance was repealed in 1986.)

Industries are also treated differently with respect to their capital cost allowances. Manufacturing industries are permitted to deduct certain machinery expenditures at a 50 per cent straight-line rate (subject to the "half-year" convention introduced in 1981 limiting the CCA rate to one-half of its usual value). Heavy construction machinery is written off at a 50 per cent declining balance CCA rate. Other industries are able to deduct certain investment expenditures at a faster rate than the true rate of economic depreciation. In Table 3.8, these CCA rates are reported by industry. The CCA rates for wholesale trade reflect a fairly significant portion of manufacturing and construction machinery held by leasing companies that are classified as part of wholesale trade. The low CCA rates for utilities reflect the inclusion of durable machinery and structures listed under Class 2.

Not only are there explicit differences in how the tax law treats industries, they are also taxed differently because they use different proportions of the various types of capital. Manufacturing, construction, utilities, and service industries tend to invest more in machinery. Manufacturing and the trade industries invest a large proportion of their funds in inventories. Land is significant only in agriculture and, to a lesser degree, in services and construction. Buildings are most important in retail trade, services, and construction industries.

Physical rates of depreciation on capital also vary by industry. Table 3.8 provides an approximate average of rates of depreciation based on the additions made to various CCA classes as published by the Department of Finance.[9] Utilities use the most durable machinery assets, while trade and services require the least durable (such as automobiles, trucks, and computers). Little variation occurs among industries with respect to physical depreciation rates for buildings.

Using the data as summarized in Table 3.8, we provide an estimate of the effective corporate tax rates on capital for each industry in Table 3.9. The higher the effective corporate tax rate, the higher the marginal rate of return to capital (gross of taxes) that needs to be earned by the industry to cover the cost of holding capital, and therefore the greater the disincentive to invest. Table 3.9 shows that considerable variation exists among industries and types of capital with respect to these tax rates. The two cases we have presented indicate that this variation exists regardless of the interest and inflation rates chosen for these calculations. In Case I, we used 1984 values of nominal interest rates (including risk) and expected rates of inflation. In general, the real interest rate (nominal interest less inflation) is relatively high in this year compared with a 20-year historical average. Case II provides estimates for the 1977-1980 period, for which we used observed nominal interest rates, which were low relative to expected inflation. This provides a guide to the variation in effective tax rates across industries when inflation and interest rates vary over time.

Our general conclusion is that the effective corporate tax rates vary significantly across assets and sectors, providing an incentive for resources to be allocated across sectors differently than would be the case in an economy where there was no corporate tax. This is illustrated in Table 3.9 where tax rates vary from −15.0 to 42.0 per cent (Case I) and −30 to 55 per cent (Case II). As shown in Table 3.9, there is considerable variation in effective tax rates both across sectors and assets. The following are the most significant differences:

1) Except for agriculture, fishing, and forestry (which use cash accounting for inventories), inventories are the most highly taxed asset. This is especially so in the construction and utilities industries, where the inventory allowance is more restricted. Buildings are generally more highly taxed than machinery, except in retail trade and service industries, which use less durable equipment such as computers, automobiles, and trucks. These assets are more highly taxed under the current tax system than are other machinery assets. Land is generally less highly taxed as an asset compared with buildings, but can be more highly taxed than machinery for some industries.

2) Agriculture, fishing, and forestry, also construction and, to a lesser extent, manufacturing and services industries are more favourably treated

---

[9]See Canada, Department of Finance, "The Theory and Empirical Methodology Underlying the Measure of Marginal Tax Rates," December 1985 background paper for Canada, Department of Finance, Budget Papers, The Corporate Income Tax System: A Direction for Change, May 1985.

**Table 3.9   Effective Corporate Tax Rates by Industry[a]
(Current Law)**

Industry	Buildings	Machinery	Land	Inventories	Aggregate
Case I					
Real cost of funds of 10.0%[b]					
Agriculture-fishing-forestry	7.7	0.4	12.8	−14.6	2.1
Manufacturing	25.3	7.6	22.9	33.6	20.5
Construction	17.3	6.7	15.1	33.5	16.0
Utilities	32.5	31.6	25.8	42.3	32.2
Wholesale trade	22.9	18.9	24.3	31.2	27.1
Retail trade	16.9	25.2	20.6	26.9	24.3
Services	15.6	23.5	15.3	28.2	20.8
Total	24.0	20.5	18.3	32.1	24.0
Case II					
Real cost of funds of 5.0%[c]					
Agriculture-fishing-forestry	5.0	−0.6	6.0	−29.8	−2.0
Manufacturing	23.8	5.9	10.1	45.1	25.8
Construction	16.6	8.5	6.9	47.4	21.3
Utilities	31.0	33.2	11.7	54.8	34.1
Wholesale trade	21.6	24.8	10.9	43.2	36.2
Retail trade	15.3	34.2	9.2	38.5	32.3
Services	15.3	31.8	7.0	40.5	26.1
Total	22.7	22.5	8.2	43.8	28.6

[a]See Table 3.2 for an explanation of the formulas used to calculate effective tax rate. The nominal cost of funds in absence of taxes used for these calculations is $R = \beta i + (1 - \beta)\rho$ where i = nominal interest rate, ρ = cost of equity finance including the risk premium, and β = debt-asset ratio. The formulas used for the calculation of effective tax rates and the gross of tax rates of return to capital are provided in footnotes to Table 3.2. For agriculture, fishing, and forestry, the gross of tax rate of return to inventory capital was calculated as $r_g = \beta i(1 - u) + (1 - \beta)\rho - \pi$ (u is the corporate tax rate). [b]Based on the 1984 nominal interest rate of 12 per cent, the cost of equity finance of 16.3 per cent, and the expected inflation rate (5 per cent). [c]Based on the 1977-1980 nominal interest rate of 10.2 per cent, the cost of equity finance of 14.5 per cent, and the expected inflation rate (7.5 per cent).

under corporate tax law. Agriculture, fishing, and forestry and services and construction benefit more from the low small business tax rate. As well, agriculture and fishing use cash accounting for inventories, thus reducing their sectoral tax rate. Construction and manufacturing benefit from accelerated capital cost allowance write-offs. Agriculture, fishing, and forestry as well as manufacturing and, to a lesser extent, wholesale trade (leasing) have benefited from the investment tax credit, which reduces the effective corporate tax rate on machinery.

3) Sectors that must hold a large portion of assets in inventories have been taxed more highly for this reason. These sectors include manufacturing, wholesale trade, and retail trade, which invest at least 30 per cent of their funds in inventories. Sectors that hold a large proportion of their assets in machinery have been less highly taxed when these assets are written off more quickly and when the investment tax credit is applied to them. This is especially so for manufacturing, construction, agriculture, fishing, and forestry, which invest over 50 per cent of their funds in machinery.

4) It is unclear whether the tax system distorts investment more across

sectors or across assets. The difference between highest and lowest effective corporate tax rates across sectors is 30 per cent (Case I) and 38 per cent (Case II). The difference in effective corporate tax rates across assets within a sector varies from 10 per cent (retail trade) to 27.4 per cent (agriculture, fishing, and forestry) for Case I and 29.3 per cent (retail trade) to 43.1 per cent (utilities) for Case II. It is difficult to measure the economic cost associated with this dispersion in effective tax rates without knowing the responsiveness of investment to the tax-adjusted cost of capital. The substantial differences in tax rates suggest that the corporate tax system could impose large economic costs by distorting the allocation of resources in the economy. We are, however, unable to provide any estimates of the economic cost arising from the non-neutral impact of the corporate tax on the basis of the size of the distortions alone. More empirical work needs to be done on the quantitative effect of these distortions on capital allocation, now that more precise measures of the distortions are coming available.

The above interindustry tax rate comparisons are only for 1984 law and do not incorporate corporate tax changes proposed in the May 1985 budget and the tax changes instituted in the February 1986 budget. Because the government also intends to revise the capital cost allowance classes, there will be further changes in tax rates. These changes are meant to reduce dispersions in effective tax rates, although our numbers suggest that for inventories, at least, such dispersions may not be fully eliminated.

This final set of calculations completes our description of the distortions imposed by the corporate tax system in Canada. The substantial variation in effective tax rates across industries and assets indicates that the corporate tax system may have an important impact on sectoral investment, costs of production, industry output, and use of resources. Recent studies in the United States[10] suggest that these effects can be quite substantial as a percentage of tax revenue raised, but further work is needed in Canada to confirm these results.

Conclusions

In this chapter, we have quantified the effect of the corporate and personal tax system on the structure of investment, financing, and domestic savings available to businesses in Canada. The provisions of the income tax system were incorporated in a measure of the effective tax rate, which was based on the arguments developed in Chapter 2. Calculations were made for the years 1963-1978 for investments in four assets undertaken by all industries; for the years 1979-1981 for six different-sized corporations and four assets; and for the year 1984 for seven industries and four assets. Our major results have been as follows:

1) For all corporations, the average effective corporate tax rate had fallen in Canada, but the effective personal tax rate on domestic ownership

---

[10]Don Fullerton, Andrew B. Lyon, and Richard J. Rosen, "Uncertainty, Welfare Cost and the Adaptability of U.S. Corporate Taxes" (1984), 86, no. 2 *The Scandinavian Journal of Economics* 229-43.

of corporate capital had risen from the 1962-1971 period to the 1972-1981 period.

2) Inventories have generally been more highly taxed while land is least taxed. This is not true for all years or for all sectors. In some cases, machinery is the least taxed asset (manufacturing and construction) or inventories are the least taxed asset (agriculture, fishing, and forestry).

3) Smaller businesses are taxed less than larger corporations because of the small business tax rate reduction available to qualifying corporations. The low tax rate does not always reduce the effective tax. A lower tax rate reduces the value of fast write-offs (capital cost allowances and interest deductions) so that some assets, such as manufacturing machinery, are more highly taxed in the hands of the small business compared with the large business.

4) Investments that tend to be debt-financed rather than equity-financed are taxed less in terms of the combined corporate and personal income tax. This is due to the deductibility of interest by the corporation, which is taxed more highly than the individual who receives the interest. The advantage of debt financing increases with higher rates of inflation.

We have also found that the effective tax rates can be sensitive to the inflation rate, and to the cost of debt and equity financing. This suggests that effective tax rates not only vary across assets and sectors but also vary over time. It further suggests that corporate and personal tax revenue collected on capital income can be a highly unstable source of revenue for the government.

In the next two chapters, we will discuss various policies that would reform the current corporate and personal tax system and remove the biases associated with the current tax system which influence the decisions made by corporations in Canada. The effective tax rates that we have presented here are background information needed to evaluate reform of the tax on capital income.

All these calculations have been made under the assumptions that the company is taxpaying and that the Canadian income tax (as opposed to any foreign tax) is binding at the margin. The first assumption implies that tax losses generated by assets that are treated liberally under the tax system can be fully written off taxable income generated by other assets owned by corporations. If tax losses could not be fully used, then our measure of effective tax rates would be higher or lower depending on the asset and history of the corporation. According to the second assumption, we ignore foreign ownership of Canadian corporations. In certain circumstances, foreign subsidiaries operating in Canada may fully credit Canadian taxes against home country liabilities. Unless the subsidiary reinvests profits in Canada, allowing it to defer payment of home country tax liabilities, the effective tax rate on subsidiary investments in Canada is not based on Canadian corporate tax law but the home country's corporate tax law. As discussed by Brean,[11] most subsidiary investment in Canada is financed by retained earnings; con-

---

[11]Donald J. S. Brean, *International Issues in Taxation: The Canadian Perspective*, Canadian Tax Paper no. 75 (Toronto: Canadian Tax Foundation, 1984).

sequently, most foreign subsidiary investment is affected by Canadian tax law.

APPENDIX
DESCRIPTION OF DATA SOURCES

The methodology used to estimate various parameters contained in the expressions for the cost of capital and effective tax rates is described in this Data Appendix. For each set of calculations, three types of estimates were made, as follows: (1) time series estimates, (2) business size estimates, and (3) industry estimates.

Financing Ratios

1) *Time series estimates*: The sources of financing capital investment were obtained from Statistics Canada, *Industrial Corporations: Financial Statistics*, Catalogue no. 61-003, which excludes agriculture, fishing, construction, government corporations, and foreign branch data. New debt was defined as the difference between year-end values of short-term and long-term loans, accounts payable, and other current liabilities excluding deferred income taxes and minority shareholders' liabilities. New equity finance was calculated by taking the difference between year-end values of paid-up capital, contributed surplus, and minority shareholders' liabilities. Retained earnings were computed as the residual change in shareholders' equity (equity excluding paid-up capital and contributed surplus).

2) *Business size estimates*: The general methodology used for these estimates was the same as for the time series estimates. The only difference was that 1977 year-end values of liabilities and shareholders' equity (stock values) were used instead of differences in year-end values (flow values). The flow values would have been preferred but the data were unavailable.

3) *Industry estimates*: The methodology used was the same as for the time series estimates except that book-value estimates of financing ratios of nonfinancial corporations based on changes in financing sources were used for 1984 (Statistics Canada, *The National Balance Sheet Accounts, 1961-1984*, Catalogue no. 13-214). This estimate was approximately 41 per cent, which was very close to the aggregate market value estimate of the ratio of the stock of debt to the stock of assets held by nonfinancial corporations.

Physical Rates of Depreciation

For all calculations, physical depreciation rates on buildings were computed using Statistics Canada, *Fixed Capital Flows and Stocks*, Catalogue no. 13-211. The machinery estimates of physical lives were based on Charles R. Hulten and Frank C. Wykoff, "The Measurement of Economic Depreciation," in Charles R. Hulten, ed., *Depreciation, Inflation, and the Taxation of Income from Capital* (Washington, D.C.: Urban Institute Press, 1981). The estimates of service lives were matched to various capital cost allowance categories. Using weights recently published by the Department of Finance ("Department of Finance estimates" in "The Theory and Empirical Methodology Underlying the Measure of Marginal Tax Rates," December 1985 background paper for Canada, Department of Finance, Budget Papers, The Corporate Income Tax System: A Direction for Change, May 1985) for gross investment in each class, a weighted average of service lives was calculated for each case.

Using the average service life (L), a declining balance rate was calculated as $\delta = 2/L$. (For a derivation of this formula, see Chapter 1, footnote 5.)

Holding Period for Inventories

For all calculations, the holding periods of each year were computed as the ratio of the average monthly value of total inventories owned to average monthly shipments (Statistics Canada, *Inventories, Shipments and Orders in Manufacturing Industries*, Catalogue no. 31-001). The inventory-to-sales ratio was also computed using *Industrial Corporations: Financial Statistics* data, which provided similar results. Because this number was less than one year in all cases, we ignored the holding period of inventories in all calculations.

Corporate Tax Rate

Depending on the calculation, the corporate tax rate was based on an aggregation of federal and provincial tax rates for small business, large business, manufacturing, and nonmanufacturing. The weights used for aggregation were based on the distribution of corporate taxable income by province, industry, and size of firm. Corporate taxable income by province (appearing in Statistics Canada, *Corporation Taxation Statistics*, Catalogue no. 61-208) was computed excluding sectors not appearing in our data (finance and resources). For each province and industry, the shares of provincial taxable income earned by small and large firms was computed, and after 1971, the share of provincial taxable income earned by manufacturing and non-manufacturing firms was also computed.

1) *Time series estimates*: We used the weights, as derived above, to compute an average combined federal and provincial tax rate for each province. Next, a weighted average of corporate tax rates by province was computed to arrive at an aggregate corporate tax rate for that year (the weights were based on the distribution of provincial corporate taxable income).

2) *Business size estimates*: The corporate tax rate was computed by comparing the corporate taxes paid to the small business tax credit and then calculating the portion of taxable income that claimed the small business tax credit.

3) *Industry estimates*: We used a weighted average of corporate tax rates across provinces for each size and industry type.

Dividend Tax Rate

The dividend tax rate was calculated for each year by first computing an average combined federal and provincial marginal tax rate on dividends (m) according to the distribution of dividends paid to each income class (derived from Revenue Canada, *Taxation Statistics*). Allowance was made for those individuals who received dividends but had a nontaxable return. The effective tax on dividends (θ) was calculated using the average marginal tax rate (m).

     1963-1971: $\theta = m - .20$
     1972-1978: $\theta = [m - S(1 + x)(1 + w)]$

where:

     w = gross-up rate
     S = federal tax credit for dividends
     x = province's tax rate on federal taxes payable.

Accrued Capital Gains Tax Rate

The tax rate on accrued capital gains was calculated so that the present value of capital gains tax payments based on realized capital gains was equal to the present value of taxes levied on accrued gains discounted at the shareowner's after-tax opportunity cost of equity finance. The formula used to calculate c was derived as follows.

Suppose an individual invests \$1 in an equity share, the price of which grows at a constant nominal rate, g, per year. The holding period of the share is Y years, after which a capital gains tax of m_c is levied on realized capital gains, which is $e^{gY} - 1$. Letting $\rho + h$ denote the shareholders' discount rate, the present value of wealth at $t = \theta$, when capital gains are taxed on a realized basis, is

$$W_R = e^{gY} e^{-(\rho + h)Y} - m_c (e^{gY} - 1)e^{-(\rho + h)Y}.$$

If the share is taxed on an accrual basis, then in each year, the capital gain ge^{gt} is taxed at the rate c. The present value of wealth with accrued capital gains taxation is

$$W_A = e^{gY} e^{-(\rho + h)Y} - cg \int_0^Y e^{gt} e^{-(\rho + h)t} \, dt.$$

Letting $W_A = W_R$, the solution for c is

$$c = \frac{m_c (e^{gY} - 1)(g - (\rho + h))}{g(e^{gY} - e^{(\rho + h)Y})}.$$

To calculate c for each year after 1971, it is necessary to estimate g, Y, and $\rho + h$. The holding period for Y was obtained by dividing the number of shares floated by the volume traded on the Toronto Stock Exchange (TSE) for each year. Because the holding period fluctuated from year to year, an average of annual holding periods was computed (10.9 years for Y).

To compute a tax rate based on what equity owners expected to face, an expected capital gains rate for g was estimated by using autoregressive integrated moving average (ARIMA) five-year projections to stock market prices. The TSE 300 Price Index of the first month of each quarter (*Bank of Canada Review*) was differenced quarterly and yearly with a first-order moving average, first-order autoregressive and yearly moving average parameters included (the residuals satisfied the Box-Pearce test for non-correlation).

The discount rate ρ + h was calculated as follows. First, the real after-tax rate of return on debt was calculated by assuming a marginal tax rate on interest of 30 per cent (see below). To obtain a risk premium for equity (h), the average risk premium was calculated using estimates taken from capital asset pricing model techniques (see below).

To calculate m_c, we used one-half of the marginal tax rate calculated for dividends (see the discussion above). An attempt was made to calculate the average marginal tax rate according to the distribution of net realized capital gains earned on equity shares. This number was, however, highly unstable, reflecting the timing differences in realization propensities.

In the zero inflation case, ρ + h and g were both reduced by the inflation rate, π, to calculate the accrued capital gains tax rate.

Inflation Rate

To estimate the expected inflation rate, an ARIMA five-year forecast using the sample method was made based on the consumer price index. A first-order and yearly moving average, and a first-order autoregressive series, calculated quarterly and yearly, was estimated. The residuals satisfied the Box-Pearce test for noncorrelation.

Tax Depreciation (CCA) Rates

Tax depreciation declining balance rates were taken to be those set out in the Income Tax Act for buildings and machinery for all years except for 1963-1966 and 1972-1981, when manufacturing machinery and/or buildings received special tax treatment. In those years, a formula was used to calculate the present value of tax depreciation based on straight-line methods.

Let Z be the present value of the capital cost allowance assuming that $1 of capital was purchased. The straight-line depreciation rate d is applied to the original purchasing price of capital for all present and future years. We assume that depreciation is claimed at the end of the year after the investment had taken place. The nominal discount rate of the firm is $r_f + \pi$. Therefore,

$$uZ = \frac{ud}{(1 + r_f + \pi)} + \ldots + \frac{ud}{(1 + r_f + \pi)^T}$$

where

$$uZ = \frac{ud}{(r_f + \pi)}(1 - \frac{1}{(1 + r_f + \pi)^T}).$$

This formula replaced $ud/(r_f + d + \pi)$ as shown in the text for declining balance methods.

In the 1963-1966 period, manufacturing was permitted a 20 per cent straight-line depreciation write-off for buildings ($d = 0.2$ and $T = 5$) and in 1963-1966 and 1972-1981, a 50 per cent write-off for machinery ($d = 0.5$ and $T = 2$). From December 2, 1970 to April 1, 1972, a special markup of 15 per cent applied to the purchasing price of capital was allowed for manufacturing investment in depreciable capital. This was incorporated in the calculation of the depreciation allowances for 1971.

1) *Time series estimates*: An average CCA rate was calculated by taking a weighted average CCA of rates of the most important classes. For buildings, most investment was in Class 3. For machinery, the most important classes were 2, 8, 10, 22, and 29. The present value of CCA allowances was calculated for manufacturing and nonmanufacturing and then aggregated.

2) *Business size estimates*: Same as for time series estimates.

3) *Industry estimates*: These calculations were based on the 1984 tax system. Consequently, they include the half-year convention used for all CCA classes (except 7 and 12). For a declining balance class, the present value of CCA write-offs was calculated according to the following formula:

$$uZ = ud/2 + \sum_{t=1}^{\infty} u(1 - \frac{d}{2})\frac{(1 - d)^{t-1}}{(1 + r_f + \pi)^t}$$

$$= ud/2 + (1 - \frac{d}{2}) ud/[(d + r_f + \pi)(1 + r_f + \pi)].$$

A similar formula was also obtained for the straight-line classes:

$$uZ = ud/[2(1 + r_f + \pi)] + \frac{(1 - d/2)ud}{(1 + r_f + \pi)}(1 - \frac{1}{(1 + r_f + \pi)^T}).$$

Investment Tax Credit

The investment tax credit rate was calculated by using the Department of Finance estimates described above in "Physical Rates of Depreciation." The rate was calculated as the investment tax credit earned divided by additions to the CCA base excluding tax credits associated with research and development.

Inventory Tax Allowance

The inventory tax allowance was based on Department of Finance estimates for the inventory allowance earned as a portion of the opening year balance of inventories.

Corporate Bond Rate

The nominal rate was calculated by taking a 12-month average of the McLeod Young Weir long-term bond yields, which provided an effective interest rate on newly issued bonds (*Bank of Canada Review*). The after-tax real rate of return on debt was calculated as $r_b^n = i(1 - m) - \pi$ where π was the expected rate of inflation and m the marginal tax rate on interest income. We estimated m = 30 per cent for the period 1961-1973. From 1974-1978, the tax rate on interest income was estimated as approximately 22 per cent with the $1,000 exemption taken into account. After 1978, the tax rate rose to about 35 per cent by 1981. We took 30 per cent as the tax rate for all years 1961-1981.

The After-Tax Opportunity Cost of Equity (ρ + h)

1) *Time series estimates*: We first estimated the before-personal-tax real return to equity by calculating the inverse of the price-earnings ratio (monthly values averaged for the year) for shares traded on the Toronto Stock Exchange (*Bank of Canada Review*). Book earnings were adjusted to take into account the impact of inflation on the replacement cost of inventories and capital as well as the reduction in the real value of the debt's principal. A three-year moving average of adjusted price-earnings ratios was computed to take into account cyclical effects on earnings. This yields a real before-personal-tax return on equity assuming that inflation-adjusted profits are a good proxy of expected earnings on marginal investment decisions (because only average earnings rather than marginal earnings were estimated, our estimate of marginal return to equity is likely biased upwards).

2) *Business size estimates*: To correct for differences in finance, the risk premium was calculated for the TSE Index 1978-1980 (approximately 7 per cent) and then adjusted for leverage. This estimate was obtained from a capital asset pricing model study done for Canadian stocks by Glen Parker, "Capital Asset Pricing Estimates: An Industry Study," (masters essay, Queen's University, 1983). It can be shown that the risk premium increases proportionately with the inverse of the equity-asset ratio:

$$h' = h/(1 - \beta).$$

Greater leverage (higher β) implies a greater degree of risk faced by the equity investor. The estimate of the risk premium using the top 300 firms on the TSE reflects the equity-asset ratio of large firms $(1 - \beta^L)$. For smaller firms the risk premium was calculated as follows:

$$h = \frac{h^L(1 - \beta^L)}{(1 - \beta^s)}$$

where β^s is the debt-asset ratio of the small-sized firms.

3) *Industry estimates*: The estimate of the cost of equity finance was taken as the 1984 interest rate earned on risk-free bonds (treasury bill rate) plus the estimated risk premium on shares traded on the TSE from 1968 to 1980: 7 per cent.

4

Reforming the Treatment of Capital Income Under the Personal Tax

The Personal Tax Base—Income or Consumption?

The issues surrounding the treatment of capital income under the personal tax primarily involve the choice of a tax base—in particular, the choice of income versus consumption as the base. The choice of the rate structure, in turn, depends on the base chosen. This chapter will discuss in some detail the policy debate over these two bases, drawing on the arguments of the important policy documents that have appeared in various countries since the mid-seventies. These include the U.S. Treasury's *Blueprints for Basic Tax Reform*, the Meade Report in the United Kingdom, and the recent report of the Macdonald Royal Commission in Canada.[1] These documents all reflect a considerable revision of thinking about both the ideals and the practicality of tax reform since the immensely influential Carter Report.[2]

The fundamental difference between the Carter view of tax reform and these more recent documents is the choice of the tax base. Following the consensus of the time, the Carter Commission took the position that comprehensive income was the ideal tax base. The basis of this position was the argument that equity required that persons be taxed according to their ability to pay, which was best measured by a broad and nondiscriminatory definition of income as captured in the slogan, "a buck is a buck." Other documents—such as the Meade Report and the U.S. Treasury's *Blueprints for*

---

[1]United States, Department of the Treasury, *Blueprints for Basic Tax Reform* (Washington, D.C.: U.S. Government Printing Office, 1977); The Institute for Fiscal Studies, *The Structure and Reform of Direct Taxation*, Report of a Committee chaired by Professor J. E. Meade (London: George Allen & Unwin, 1978) ("the Meade Report"); Canada, *Report of the Royal Commission on the Economic Union and Development Prospects for Canada* (Ottawa: Department of Supply and Services, 1985) ("the Macdonald Report").

[2]Canada, *Royal Commission on Taxation* (Ottawa: Queen's Printer, 1966) ("the Carter Report"). See also, United States, Department of the Treasury, *Tax Reform for Fairness, Simplicity, and Economic Growth* (Washington, D.C.: the Department, November 1984) ("Treasury I"), and United States, Office of the President, *The President's Tax Proposals to the Congress for Fairness, Growth, and Simplicity* (Washington D.C.: U.S. Government Printing Office, May 1985) ("Treasury II"). The 1984 and 1985 proposals of the U.S. Treasury have adopted a philosophy more akin to the Carter Report than to the earlier documents. Treasury I and II, however, reflect primarily political flexibility and expediency more than they indicate any reversion to the principles of Carter. See Charles E. McLure Jr., "Rationale Underlying the Treasury Proposals," in *Economic Consequences of Tax Simplification* (Boston, Mass.: Federal Reserve Bank of Boston, 1985), 29-48.

Tax Reform cited above—have opted instead, with varying degrees of conviction, for a tax based on consumption or its equivalent.

As was discussed in the first chapter, we can detect three reasons why consumption is advocated as a tax base. One has to do with administrative simplicity. It has been increasingly recognized that the ideal comprehensive income tax base advocated by Carter is simply unattainable on practical administrative grounds. Comprehensive income taxation requires that all returns on assets, whether received in money or in an imputed form, be included in the tax base. It requires that these returns be included on accrual rather than on realization. And, it requires that they be purged of any purely inflationary components. All these requirements pose administrative difficulties and imply that any income tax system will necessarily favour some assets at the expense of others. For example, the ideal tax system would tax the imputed rent on all consumer durables (including owner-occupied housing), would tax the imputed returns on investment in human capital, and would even tax the imputed return on cash balances. The existing system does none of these, and it is apparent that to do so would be very difficult. Similarly, the ideal income tax system would tax all capital gains on all assets as they accrue, and it would have to index them and other sources of capital income (dividends, interest, rent, etc.) fully for inflation. Savings in pension funds would have to be taxable. Personal business income would have to be taxed on a proper accrual basis with the appropriate deduction for true economic depreciation. These requirements are all difficult to achieve both for administrative and for practical political reasons. Thus, an ideal comprehensive system is an unattainable ideal. As will be discussed in this chapter, these difficult problems do not arise with the consumption-based tax. It is relatively simple to administer and avoids discriminatory treatment that the existing system imposes on assets of different sorts.[3]

A second reason for advocating consumption as a base for personal taxation is the equity argument. There are various ways of putting it, but the most fundamental is as follows. Equity requires that the taxes that people pay be based on how well-off they are, or as economists say, what their utility level is. What ultimately determines how well-off people are is the amount of consumption they enjoy. Thus, aggregate consumption ought to be the tax base. Another way to put it is that taxes should be based on what is taken out of the social pot (consumption) rather than what is contributed (income). Yet another way to put it is to say that consumption should bear the same tax whether it is done today or sometime in the future. As discussed later, an essential difference between an income tax and a consumption tax is that, under the former, future consumption bears a heavier tax than current consumption. For these reasons, there are equity arguments in

---

[3]There are some problems common to both that do not involve capital income: leisure, household production, the treatment of family, etc.

favour of a consumption-based tax, although, as with all equity arguments, it is ultimately a matter for value judgment.[4]

These arguments concern the tax base only, not the rate structure, and it is important to keep those two distinct. A disadvantage often attributed to the consumption tax is its alleged regressivity. It is argued that a consumption tax would hurt the poor and help the rich since the poor consume a higher proportion of their income than the rich. This argument ignores the fact that the choice of rate structure is independent of the choice of base. A move to a consumption tax could be accompanied by a change in the rate structure so as to achieve the same degree of progressivity if desired.

The third reason for advocating consumption taxation concerns efficiency. A consumption tax removes the distortion on capital markets that exists with the income tax, since the latter taxes the return to savings while the former does not. This efficiency argument is not an unambiguous one. The distortion on capital markets is not the only distortion resulting from personal taxation. Under both consumption and income bases, labour markets are distorted as well. The move to a consumption base is likely to increase the labour market distortion, since the smaller consumption tax base means one must have higher tax rates to raise the same revenue.[5] In principle, the efficiency effects could go either way, depending on whether the capital market distortion is more serious than the effect on the labour market. Consumption tax advocates point to some recent simulation work that suggests that existing capital market distortions in the United States may be considerably larger than was formerly believed.

We have come to the view that, on balance, these arguments are compelling, and that a full-fledged consumption-based personal tax would be preferable to the present, imperfect income tax. The remainder of this chapter seeks to do two things. First, it elaborates in more detail the equity and efficiency arguments and the administration and design of a consumption tax. Second, we consider what sorts of reforms would take us from the present system to a consumption tax, bearing in mind that, to the extent possible, one may want to do this in a way that is neutral in regard to both revenue and distribution.

The Design of a Consumption Tax

Our interest is in the choice and measurement of a consumption *tax base*. The further problem of going from the tax base to taxes payable is not of particular concern. The issues surrounding the appropriate forms of deductions and exemptions, the treatment of the family unit, and the rate structure raise questions of horizontal and vertical equity not unlike those

---

[4]One interesting attempt to avoid this value judgment was the following argument. If one views lifetime as the appropriate time period over which tax liabilities should be assessed, the consumption base and the income base are the same thing in the sense that the present value of consumption will equal the present value of income; they differ only in their timing.

[5]This is not necessarily so in the long run. If the consumption tax base increases real income significantly because of an increase in capital formation, the tax base could increase.

encountered under the comprehensive income tax. We, therefore, restrict our discussion to the imputation of a tax base.

In principle, the tax base for a consumption tax should be an unambiguous concept—it is simply the stream of consumption over time measured either directly or indirectly (by subtracting changes in accumulated wealth from the flow of income). The latter is the preferred method because of the administrative difficulties of measuring consumption directly. There are, however, a number of subtleties involved in putting such a tax base into practice. In this section, we lay out the basic accounting procedures that would be appropriate for arriving at a measure of consumption as the tax base.

We also point out some alternatives to the pure consumption tax base that are equivalent in present value terms. These alternatives will be considered because of two fundamental difficulties that arise in using consumption as a tax base. The first is that when some consumption takes the form of consuming the services of durable goods, there are difficulties in measuring the flow of these consumption services, since no market prices exist to measure them directly. The second is that the time profile of taxable consumption may be unsuitable as a tax base either because of the liquidity problems involved in paying taxes when consumption is being financed out of borrowing, or because the time stream is not level so that the progressivity of the tax system would make some form of averaging desirable. The alternatives we consider are ways of avoiding either of these two problems. We begin by considering the simplest of cases, in which all consumption is of the nondurable type. We then introduce the existence of durables.

At the outset, it is useful to state explicitly the general manner of dealing with inflation. There are two general ways of proceeding. The first is to define the tax base in *real* terms—that is, as *real consumption*. Since we are measuring consumption indirectly by subtracting additions to wealth from comprehensive income, this method would involve indexing both the measure of comprehensive income and wealth changes so as to obtain real values for each. Needless to say, this would be administratively complex to do and fortunately can be avoided. The second alternative, and the one we follow, is to measure consumption in nominal terms, but to index the rate structure and exemption-deduction system. With this procedure, all income is in nominal terms and all savings deductions are in nominal terms. There is no need to index capital income to reflect changes in the real value of assets as there is under the comprehensive income tax base. This provides a significant administrative advantage to the consumption tax over the income tax—no part of the tax base need be indexed.

Case 1: All Consumption Is on Nondurables

The principles involved in this case are quite straightforward and follow from the simple accounting identity governing the individual's consumption opportunities in a given tax period:

$$C_t = Y_t + rW_t - \Delta W_t$$

where Y_t is nominal noncapital income earned in period t (including labour income, inheritances, etc.), r is the interest or dividend payment received per dollar of accumulated wealth, W_t is accumulated wealth, and ΔW_t is the change in the nominal value of accumulated wealth (that is, nominal savings). Notice the important point that since C_t is current consumer expenditures, both capital income, rW_t, and savings, ΔW_t, can be measured on a cash flow or realization basis rather than on an accrual basis. That is, under accrual accounting, accrued capital gains appear equally as capital income and wealth increases, and wash out in the consumption identity; consequently it is not necessary to measure them separately.

This implies that from an administrative point of view, the tax base is reasonably simple to administer. Despite the fact that income must be measured as part of the procedure for calculating consumption, one can argue that this system is in fact simpler to administer than the comprehensive income tax for two reasons. First, as mentioned, capital income need not be indexed under a consumption tax, but it must under an income tax. Under a consumption tax, if a consumer gets inflationary capital income and consumes it, he is taxed; however, if he saves it to maintain his real wealth intact, it is deducted. Second, the income tax should include accrued rather than realized capital gains in its base, while under the consumption tax there is no need to measure accrued capital gains. An additional administrative cost involved with a consumption tax is in accounting for savings, both positive and negative. In practice, this involves keeping an ongoing account of wealth holdings. We return to this problem later.

Let us summarize this case in a simple numerical example that we shall carry through to following sections. Suppose that, after an initial period, a consumer earns wage income of $20,000 per year during his lifetime. Suppose also that he acquires an inheritance of $100,000 in the first period and that the nominal interest rate is 10 per cent. Inheritances enter the tax base, since they are a source of consumption, but savings from inheritances are deductible. Suppose also that he consumes a gradually increasing amount each year equal to his total interest income and plans to leave the rest as a bequest. We assume that because the giving of bequests is not considered an act of consumption it has no tax consequences for the donor. (We return to the problem of bequests later.) His taxable consumption is calculated in Table 4.1. Notice that it rises in nominal terms from $10,000 in the first year by $2,000 each year until in year 70 it is $148,000. His accumulated wealth at that time is $1,480,000, which is left as a bequest and becomes taxable income for his heirs. Of course, if some is given inter vivos to his heirs, it will be added to the tax base of his heirs at that time, and they, rather than the donor, will receive the interest income.

Two difficulties ought to be pointed out at this point, both arising from the gradually increasing tax base. The first is that, assuming a progressive tax structure, some form of tax averaging is desirable for reasons of horizontal equity. For example, if two consumers have the same total amount of

Table 4.1   Tax Base Calculation with No Durables

	Year			
	1	2	5	70
	dollars			
Income:				
Wages + inheritance	100,000	20,000	20,000	20,000
Capital	10,000	12,000	18,000	148,000
Less: savings	−100,000	−20,000	−20,000	−20,000
Consumption tax base	10,000	12,000	18,000	148,000
Capital-income-exempt base	100,000	20,000	20,000	−1,460,000

tax base over a series of years, but one's tax base fluctuates while the other's is steady, the one with a fluctuating tax base is liable for more total tax under a progressive rate structure with no averaging. The additional tax incurred when the base is higher than average outweighs the tax reduction when the base is lower than average. Since over this period, both can consume the same amount, they should be taxed the same amount. Second, in the absence of averaging, the progressive tax rate applied to consumption increases over time, presumably even if the tax structure itself is indexed. This means that the relative price of present versus future consumption will be distorted by the tax system and therefore the consumer's savings decision will be distorted. A system of averaging avoids both these problems, the first one being an equity problem, and the second an efficiency problem.

Consider now an alternative tax base often advocated in the literature, which has the property that the present value of the tax base is identical to that of the above consumption tax but its time profile is different. That base is a comprehensive income with capital income exempt. The difference between this system and the one above is that savings are no longer deductible but capital income is excluded from the tax base. In the notation of the previous example, the tax base is simply Y_t, noncapital income (including inheritances and gifts received). As can be seen from the accounting identity above, the base Y_t differs from the base C_t by the amount ($\Delta W_t - rW_t$)— that is, by the acquisition of wealth less interest (or other capital income) receipts.

The present value equivalence between these two bases should be readily apparent. The difference lies in the way they treat assets. The consumption base falls by the value of the asset when an asset is acquired. It then rises later on by the principal plus interest accumulated when the asset is sold. Since the present value of principal and interest equals the initial value of the asset, exempting capital income but not allowing savings to be deducted, as is done under the capital-income-exempt system, will leave the tax base unchanged in present value terms. This equivalence holds because we expect all future returns on an asset to be capitalized into its purchase price so that the purchase price of the asset just equals the present value of future capital income plus principal. If this does not happen, say, because of unexpected windfall gains, the equivalence of the tax bases in present value terms may not be satisfied. We return to that below.

Notice, again, that all accounting can be done on a realization basis rather than on an accrual basis and that inflation indexing is unnecessary. Since accrued capital income that is not realized but is saved is a component of both ΔW_t and rW_t, it cancels out. Once it is realized and not saved, the fall in ΔW_t just equals the realized capital income, so that it is appropriately subtracted from the tax base. Similarly, indexing is not necessary, since the component of nominal capital income attributed to inflation is just the part of ΔW_t that ought not to be included as a real addition to wealth. Since the two just cancel out, no further account need be taken of inflation in arriving at the base.

One difficulty with this formulation is that additions to wealth due to inheritances and gifts are taxable when they are received regardless of whether or not they are saved. Similarly, reductions in wealth due to gifts either at death or inter vivos are tax deductible, since they represent reductions in wealth. There could very well be significant negative taxable income at death under such a system. Such a difficulty did not arise under the consumption base defined above.

The last row in Table 4.1 indicates the tax base under a system where capital income is exempt. The present value of the stream in the last row discounted at 10 per cent just equals the present value of the stream in the second last row. Note that the time profile of the tax base under such a scheme can be quite lumpy, being especially high when inheritances are received but negative when bequests are left. In addition, if the stream of labour income is uneven over the taxpayer's lifetime, so will be the tax base.

Neither of the above two bases is ideal from an averaging point of view, although both would serve adequately if some form of automatic averaging were done on the taxpayer's behalf. Presumably such an averaging scheme would work better under the pure consumption tax than under the capital-income-exempt system, since the latter involves averaging backwards the as yet unknown negative tax payments owing on death. A close look at the distinction between these two tax systems, however, suggests a way in which they can be combined so that the individual can do his own lifetime averaging, at least in principle.

The main difference between the two is the manner in which asset accumulation and the interest thereon are treated. Under the pure consumption tax, asset accumulation is tax deductible, while interest earned is taxed when spent. Asset disposals are taxable. Under the capital-income-exempt system, asset accumulation is not deductible, asset disposals are not taxable, and interest earned (or owing) is not taxable. Each scheme gives rise to a particular flow of tax base, generally not a level one over the lifetime. Thus under a progressive tax structure, both will distort the savings decision and be horizontally inequitable.

It would be possible, in principle, to design a tax base that had the same present value as the pure consumption base, but with a level stream of consumption, by combining the pure consumption system with the capital-income-exempt system. This could be done by treating some assets as under the pure consumption tax (call them *designated assets*, following the U.S. Treasury's *Blueprints*[6]), and the rest as under the capital-income-exempt tax. Provided the taxpayer faces no capital market constraints, he can always organize his asset accumulation so that the tax base is level over his lifetime. Such a system would then combine the virtues of consumption taxation (that is, removal of the savings distortion) with perfect averaging. By giving the consumer a choice between treating particular assets on a designated basis and others on a capital-income-exempt basis, some of the other difficulties of each of the systems mentioned above are also avoided. For example, only those assets that are designated have to be continually accounted for. The consumer can designate or register assets that he intends to hold for a long time, much like the current registered pension and retirement savings plan accounting, while those that he may want to turn over frequently, or that are small, can be left undesignated and simply unaccounted for. Similarly, the problem of bearing taxes on inheritances (and having negative tax liabilities on bequests and gifts) can be avoided simply by designating the assets inherited on receipt. Thus, combining these two systems has definite advantages.

Relying on the taxpayer to allocate his assets between designated and nondesignated forms for purposes of *self-averaging* is not without its difficulties. It not only requires that the individual be able to borrow and lend fully against his future lifetime income, but it also requires perfect foresight concerning his future stream of expenditures and bequests and concerning the tax structure. It also requires that designated loans be possible and that they be treated symmetrically by the tax system (that is, added to the tax base when made and deducted as principal and interest are repaid). Two alternatives to self-averaging exist. One is to institute a central system of automatic or general averaging. This would average tax rates for a taxpayer after consumption is realized (ex post), while self-averaging does so before consumption is realized (ex ante). The latter requires foresight, while the former does not. The other alternative is to have constant *marginal* tax rates and thereby compromise the desired tax structure. It is, of course, possible to have progression in the tax system while maintaining constant marginal tax rates. This discussion on averaging ignores the fact that there may be other criteria the taxpayer or the government will use in deciding how to treat different assets, including administrative simplicity. These will be discussed below.

Case 2: Some Consumption Is from Durable Goods

Much consumer expenditure is on durable consumer goods such as housing, cars, clothing, furniture, and appliances. In all of these cases there is a distinction to be drawn between consumer *expenditures* and consumption *services*. The ideal consumption tax should presumably fall on consumption per se—that is, on the imputed services of consumer durables. It is con-

---

[6]Supra footnote 1.

sumption services that yield utility for the consumer and that is what the consumer ultimately chooses over his lifetime. The difficulty with taxing consumption services is that their value is not directly observable in the sense of having a market price associated with them. The alternative of taxing expenditures as they occur has the disadvantage of yielding a lumpy stream of tax base. Let us begin by examining the alternatives using a simple example.

Consider first the case of using the imputed services of consumer durables as the tax base. We shall simply refer to this as the *consumption services base*. Under the consumption services base, the treatment of financial asset accumulation is exactly as earlier, as is the treatment of nondurable expenditure. Financial wealth accumulation is tax deductible from comprehensive (nominal) income, while capital income is taxable if not saved, both on a realization basis. Now, however, there is an additional type of asset to consider—the real asset yielding consumption services. Under a consumption services base, expenditures on this real asset (for example, housing) are deductible when made, just like savings. The imputed consumption services ought, however, to be taxable while the durable is used. When the durable is sold, its sale value must be added to the tax base, since it is just like a running down of wealth (dissaving). Of course, it is the nominal sale value that must be included. There is no need for inflation accounting here, except for indexing the statutory tax brackets and standard deductions. In the numerical examples of this section, we simply ignore inflation by assuming that there is none.

Table 4.2 extends the example of Table 4.1 to the case in which an individual purchases a house for $80,000 and finances it partly with a mortgage. In this case, $50,000 of the $100,000 inheritance is used to acquire equity in the house while a mortgage of $30,000 is taken out to finance the

Table 4.2   Tax Base Calculation with Durable Goods

			Year		
	1	2	5	10	70
			dollars		
Income:					
Wages + inheritance	100,000	20,000	20,000	20,000	20,000
Interest received................	10,000	7,000	13,000	23,000	148,000
Less: mortgage interest	—	−3,000	−3,000	−3,000	—
Imputed rent	—	8,000	8,000	8,000	—
Less: savings:					
Financial assets	−50,000	−20,000	−20,000	−70,000	−20,000
Housing purchase	−80,000	—	—	80,000	—
Mortgage finance	30,000	—	—	−30,000	—
Consumption services base..........	10,000	12,000	18,000	28,000	148,000
Consumption base:					
mortgage designated	90,000	4,000	10,000	−60,000	148,000
Consumption base:					
mortgage undesignated	60,000	7,000	13,000	−27,000	148,000

remainder. For simplicity, it is assumed that the mortgage is not amortized but is paid back entirely in year t = 10, the year the house is sold (and the household becomes a renter). By assuming that all other consumption is on nondurables, we can ignore all other consumer durables. The individual again earns $20,000 per year starting in year 2, and the interest rate is constant at 10 per cent.

This example has been set up so that the stream of consumption services is identical to what it was before. In year 1, an inheritance of $100,000 is received, which enters the tax base. Of that $100,000, $50,000 is saved as financial wealth and thus deducted, while $30,000 is borrowed via a mortgage and added to the tax base. The acquisition of a house for $80,000 is then deducted, since it is a form of wealth acquisition. These transactions are assumed to take place at the end of the first period, so that the individual's consumption is $10,000.

In the second period, the individual obtains an imputed rent on his house of $8,000 ($80,000 × 0.10), where we have assumed zero depreciation. All else is as before except that the interest on financial wealth owned is now $7,000, from which must be deducted the payment of mortgage interest.

In year 10, the year in which the house is sold, the proceeds of the house sale of $80,000 are added to the tax base. Since $30,000 is used to repay the mortgage principal and $50,000 to acquire financial wealth, these are deducted. Otherwise, the accounting is as before.

Although this is an ideal consumption services base, there are two difficulties with it. First, as before, the consumption stream is not level; consequently, in the absence of further averaging, the system will be inequitable and will also distort the savings decision. Second, there is an obvious measurement problem here, since imputed rent, which is not directly observable, must be added to the tax base. The only way to avoid this measurement problem is to adopt a tax base that does not require accounting for the "capital income" of the asset. This can be achieved by treating housing (and other consumer durables) on a capital-income-exempt basis. Expenditures on acquiring a durable for one's own use would not be tax deductible, and imputed rents from the durable would not be taxable, nor would the proceeds of the sale of the durable asset. In other words, the acquisition of equity in a durable would have no tax consequences whatsoever. Notice that this is the method by which durables are currently treated under the Canadian tax system. It is also important to note that the present value of the tax base obtained when durables are treated in this way is equivalent to the present value of the tax base when the services of durables alone enter the tax base under the assumption that the implicit rate of return on the durables equals the market interest rate.

Financial asset transactions accompanying ownership of the durable asset are treated like any other financial transaction involving changes in the financial wealth of households. Thus, they can be treated on either a designated basis or a capital-income-exempt basis. For example, suppose the individual takes out a mortgage to help finance the acquisition of the house.

Treating this on a capital-income-exempt basis would imply that the mortgage has no tax consequences. The initial acquisition does not enter the tax base, and subsequent interest and principal repayments are not tax deductible. Treating the mortgage on a designated basis is a bit novel. Instead of being a designated asset (as with RRSPs), it is a designated liability or loan. Because the acquisition of the mortgage represents dissaving, it is *added* to the tax base. Subsequent interest and principal payments are then deductible for tax purposes. The advantage of giving choice in this regard is that by choice of designation or otherwise the individual can influence the time profile of his tax base (that is, self-average) without affecting its present value.

The difference in the time profile of the tax base under these two options with respect to the mortgage is illustrated in the last two rows of Table 4.2. The difference between these two profiles is simply that when mortgages are treated as designated liabilities, the tax base is moved forward in time, but its present value remains the same. In these examples, other assets are all treated as designated. The consumer can even out his time stream of tax base by treating some savings on a capital-income-exempt basis.

In summary, the two basic ways of designing a consumption tax base are equivalent in present value terms. The difference in these concerns the manner in which savings and asset income are treated. In one system, assets are *designated* (or registered). Increases in asset holdings are tax deductible, while running down asset holdings (including their accumulated interest) is taxable. The acquisition of liabilities is treated symmetrically with assets but is taxable rather than deductible. In the other system, assets are not designated, or, as referred to in the U.S. Treasury *Blueprints*,[7] are *tax prepaid*. Assets treated on a prepayment basis are not deductible when acquired and neither principal nor interest is taxable when received. Both systems measure income and savings on a nominal cash flow basis and there is no need to index any part of the base for inflation. There is no reason why a consumption tax system cannot incorporate both methods—that is, allow some assets to be designated and others to be tax prepaid. In fact, assets whose return comes in an imputed form must be treated on a prepaid basis for practical reasons (for example, consumer durables, cash balances, or insurance). Similarly, consumers may wish to hold some assets, such as liquid ones, in tax prepaid form to avoid the administrative costs of keeping records of all transactions involving them. More generally, the taxpayer may wish to vary the proportion of assets held in the two forms in order to even out his tax base over time for averaging purposes. Alternatively, the authorities could institute an automatic general averaging system that averages ex post.

The consumption tax avoids many of the difficult administrative complexities of an ideal comprehensive income tax including the requirement to measure capital gains on accrual, the need to index capital income, and the

---

[7]Ibid.

need to measure imputed rents on consumer durables and other assets yielding services directly.

Some Special Design Issues and Problems with the Consumption Tax

Any personal tax base is bound to have its subtleties and complications, and the consumption tax is no exception. The following section reviews some of the issues that arise with particular sorts of assets and some more general difficulties with the consumption base that have design implications. With many of these issues, the problems that are addressed are also present with the income base.

Integration with the Corporate Income Tax

The need for integration of the corporate and personal income taxes depends ultimately upon the rationale for the corporate tax and is independent of whether or not the personal tax base is income or consumption. We argue in Chapter 5 and elsewhere[8] that there are two main reasons for taxing the income of corporations. One is to tax the pure profits of the firm. The other is to withhold capital income at source when it is difficult to tax this income at the personal level such as in the case in which foreigners own the corporation or the owners of the corporation postpone personal tax liabilities by reinvesting income in the corporation. The withholding function loses part of its justification under a consumption tax, since the capital income generated is not liable for tax if the owners are domestic. If foreign countries also adopt a consumption tax, the rationale for withholding is reduced even more.

If the object of corporate taxation is to tax pure profits earned by businesses, there is little need for integration. No personal tax credits need to be provided for corporate taxes paid, since the tax credits would undo the pure profits tax. Dividends and interest received by individuals would be included in income when realized. Capital gain income would be properly accounted for on realization, since the individual deducts the cost of the investment and is taxed on the market value when the asset is sold. A clear advantage over comprehensive income taxation is that there would be no need to calculate accrued capital gains or to index the prices of capital goods for inflation. Consumption taxation thus has clear advantages over comprehensive income taxation.

If the object of the corporate income tax is to withhold capital income at source, the government could, in principle, withhold against all types of income accruing to investors, including interest income. If so, the ideal would be to pay a tax credit at the time when interest, dividends, or capital gains are realized. Realized capital gains (or losses) would have to be

---

[8]Robin Boadway, Neil Bruce, and Jack Mintz, "The Role and Design of the Corporate Income Tax" (1984), Vol. 86, no. 2 *The Scandinavian Journal of Economics* 286-99.

calculated in order to assess the tax credit. Also, the tax credit must be paid to the individual even though capital income is explicitly or implicitly tax exempt. One of the difficulties of providing a tax credit for capital gains is that some of the capital gain income on equity shares may bear little relation to the firm's changing profitability taxed at the corporate rate. For example, windfall capital gains or losses may arise from revised expectations on the part of investors with regard to the firm's prospects. In this case, the capital gain is not generated from corporate retained earnings that have had corporate tax deducted from them. Thus, in principle, there should be no credit.

Unincorporated Business Income

We considered earlier the case of taxpayers investing in one sort of real asset—consumer durables. They may also invest in the physical capital of their own unincorporated businesses. The returns to this investment accrue as business income to the taxpayer, which is a form of capital income. In principle, investment in unincorporated businesses may be treated either as a designated asset or as a tax-prepaid asset. In practice, the latter is difficult to implement. To do so requires that the capital income of the unincorporated business be tax exempt, which is impractical, since it is not easy to distinguish between capital and labour income in unincorporated business. Owners would have an incentive to have labour income masquerade as capital income so that it would be tax exempt. Therefore, for practical reasons, one would have to treat unincorporated business income as a designated asset, which is equivalent to taxing it on a cash flow basis. The same may also be true for corporations held at non-arm's-length.

Rents and Pure Profits as a Component of Capital Income

For the treatment of assets on a designated basis and on a tax-prepaid basis to be equal, the present value of both the acquisition cost of an asset and its future repayment of principal and capital income must be the same. In the case of assets whose capital income yields a rate of return equal to the competitive market rate of return, this equivalence will obviously hold. Some assets will, however, yield rates of return above the market rate. One important reason for this higher yield is that some assets have rents or pure profits as part of their capital income. For example, the ownership of resource properties may well yield substantial rents as a return. The existence of such rents will yield to some persons a rate of return above the market rate of interest. Similarly, the existence of monopoly profits will result in a rate of return on assets above the market rate of return.

It may not be at all obvious to whom such rents accrue. Once an asset is discovered to have rents associated with it, presumably those rents will be capitalized into the value of the asset. The person who owns the asset when the rents are capitalized will reap their benefit either by selling the asset and obtaining a capital gain, or by holding the asset and receiving the rents as an income return. In either case, if the asset is held in the designated form, the rents will eventually be taxed when they are removed for consumption purposes. If the assets are held in the tax-prepaid form, however, the rents will escape taxation when they are eventually consumed, because all capital income, including the rents, is tax exempt. Thus, the two tax bases will not be equivalent in present value terms. For persons who purchase rent-yielding assets after the rent has been capitalized, the equivalence will remain. In this case, however, someone in the past has received the benefits of the capitalization, and for them the two bases will not be equivalent.

Put in a slightly different way, when there are pure rents, the designated asset method of treatment will always be equivalent to a consumption tax. The tax-prepaid method of tax accounting will not. Therefore, one might argue that assets that are liable to yield rents ought to be treated on a designated basis. In the most general sense, any equity asset can yield pure profits. Thus, if one wants to be sure of capturing all rents at the personal level, one may want to insist that equity assets all be designated.

The alternative to treating all equity as designated, other than forgetting about the problem of including rents altogether, is to tax such rents at the corporate level. As we shall discuss in the next chapter, this is a rather clumsy way to solve the problem because, to the extent that corporate equity is held in designated form, one would have to integrate its rent income with the corporate tax. This is difficult to do, since one cannot readily identify that part of the return to designated assets that consists of rents.

To the extent that assets that yield a return in kind (for example, housing) may also earn rents, the consumption tax will not be successful in taxing them. Since these assets must necessarily be treated on a tax-prepaid basis, any rents they earn above the normal rate of return on capital will go untaxed. This is unfortunate. Exactly the same problem, however, would arise under a comprehensive income base, since it is difficult to measure the imputed rent on housing.

Loss Offsetting

In order not to discriminate against risky enterprise and small growing businesses, the tax system should treat negative tax liabilities symmetrically with positive ones. That is, it should have full loss offsetting, preferably in the form of full refundability of losses. From the point of view of unincorporated businesses, this not only prevents the tax system from discouraging investment in growing businesses and risky assets, it also assists in the problem of financing faced by small firms who may not otherwise have as easy access to capital markets as large firms. More generally, refundability is essential to ensure that households can take full advantage of self-averaging.

Governments are notoriously reluctant to introduce refundability into the tax system because of their fear of the revenue consequences. This is a short-sighted view of government revenues. The need for refundability arises when tax liabilities of a taxpayer are moved backward in time. The refundability of tax liabilities is accompanied by tax revenues that the government can expect to receive in the future. Although it is true that the exact amount of future taxes cannot be known with certainty, the government can count on receiving the expected value of future tax liabilities on average. Therefore, the revenue implications of refundability should not be of great concern unless the government borrows at less favourable terms than households.

Windfall Gains and Losses

One of the more difficult problems with a consumption tax system is that if unexpected windfall gains or losses occur on assets held, those losses are treated differently ex post under the designated asset method than under the tax-prepaid method. As designated assets, they enter the tax base when the asset is dissaved for consumption. To put it another way, the present value equivalence breaks down between the two methods of implementing a consumption tax.

With the designated asset, the government shares the riskiness of windfall gains and losses with the investor. If the asset value rises or falls, the gain or loss is fully included in the tax base. With the nondesignated asset, however, the government does not share any risk with the investor. When the investor disposes of his asset, the value of the sale is not included in the tax base. In this latter case, the government shares neither the gains nor the losses arising from risky investments. Note that taxpayers may be inclined to use registered assets for risky investments in any case, if full loss offsetting is permitted in the personal tax system.

If assets are prone to windfall gains and losses, it might be argued that these assets should be confined to designated asset treatment anyway, so that consumption out of the windfall gain is fully taxed. The difficulty is that it is impossible to know ex ante what assets are likely to be prone to windfall gains or losses. If it is known that an asset may get a windfall gain or loss, that potential windfall will already be capitalized to some extent into the price of the asset, so the problem is lessened. Some authors[9] have suggested that all assets whose return can come partly in the form of capital gains should be treated on a designated basis. This includes basically all long-term assets and leaves the more liquid assets to be treated on a tax-prepaid basis.

The problem of windfalls combined with the earlier problems of rents and unincorporated businesses discussed in previous sections together comprise a strong argument for requiring that equity assets be held in the designated form. This would ensure that rents and windfall gains and losses that are consumed enter into the tax base. It would also prevent

---

[9] J. Davies and F. St.-Hilaire, *Reforming Capital Income Taxation in Canada: Efficiency and Distributional Effects of Alternative Options* (Ottawa: Economic Council of Canada, forthcoming).

shareholders in a corporation from having labour income masquerade as capital income in order to avoid personal taxation, as they might have an incentive to do under the tax-prepaid method.

International Issues

Consumption taxation raises three international tax issues: (1) the tax treatment of individuals entering or leaving Canada, (2) the taxation of foreign investment income accruing to Canadian residents, and (3) the taxation of income earned in Canada by foreigners. We shall consider these in turn.

If an individual migrates from Canada, he is no longer consuming from the point of view of Canadian tax authorities, and, in principle, assets withdrawn should not be taxed. (In fact, taxes prepaid on assets owned should be repaid.) But so that there be no incentive to retire abroad, taxes should be imposed on designated assets withdrawn at the time the individual leaves if other countries do not have consumption taxes. Some system of averaging will be important here. On the other hand, taxes need not be imposed on tax-prepaid assets.

If other countries also had consumption tax bases, international tax crediting arrangements could be agreed to, such that tax liabilities were paid in the country in which consumption actually occurred. Thus, persons could roll over designated assets in one country to those of another without any tax consequences. In the case of prepaid assets, a tax refund should in principle be made available on tax-prepaid assets when an individual leaves a country for another one in which consumption taxation is in effect. In practice, such a system would be very difficult to administer because of the need to keep records of assets accumulated in prepaid form. On administrative grounds, a simple rollover of prepaid assets might be preferable as well. This would ensure that migration decisions would not be interfered with, but there would be a revenue loss from countries with net in-migration to those with net out-migration.

Foreign assets held by Canadian residents can be treated as any other assets are. They may be designated, in which case income upon realization should be included in the tax base and any investments made in foreign assets should be deductible. If they are tax prepaid, their acquisition is not deductible and their capital income is not taxable. If foreign taxes have been paid on acquisition by Canadian residents, they should be deductible from the Canadian tax base.

Capital income accruing to foreigners is a little more difficult. On the one hand, if Canada is truly on a consumption base, it can be argued that capital income accruing to foreigners should be exempt. On the other hand, if foreigners continue to tax capital income in their own tax bases, including capital income accruing to Canadians, failing to withhold tax against foreigners in Canada may simply amount to transferring potential tax revenues to foreign treasuries. In any case, this is all subject to international tax treaty arrangements.

The Treatment of Bequests

The existence of bequests and inheritances poses exactly the same problems for a consumption tax base as for an income tax base. In practice, bequests can be expected to be larger under a consumption tax because of the removal of the distortion on saving, and therefore there may be a greater desire to tax them. In either case, the tax treatment of bequests depends essentially upon whether or not bequests are considered an act of consumption by the donor or not. If they are not, the giving of bequests should not be taxable under either base. Inheritances pose no such problem. Most observers agree that they are a source of income that ought to be included in the tax base unless tax has been prepaid on them. Let us consider the alternative ways of thinking of bequests first, and then turn to the tax design implications afterwards.

According to one view of bequests, they are simply unconsumed wealth left to heirs, perhaps unintentionally or simply because wealth was not all consumed, for precautionary reasons or because of capital market imperfections. In this case, the bequest would not be viewed as an act of consumption, and so would not be liable for tax. The other view regards bequests as being left intentionally at death to satisfy an altruistic urge of the donor. The donor is said to derive utility from the leaving of the bequest. Since this utility is indistinguishable from that derived from using the wealth for one's own consumption, this decision to leave a bequest should be treated on a par with other forms of consumption and should be taxed as such. The implication is that the bequest could be taxed twice; once in the hands of the donor as his "consumption," and again in the hands of the heir if it is consumed by the heir.

The decision as to whether to treat bequests as consumption or not essentially involves a value judgment; however, there are some practical issues involved as well. First, even if one views intentional bequests as acts of consumption, it will always be the case that some bequests are unintentional, and one may not want to view those as acts of consumption. Because it is practically impossible to distinguish intentional from unintentional bequests, if one wishes to tax intentional bequests, in practice one must tax all bequests, intentional or otherwise. Second, the decision whether or not to tax bequests has resource allocation implications as well. Taxing bequests will discourage the giving of bequests and will therefore reduce the level of savings and capital accumulation in the economy. On the other hand, the taxation of bequests also has redistributive effects that some may find attractive. For example, they allow the tax system to tax dynastic wealth which is passed from one generation to another and which, if not consumed, would not be taxed at all under a consumption tax system. It is worth repeating, however, that these issues are not peculiar to a consumption tax base. Exactly the same issues concerning the taxation of bequests are present under income tax systems, although the magnitude of the problem may differ. As well, the making of gifts inter vivos raises exactly the same problems.

Suppose bequests and gifts are not treated as consumption. Assets held in the designated form at death need not enter the tax base of the deceased, but should be included as income by the inheritors. The inheritors may then choose to leave them in a designated form, in which case they are immediately deductible. Thus, a rollover of designated assets from donor to heir has no tax consequences until the heir chooses to consume them. For tax-prepaid assets (such as houses), the issue is slightly more complicated. In principle, the tax should be rebated on the asset, and the total inheritance plus tax should enter the tax base of the heir. In practice, this is impractical. It would involve evaluating prepaid assets, such as housing, whenever they pass from one generation to the next. It would also involve keeping records of tax-prepaid assets, one of the things that the consumption tax system is trying to avoid. Instead, a simpler procedure is to allow the assets to pass from bequeather to inheritor with no tax consequences whatsoever. That is, the inheritor does not include the asset in his tax base when received, and is not liable for taxes on the capital income earned by the asset. The tax has already been prepaid when originally purchased. Of course, this is not completely ideal, since the tax rate applicable to the original purchaser of the asset may not be appropriate for the inheritor.

Treating the bequest simply as an act of consumption has an additional tax implication. The estate of a donor should be fully taxable over and above the measures mentioned above. By the same token, any gifts given during one's lifetime should be fully treated as consumption and taxed.

Educational Expenditures and Human Capital Accumulation

Yet another form of investment that may be undertaken by taxpayers is investment in human capital, such as by formal education. This investment involves two sorts of costs—forgone earnings (that is, the cost of time) and monetary costs (tuition, books, supplies, transportation, and so on). Studies have indicated that forgone earnings are the most important of these costs. If expenditures on education were solely an investment, the returns would be in the form of higher earnings afterwards.

Practicality requires that investment in human capital be treated on a designated or cash flow basis under a consumption tax. To treat it on a prepaid basis would require being able to measure the returns to human capital investment. This would require attributing the correct portion of earnings to returns on human capital investment and would also involve including the full costs of human capital accumulation in the tax base, such as forgone earnings. While the prepaid approach is clearly impractical, treating investment in human capital on a cash flow basis is straightforward. All monetary costs of education would have to be deductible. In addition, forgone earnings would have to be tax deductible, as they are implicitly now. Finally, all returns to human capital would have to be taxable, again as they are now. In fact, the present income tax system basically treats human capital accumulation on a cash flow consumption-tax basis now. The difficulty of imagining how it could be otherwise is one of the reasons why comprehensive income taxation is such an impossible objective. A truly comprehensive income tax would not allow the costs of acquiring human capital, whether forgone earnings or monetary costs, to be deducted.

There are a couple of difficult conceptual problems involved in the treatment of human capital. One is the fact that some of the benefits of educational expenditures by nature involve consumption. Either the education process itself is partly consumption, or some of the returns to human capital are imputed returns (working conditions, etc.). To the extent that this is the case, the expenditures should not be tax deductible. Obviously, it is impossible to sort out which of the educational expenditures are for consumption purposes and which are for investment. Thus, for practical reasons, all must be treated as investment and be deductible on a cash flow basis. Again, however, these problems are not unique to the consumption tax; the very same problems arise under the income tax.

The second problem is that to the extent that education is paid for by a parent, it may be viewed as a gift. How the tax system treats these expenditures depends upon how one views gifts. If gifts are not considered as consumption, the education expenditures of the parent should be deductible on a cash flow basis as in the case of a designated asset. If bequests are viewed as consumption by the parent, the costs of education should not be deductible. The treatment of the beneficiary is the same in either case.

More generally, one could argue that the ownership of all human capital, whether accumulated by investment or endowed at birth, should be treated the same as the ownership of any other type of capital for tax purposes. Under consumption taxation, inherited human capital would enter the tax base when wages are received and consumed. Comprehensive income taxation would require that the imputed return on human capital enter the tax base as it accrues. This is impossible because it is difficult to measure the depreciation of human capital.

The Consumption Tax and Equity

Equity arguments are central to any discussion of personal tax design, since personal taxation is a prime method by which governments carry out redistributive policies. Indeed, the Carter Report[10] elevated equity to the prime consideration in the design of a personal tax base. Unfortunately, equity is an elusive concept. The implementation of equity objectives must necessarily involve value judgments. That being the case, perfectly reasonable people may disagree with one another over the definition of equity. What we present here is the equity case for consumption taxation that recognizes that the arguments are not clear cut. Instead, the idea is to try to persuade the reader that consumption is the most equitable personal tax base.

The argument is ultimately based upon an individualistic view of social welfare that economists often adopt. Social welfare is taken to depend upon

---

[10]Supra footnote 2.

the welfare or *utility* achieved by individual members of society. In particular, social welfare is thought of conceptually as the welfare of all individual members somehow aggregated. The means of doing the aggregation is sometimes referred to as the *social welfare function*. To arrive at aggregate social welfare, one first must have a means of measuring individual welfare in a manner that is comparable across individuals. That is, one wants to have an index of individual welfare that will serve as a scale for comparing welfare levels across individuals. Using such a scale, one should be able to say one individual is better off than another, though not by how much. Next, given this index for measuring individual welfare, one should have a way of aggregating the welfare of individuals at different levels to arrive at social welfare. That is, there must be a weighting scheme to apply to different levels of individual welfare. This second stage involves more than being able to compare levels of utility across individuals. It involves stipulating by how much one individual is better off than another.

Tax policy on the personal side involves a decision as to how to allocate across individuals the burden of transfers of spending power from the private sector to the public sector. Conceptually, one would like to select the tax structure that reduces social welfare the least. In principle, this requires some notion of the effects on individual utility of various tax structures. An allocation of tax revenues across individuals that is based upon utility levels is a natural consequence of this.

Applying these principles in practice is not a straightforward matter. Tax policy discussion rarely takes place at the level of generality of the social welfare function. Tax policy economists tend instead to separate the analysis of the social welfare effects of various tax policies into various subcomponents. First, there is a tendency to distinguish between the effect of tax policy on the size of the "pie" and its effect on the distribution of the pie among individuals—that is, upon the efficiency effects of taxes and the equity effects. This is a fictitous division, since efficiency and equity are inextricably interwoven. An attempt to change the redistributive effects of taxes will simultaneously affect the size of the pie. Thus, a trade-off between efficiency and equity goals is always lurking behind both efficiency and equity arguments. Nonetheless, we will follow that sequential procedure here by dealing in this section with equity and in the next section with efficiency.

The equity arguments themselves are frequently divided into two conceptually distinct components—*horizontal equity* and *vertical equity*. A tax system that is horizontally equitable treats equals equally. That is, two persons who are equally well-off in the absence of the tax should be equally well-off in its presence. Equivalently, persons who are equally well-off should pay the same tax.[11] A precondition for implementing horizontal

---

[11]This notion of horizontal equity is widely accepted in the literature. For further discussion, see Martin S. Feldstein, "On the Theory of Tax Reform" (July-August 1976), 6 *Journal of Public Economics* 77-104; and Richard A. Musgrave, "ET, QT and SBT" (July-August 1976), 6 *Journal of Public Economics* 3-16.

equity is to have a way of comparing levels of welfare across households. A measurable index of welfare would be appropriate. Such an index could serve as the base for personal taxation, perhaps with a suitable set of exemptions to make it comparable across individuals with different personal characteristics (dependants, disabilities, and so on).

Vertical equity concerns the treatment of unequals—that is, persons at different levels on the index of well-being. A tax system is vertically equitable if it reduces welfare by appropriately differing amounts for persons at different levels of welfare. Implementing vertical equity involves more than simply comparing levels of welfare: it involves a judgment as to how much a person's welfare is changed for changes in their index of welfare. That is, it involves attaching an appropriate weighting scheme to changes of individual welfare levels, taking due account of the equity-efficiency trade-off in tax policy. Given an index of welfare, the implementation of vertical equity involves primarily a choice of rate structure. The joint implementation of horizontal and vertical equity involves the simultaneous selection of a tax base corresponding to some index of utility and a rate structure.

Although ideally one can identify the choice of a base with horizontal equity and the rate structure with vertical equity, and although the base can, in principle, be chosen quite independently of the rate structure, in practice, actual tax reforms made for vertical equity purposes often violate horizontal equity norms, and vice versa. For example, changes in the tax base for the purpose of achieving horizontal equity in the tax system may reduce the vertical equity in the system unless accompanied by offsetting changes in the rate structure. Thus, even though the base and the rate structure can be chosen independently, the appropriate structure for one will not be independent of the choice of the other. This will be important to bear in mind when evaluating alternative personal tax bases. The degree of progressivity in the rate structure required to attain a given amount of vertical equity or redistribution will depend on the choice of the base.

In the context of the income versus consumption tax question, the concept of horizontal equity has commonly been used to justify the comprehensive income base. Specifically, the Carter Commission argued that the source of one's income, whether from capital or labour, should be irrelevant in determining the tax liability. All sources of income provide equivalent ability to pay taxes. The consumption tax seems to violate this criterion since, under certain circumstances, it is equivalent to an income tax that exempts capital income. If, however, one adopts horizontal equity in terms of utility, rather than income or ability to pay, the picture is quite different. A reasonable interpretation of horizontal equity is that the means of obtaining utility—present consumption, future consumption, or bequests—should be irrelevant in determining the tax burden of the household. The income tax, which penalizes the household that prefers future consumption or bequests, is horizontally inequitable by this criterion, whereas the consumption tax, if proportional at least, satisfies horizontal equity in this regard. To put it another way, an index of utility should reflect the items that actually generate utility for the household. Those things include consumption (what one takes out of the social pot) rather than income (what one contributes).

In technical terms, any base that is the present-value equivalent of the stream of consumption undertaken by an individual is a suitable "money metric" or index for measuring the welfare level of individuals. For readers with some technical training in economics, this can be illustrated geometrically. (Other readers may prefer to skip over this paragraph and the next one.) Consider a taxpayer who, over a two-period length of time receives a stream of wage income and converts it into a stream of consumption by using capital markets for saving or dissaving. Figure 4.1 depicts the preferences of the individual as a set of indifference curves, the stream of wage earnings in the first and second period (E_1, E_2), the budget line with a slope of $(1 + r)$ indicating the ways in which the taxpayer can transform E_1 and E_2 into an alternative stream of consumption, and the chosen consumption point C_1, C_2. The present value of the stream of consumption (C_1, C_2) and the stream of earnings (E_1, E_2) discounted at the interest rate r is W. This is the present value of a tax base that uses consumption. It is independent of the time pattern of the stream of earnings of the household. Any combination of (E_1, E_2) lying on the budget line shown gives rise to the same combination (C_1, C_2) and yields the same level of welfare for the taxpayer. Also, any stream of (E_1, E_2) to the southwest of the budget line gives a correspondingly lower level of (C_1, C_2) with a lower present value. The opposite holds for (E_1, E_2) to the northeast. A consumption tax base is a proper measure of the level of welfare of the taxpayer since its present value provides a correct ranking of the level of utility achieved.

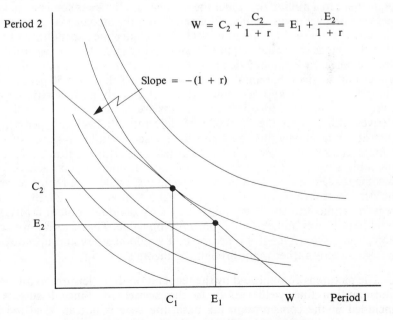

Figure 4.1   Consumption as an Index for Utility

An income tax does not have this property. In particular, two alternative streams of earnings that give rise to exactly the same stream of consumption (C_1, C_2) yield different tax bases and tax liabilities. For example, if the earnings streams are identical (C_1, C_2), the present value of the tax base is W since there are no savings and no capital income to include in the base. However, the earnings stream (E_1, E_2) gives rise to a tax base that includes not only E_1 and E_2 but also the interest income earned on the savings $(E_1 - C_1)$. This income is $r(E_1 - C_1)$. This is included in the tax base in period 2 and, although the same consumption stream (C_1, C_2) is obtained, the latter person's tax liabilities will be higher than the first person's. Persons earning income early in life are discriminated against. Indeed, it is possible that a person with a higher present value of consumption than another has a lower present value of tax liabilities than the other. It is for this reason that the income tax is said to be horizontally inequitable. This same argument can be extended to more than two periods.

A commonly encountered contrary argument is that the taxation of income saved is appropriate because such savings represent economic power in the form of potential command over goods and services and that such wealth provides a source of welfare over and above consumption. The applicability of that argument requires a value judgment. A related argument suggests that a consumption tax is vertically inequitable because it treats a millionaire miser in the same way as a pauper. This view seems to us to be invalid. At a most basic level, one wonders why the tax system would wish to penalize somebody who produces goods but doesn't consume them! More to the point, however, a millionaire under an expenditure tax is not equivalent to a millionaire under the income tax. Suppose someone in the 50 per cent bracket earns a million dollars. Under the income tax, at most he or she could acquire a net worth of $500,000. Under the expenditure tax, it is true that he or she could acquire $1 million in assets. But net worth should still be correctly estimated at $500,000, since that is all the·command over goods and services that a million dollars allows if there is a 50 per cent consumption tax. It is apparent that there is effectively no real difference between the two taxes in this regard unless for some reason the individual derives utility from the $500,000 of deferred tax liabilities per se. One plausible reason why this could give the household utility is the existence of capital market constraints, but the existence of such constraints does not, unambiguously, diminish the merits of the consumption tax relative to the income tax. For example, a proper income tax would require that a wealth-holder pay taxes on accrued gains on wealth that are not realized. Another reason, as mentioned above, might be that individuals obtain utility from wealth itself over and above its consumption value. That is a view we do not accept ourselves. Even if it is accepted, it would be more appropriate to tax wealth directly rather than through the income tax.

The picture is complicated by the recognition that "leisure" is an item of consumption that yields utility to the household. Since leisure is not included in the consumption tax base, the base is not an ideal index of welfare. It will be horizontally inequitable, because two persons with the same consumption but differing amounts of leisure will be treated identically. This imperfection also exists in the income base, which similarly excludes leisure from comprehensive income. Futhermore, the problem applies not only with leisure, but with other forms of imputed consumption, such as the production of consumption services within the household.

Given this imperfection in the tax base, it is no longer necessarily the case that the consumption base as defined here is superior to the income base on equity grounds, even given that full consumption is what one ideally wishes to tax. For example, suppose that future consumption and leisure are complementary, which is conceivable since much leisure is taken in the form of retirement. Since the income tax taxes future consumption relatively heavily, this can be viewed as an indirect way of taxing leisure if the two are complementary. In this case, the income tax could be superior as a tax base to the consumption tax. Unfortunately, it is virtually impossible to verify this argument. Not only is it difficult to say whether future consumption and leisure are complementary, it is even more difficult to detect the relationship between future consumption and other forms of nontaxed imputed consumption such as household services. Because the argument could easily go either way, it is impractical to use this as a basis for tax policy.

It is often asserted that the progressive income tax is more equitable than the progressive consumption tax on vertical equity grounds as well. The argument is simply that the proportion of income consumed falls with income, so that the application of a progressive rate structure will be relatively more redistributive using the income base than the consumption base. This argument is invalid for two reasons. First, the observation that the proportion of income consumed falls with income is misleading. For one thing, it is an empirical observation based on cross-section data that incorporates the so-called regression fallacy. To the extent that observed income includes a transitory component that is greater than or less than permanent income, the observation of falling propensity to consume income will be observed, since a larger proportion of transitory income is saved. Another problem, related to this, is that a good part of the distribution of income observed at any moment reflects the age distribution of the population. It is well known that income varies systematically over the life cycle, much more so than consumption does. If one looks at the distribution of lifetime income across households, it is far less dispersed than is the distribution of current income. Furthermore, the proportion of lifetime income consumed probably varies little across households. If this broader concept of income is adopted for determining the level of a household's utility, a progressive tax on consumption seems more appropriate than a progressive tax on current income, which may bear little relation to lifetime income for many households.

A second major reason why the above comparison of vertical equity between consumption and income taxes is invalid is that it ignores the fact that the choice of rate structure is independent of the choice of base. Any degree of progressivity can be obtained under either tax by appropriate selection of a rate structure for each.

The Consumption Tax and Efficiency

Taxes will introduce inefficiencies into the market economy by imposing distortions in the pricing mechanism. Taxes impose distortions by causing the price that demanders pay for an item (the demand price) to exceed the price that suppliers of the item receive (the supply price). Whenever such a distortion exists, some of the potential "gains from trade" are being forgone. That is, if the demand price exceeds the supply price because of a tax, the amount of money demanders would be willing to pay for an additional unit of the item exceeds the amount suppliers would willingly accept. Therefore, society could gain from producing more, and would continue to gain until the demand price and supply price were equal. The magnitude of the gain depends upon both the size of the tax distortion and the amount by which the item would have to increase to extinguish the differential (that is, the elasticities of supply and demand for the product). The gain also depends, in a complex way, upon whether there are distortions in other markets. If the quantity of an item increases as a result of a reduction in a tax on the good, and if this induces a reduction in an item elsewhere that has a tax distortion on it, the loss incurred elsewhere will have to be set against the gain from the increase in output of the first item.

Both the income and consumption taxes are broadly based taxes. Thus, the distortions they impose operate on broadly defined economic activities. The primary difference in the distortions imposed by the two taxes concerns their effect on capital markets. Put simply, the income tax imposes a distortion on capital markets; the consumption tax does not. Putting the function of the capital market in terms of commodities, the commodity being traded on capital markets is future consumption. On the demand side, savers are demanding future consumption by forgoing present consumption. The "price" of future consumption in terms of present consumption is the reciprocal of one plus the interest rate that savers face on capital markets. The suppliers of future consumption are the firms that undertake investment with the funds supplied by savers. They use these funds to finance production processes that convert present resources into future consumption goods. The rate at which the marginal investment project uses current resources to produce future consumption goods is the reciprocal of one plus the interest rate facing investors.

The income tax, by taxing interest income, drives a wedge between the interest rate received by savers and the rate of return on investment by firms. That is, it makes the price of future consumption by savers higher than the cost of producing future consumption in the market. It therefore distorts the market for future consumption. The consumption tax imposes no such tax on capital markets. Because it treats future consumption just like present consumption, it does not distort capital markets.

If this were the only distortion of concern, the gain in efficiency would depend upon the elasticity of demand for future consumption with respect to the interest rate (which is not the same thing as the elasticity of supply of savings, since savings is not the quantity of future consumption but its value).[12] The measurement of this elasticity, and therefore of the efficiency effect of income taxation, is notoriously difficult.[13] The efficiency gains from removing the distortion are therefore very much up in the air.

Some recent simulation results[14] have suggested that the gains from removing the tax distortion on capital markets could be sizeable indeed, as much as 10 per cent of GNP per annum in the long run. Unfortunately, such measures, even if they are legitimate, incorporate more than the pure efficiency gains of removing tax distortions. They also include a wealth effect that arises when one substitutes a consumption tax for an income tax and that induces aggregate savings and capital accumulation to rise. In these simulations, the consumption tax system is assumed to be of the designated asset form. Very briefly, the source of this wealth effect is that the two taxes collect their revenues at a different point in the life cycle of the taxpayer. In particular, tax liabilities under the consumption tax occur later in life than under the income tax. This implies that a household that faces an income tax over its lifetime will save less than a household facing a consumption tax of equal present value, simply because of the fact that tax liabilities later in life must be planned for, and tax savings occur early in life. When the transition is made from the income base to the consumption base, however, those part way through their life cycles at the time of the transition will face higher than expected taxes, which will come largely from lost consumption. Therefore, during the transition there are consumption losses, though in the long run future generations are better off. These wealth effects are not really part of the efficiency effects of the tax change, but would arise under any change in the life cycle incidence of government taxes and transfers, including changes in national debt and changes in public pension schemes.[15]

Notice, however, that the distortion imposed by the ideal comprehensive income tax on future consumption, and avoided by the consumption tax, applies to much more than the market for private sector investment. There are two other important investment decisions that are distorted by the com-

---

[12]On this, see M. S. Feldstein, "The Rate of Return, Taxation and Personal Savings" (September 1978), 88 *The Economic Journal* 482-87.

[13]Recent work for Canada supports the view that savings are quite responsive to interest rate changes. See C. M. Beach, R. W. Boadway, N. Bruce, and G. Ansong, *Taxation and Savings: Some Life-Cycle Estimates for Canada*, Discussion Paper no. 622 (Kingston, Ontario: Institute for Economic Research, Queen's University, 1985).

[14]Lawrence H. Summers, "Capital Taxation and Accumulation in a Life Cycle Growth Model" (September 1981), 71 *The American Economic Review* 533-44; Alan J. Auerbach, Laurence J. Kotlikoff, and Jonathan Skinner, "The Efficiency Gains from Dynamic Tax Reform" (February 1983), 24 *International Economic Review* 81-100. Recent work by Gauthier has shown that the size of this gain in an open economy setting could be less depending on the nature of international tax treaties and the behaviour of foreign governments; see Denis Gauthier, *Taxation and Life Cycle Savings Behaviour in a Small Open Economy*, Discussion Paper no. 306 (Ottawa: Economic Council of Canada, 1986).

[15]For a fuller discussion of this, see Robin W. Boadway and W. Steven Clark, "The Government Budget, the Accumulation of Capital and Long Run Welfare," in John Sargent, Research Coordinator, *Fiscal and Monetary Policy*, Collected Research Studies of the Royal Commission on the Economic Union and Development Prospects for Canada, Vol. 21 (Toronto: University of Toronto Press, 1986), 257-94.

prehensive income tax. One is the investment by households in consumer durables. The other is investment in human capital. But these are of lesser concern in practice because, as we have argued above, actual income tax systems never include the rate of return on either consumer durables or human capital in the tax base. Both are already treated on a consumption tax base so are not tax-distorted. In fact, we should be comparing the consumption tax with an imperfect income tax in which significant inter-asset distortions exist because of the fact that the return on some assets is being taxed while that on others is not.

One caveat applies to the conclusion that consumption taxes do not distort the market for future consumption. That will only be the case if the tax rate applicable on future consumption is the same as on present consumption. If the consumption tax is applied at progressive rates, constancy in tax rates will arise only if the tax system allows for lifetime averaging, either self-averaging by the household's choice between designating assets or prepaying taxes on them, or a system of centrally imposed general averaging. To the extent that full averaging does not exist, even the consumption tax will impose some distortion on future consumption.

The efficiency argument for consumption taxation becomes much less clear cut when one recognizes that the market for future consumption is not the only broad activity that personal taxes can distort. The other broad incentive effect concerns the choice between goods and leisure (or, more generally, nonmarket activities). It is well known that the income tax favours the acquisition of utility through leisure, since such a nonmarket activity is untaxed. The consumption tax involves exactly the same distortion. The actual inefficiency from this distortion may, in fact, be larger with the consumption tax, because in order to yield the equivalent tax revenues, the consumption tax rate must, on average, exceed that of the income tax. The reason is that the tax base is smaller under a consumption tax since savings are sheltered. In an ongoing economy, savings can be positive in every period; thus some tax revenues are, in a real sense, continually deferred. This means that, in isolation, the disincentive to consume goods relative to leisure is likely to be greater under a consumption tax than under a *comprehensive* income tax. Of course, actual income taxes allow for so many deductions that, in practice, the average tax rate need not be raised much under a consumption tax relative to the existing income tax.

The combined effect on the timing of consumption (that is, savings) and the goods-leisure choice means that the efficiency effect of consumption versus income taxation is ambiguous, a priori. Recall that the consumption tax is likely to involve a smaller (or non-existent) distortion of the saving decision but an equal (or larger) distortion of the goods-leisure decision. As is well known, from the theory of the second best, it is not clear under these circumstances that the consumption tax is better than the income tax. The results of Corlett and Hague[16] are relevant here. They showed that a

---

[16]W. J. Corlett and D. C. Hague, "Complementarity and the Excess Burden of Taxation" (1953-54), 21 *Review of Economic Studies* 21-30.

divergence away from equal taxation of two commodities (in this case, present and future consumption) will yield a welfare improvement if the tax rate is increased on the commodity that is least substitutable for the third untaxed good (leisure).

In the consumption versus income tax question we have, at a minimum, four goods: present consumption, present leisure, future consumption, and future leisure. Leisure is untaxed regardless of when it is undertaken. It is, however, well known that there is an incentive, consistent with economic efficiency, for the household to concentrate leisure later in its life when work is least productive. Such retirement is tolerable and desirable to the household only if accompanied by goods such as food, housing, recreation equipment, and travel. In this context, an incentive to consume leisure is also an incentive to retire early and to save enough to do so. Thus an income tax, by taxing future (retirement) consumption more heavily, may actually be more efficient than a consumption tax.

The efficiency case for consumption taxation requires that one weigh the effects of the elimination of the tax on capital markets against the higher tax on leisure. As the theory of second best reminds us, it is ambiguous on theoretical grounds whether efficiency is improved when one distortion is removed from an economy in which other distortions exist. The existing empirical evidence on the relative magnitudes of labour and capital market distortions and their associated deadweight losses does not provide conclusive evidence here. There is, however, another sort of argument that lends weight to the importance of removing tax distortions on capital markets. The argument is that in mixed economies like that of Canada there are forces at work that tend to reduce saving below its socially efficient level. In economics jargon, there are "external benefits" associated with saving that are not accounted for when households decide on their own savings.

These externalities are of two sorts. One, associated with the works of Marglin and Sen,[17] is that savings for future generations provide benefits not only to the individual saver, but also to other members of the saver's own generation. Since there is no incentive for savers to take these benefits into account, there will be a tendency to save too little for future generations. The existence and magnitude of this externality depend upon both the existence of rational bequest behaviour by households and the existence of some altruistic urge by present generations for the collective well-being of future generations. It is difficult to assess empirically the strength of these arguments.

From the political economy viewpoint, there is another sort of externality involved in savings. The argument is that if households do not save for their own retirement, there is a reasonable expectation (borne out by actual policies) that the modern welfare state will provide for them to some

17Stephen A. Marglin, "The Social Rate of Discount and the Optimal Rate of Investment" (February 1963), LXXVII *Quarterly Journal of Economics* 95-111; Amartya K. Sen, "Isolation, Assurance and the Social Rate of Discount" (February 1967), LXXXI *Quarterly Journal of Economics* 112-24.

extent. This expectation reduces the incentive or the urgency of providing for one's own retirement. There is, thus, a sort of moral hazard problem. People are induced not to provide for their own retirement (except, say, in assets such as housing that yield no observed rate of return), but to rely on the next generation to provide some income for them. They will thus under-save. Any additional incentive that the tax system could provide for them to save on their own behalf will reduce their reliance on transfers from the next generations. Again, it is difficult to establish whether persons actually behave in this way. There is, however, considerable evidence that a large proportion of households do not, in fact, save adequately for their own retirement.[18]

Another minor issue concerns intergenerational transfers. Under an income tax, the income transferred to heirs is taxed when the generation bequeathing it earns it (except when such income is tax exempt, as in the case of housing). Under a consumption tax, it would be necessary to add inheritances of designated assets to the tax base of the recipient. Of course, the amount of the inheritance saved would be deductible. Since this involves a tax deferral, the consumption tax would favour bequests relative to the income tax. Unless some social cost is associated with bequests, this would be efficient. If there were such social costs, an estate tax rather than an income tax would be warranted.

The preceding discussion was based on the implicit assumption that capital markets are perfect, so that taxpayers face no imperfections in the form of borrowing constraints: that is, the taxpayers can borrow against anticipated lower taxes in the future. It is sometimes suggested that the consumption tax would decrease efficiency in the presence of such borrowing constraints. For example, individuals who find it desirable to borrow in order to consume in excess of income now would need to borrow more in order to meet the consumption tax liability. With borrowing constraints, individuals would be forced further away from their desired consumption level by the consumption tax. This argument is largely based on taxing consumption as it occurs (that is, under the designated asset method). To the extent that the tax prepayment method is used, the problem is not much different from that faced under an income tax, except that the rates are liable to be higher with a consumption tax.

Nevertheless, the net effect of the consumption tax is to increase the "liquidity" of the private sector. Individuals are allowed to save not only their disposable lifetime income, but also the taxes they owe the government. For example, an individual facing tax rate t and earning $1,000 could save only $(1 - t)$ $1,000 under the income tax, but the full $1,000 (assuming tax rates are not adjusted) under the consumption tax—that is, their own $(1 - t)$ $1,000 and the $(t \times$ $1,000) they owe the government.

To summarize, unlike the case with the administrative cost and, in our view, equity arguments, the efficiency case for consumption taxation is

---

[18]See, for example, P. A. Diamond, "A Framework for Social Security Analysis" (December 1977), 8 *Journal of Public Economics* 275-98.

ambiguous. It all depends upon how one weighs the advantages of removing the distortion on capital markets against the disadvantages of increasing the distortion on labour markets. Of course, one must remember that the distortion on capital markets under an income tax has two aspects to it. Not only does such a distortion exist, but it exists in a very uneven manner across types of investment since some (perhaps most) types of investment are treated on a consumption tax basis and others on an income tax basis. This can lead to a misallocation of savings across types of assets that can be as important as a broadly based capital market distortion.

Reforming the Existing Personal Income Tax

In our view, the case for basing personal taxation on consumption is compelling. There remains the practical policy problem of how to get from the existing personal income tax to the consumption tax. This task is made easier than one might expect by the fact that the existing personal tax is already very close to a consumption tax, probably much closer than it is to a comprehensive income tax. Some forms of savings and investment are already treated on a consumption tax basis. These include the acquisition of consumer durables (including housing), investment in human capital, and the holding of assets that yield a rate of return in kind (cash balances, insurance, etc.). Various means of sheltering capital income from personal taxes treat savings on a near-consumption-tax basis. These include the various means of saving for retirement (RRSPs, RPPs, DPSPs, etc.) and the $1,000 capital income exemption.

Nonetheless, the present system deviates from a consumption tax base in some important respects. Following is a list of changes to the personal tax base that, if made, would turn the present system into a full-fledged consumption tax:

1) *Designated assets.* All restrictions would have to be removed on both contributions and withdrawals to registered vehicles such as RRSPs and RPPs. There should be no limits on contributions in any given year and no limits on withdrawals. There should be no requirement to take the proceeds in the form of an annuity, although that option should be open. The possibility of bequeathing designated assets should exist, in which case recipients could either keep them in designated form or withdraw them and be subject to tax. There should also be an option of making designated loans for income-averaging purposes. These measures are not as radical as they may seem since the liberalization of contributions proposed in the May 1985 budget comes close to removing effective contribution limits for a large part of the population.

2) *Tax prepaid assets.* The capital income exemption limit of $1,000 should be abolished. All income accruing to nondesignated assets should be tax exempt. It may be desirable to stipulate that certain types of assets must be treated on a designated basis, particularly those financial assets prone to unexpected capital gains. Whether or not one views this as a priority depends upon how seriously one is concerned with the need to include unex-

pected capital gains and rents in the tax base ex post. We would argue that equity assets should be required to be designated.

3) *Unincorporated business income.* Unincorporated businesses should be treated on a cash flow (designated) basis. All revenues should enter the tax base when received, and all expenditures should be fully deductible when paid for, including capital expenditures. There should be no other capital deductions such as interest or depreciation. It is important that there be full loss offsetting in the tax system by refundability of negative tax liabilities or the equivalent.

4) *Integration with the corporate tax.* To the extent that the corporate tax is used for withholding purposes rather than to collect rents (see Chapter 5), the tax should be fully integrated with the personal tax. Full credit should be given to shareholders for taxes withheld from them at source. If other nations were to adopt a consumption base as well, it might be desirable, by tax treaty, to abolish the use of the corporate tax for withholding altogether. The design of an integration system will be dealt with more fully in the next chapter.

The above changes represent those that would have to be made to move the present tax base all the way to a consumption tax base. To preserve the existing degree of vertical equity in the tax system, the rate structure would have to be changed as well. In particular, one would expect it to be made more progressive. The system of indexing exemptions and tax brackets for inflation should remain in place. If these reform measures are viewed as being too drastic to be done all at one time, incremental advantages that move the system in the direction of a consumption tax would be possible. This is what has been happening in recent years. Of course, until one gets fully onto a consumption base, the administrative and equity advantages of the tax are not being reaped.

There may, however, be a good reason for making the move to a consumption tax gradual rather than abrupt. Any tax reform is going to lead to transitional windfall gains and losses. In the case of moving to a consumption tax, those who have accumulated assets in the expectation that the income on those assets will be taxed will obtain a windfall gain. This gain, which reflects a fall in tax liabilities to this older generation of asset holders at the time of the change, will be partly offset by an increase in tax liabilities to the younger wage earners who find their tax rates rise in order to keep government revenues balanced. After the transition, of course, everyone may be better off as capital accumulation will be higher overall for the economy. But during the transition there will be these windfall gains and losses.[19]

There are two ways of addressing this problem of transition, both of which amount to lengthening the period of transition. One is simply to introduce the tax change gradually, thereby spreading the transition costs

---

[19]For one analysis of these, see Auerbach, Kotlikoff, and Skinner, supra footnote 14.

over a longer period of time. The other is to change the tax structure abruptly, but at the same time to use public debt in the short run to avoid the large intergenerational redistribution that would accompany the tax structure change. This use of debt policy would spread the costs of transition across more generations. One's views concerning whether the transition ought to be a policy problem depend upon how one weighs the long-run gains from the tax reform to all future generations against the short-run costs to those generations alive during the transition.

One final policy issue should be addressed, and that is the relationship between the personal tax system and other related taxes, especially indirect taxes and payroll taxes. The latter two taxes are both closely related to consumption taxation, and they are both the subject of ongoing reform discussion. In the case of indirect taxation, the issue currently concerns the substitution of a multistage tax, such as a value-added tax (VAT) or its equivalent, for the existing system. For payroll taxation, the question is the extent to which social programs (unemployment insurance, pensions, health care, etc.) ought to be financed from general taxes rather than payroll taxes. A brief discussion of these taxes is warranted, at least insofar as they have implications for consumption taxation (or vice versa).

Consider first the VAT. If designed properly (that is, to exclude producer durables), it is equivalent to a proportional tax on consumption.[20] Therefore, from a purely economic point of view, it seems redundant to have it in a system of taxation that includes a personal consumption tax. The government can accomplish the equivalent of the VAT by a simple proportionate increase in rates. In doing so, it avoids the collection and compliance costs of an entire tax system applicable to every transaction in the economy. Some of these compliance costs can be reduced by an alternative form of multistage tax known as a business transfer tax (BTT). This is a tax on all businesses that uses as a base total revenues less capital purchases less costs of nonlabour current inputs. It can also be levied on a destination basis. The cost saving comes from the fact that businesses pay taxes only periodically and use the accounting data they already require for income taxes. To a certain extent, they can avoid the use of invoices under the ordinary VAT.

Besides being redundant from an economics point of view, the VAT (or BTT) also has the drawback that the provinces may see it as an invasion of one of their existing tax fields. It might be far better to attempt to negotiate a tax collection agreement in this area to avoid unnecessary duplication by the two levels of government.

One final drawback of introducing a multistage commodity tax in place of the existing manufacturers' sales tax is what might be referred to as the political economy argument. The VAT or BTT constitutes a broadly based tax which though ultimately equivalent to a proportional consumption tax

---

[20]This assumes that the tax is levied on a destination basis. If it were levied on an origin basis, it would be equivalent to a tax on production.

might not be perceived as such by the public because of its relatively hidden nature (especially in the BTT form). It may thus constitute a revenue source from which government can easily finance expenditure increases. Some may object to that. Some may also object, on equity grounds, to the fact that the tax may constitute a reallocation from progressive personal taxation to proportional commodity taxation.

In practice, a VAT would not exactly correspond to a general consumption tax. For one thing, by exempting specific commodities, or giving preferential rates to some, the VAT is capable of a form of progressivity that the personal consumption tax is not capable of replicating. The latter achieves progressivity by exempting a given amount of total expenditures and applying progressive rates to the rest. To the extent that one wishes to discriminate by type of consumption (food, clothing, etc.), a VAT is useful.[21]

There are some problems with administering the VAT in particular cases. One concerns the treatment of durables. Since consumption of services from durables cannot be measured and taxed directly, the VAT must tax the purchase of new durables directly, which is equivalent to a tax-prepaid form of consumption taxation. A difficulty arises here in the case of the existing stock of housing acquired before the VAT was in effect. If only new acquisitions of durables are taxed, these used houses are effectively tax exempt. One partial measure to help alleviate this is to levy the VAT on the resale of houses that have not previously borne the tax. Another problem concerns the taxation of certain services such as financial services and shipping. In these cases, it is difficult to measure the value of services consumed. These problems would not arise under personal consumption taxation.

Similar issues arise with payroll taxation. In one sense, payroll taxation is equivalent to the prepayment method of consumption taxation since it is like an income tax system that exempts capital income. Furthermore, payroll taxation can be designed with a progressive rate structure. Payroll taxation, however, cannot be fully equivalent to consumption taxation since it does not have the flexibility of choice between prepayment and designated treatment of savings. All savings are implicitly treated on a prepayment basis, which precludes the use of the designated method for those important situations when it is desirable—particularly the taxation of unincorporated business income. In the case of unincorporated businesses, payroll taxation is difficult to apply since one cannot readily distinguish between wage and capital income. Furthermore, precluding the use of designated assets effectively prevents households from self-averaging. For these reasons, the use of payroll taxes to collect general revenues seems to be dominated by consumption taxation.

In summary, not only is the consumption tax desirable in terms of administrative simplicity and equity (and possibly efficiency), it is also a

---

[21]The arguments for and against using both indirect and direct taxation for vertical equity purposes may be found in A. B. Atkinson, "Optimal Taxation and the Direct Versus Indirect Tax Controversy" (November 1977), X *Canadian Journal of Economics* 590-606.

very feasible reform. The existing system is very close to it already. To go all the way would involve primarily loosening the restrictions on registered savings, making the capital income exemption limitless, and presumably changing the rate structure. That is our agenda for personal tax reform.

5

Reforming the Corporation Income Tax

Introduction

In this chapter we discuss issues in the reform of the corporate tax in Canada. Such a discussion first requires a clear understanding of the underlying rationale for taxing corporations. Such an understanding, which is often missing in public discussion of corporate tax reform, is a precondition for forming a view of the ideal corporate tax system toward which any reform should be moving. We saw in the last chapter that the underlying principles surrounding personal tax reform were well understood and subject to academic and professional, if not public, debate. This is not the case with corporate taxation. Corporate tax reform has often tended to proceed piecemeal without any clearly stated ultimate rationale. One of our main purposes here will be to outline carefully the rationale for the corporate tax and the ideal corporate tax that would satisfy this rationale. Our perception of the role for the corporate tax will very much determine our views about the ideal corporate tax, and thus about corporate tax reform.

At the outset, it is worth emphasizing that a discussion about the ideal corporate tax cannot proceed in isolation from the structure of the rest of the tax system. In particular, the ideal corporate tax depends critically upon three features of the more general tax environment. First, it depends upon the tax system used at the personal level. For example, we shall argue that if the personal tax is consumption-based, there is no need to use the corporate tax as a device for withholding against retained earnings in corporations that generate accrued capital gains at the personal level. Similarly, the form of the ideal corporate tax under a personal consumption tax system will be seen to depend upon whether or not equity assets are held in the designated form.

Second, the design of the corporate tax depends upon the nature of foreign corporate and personal tax systems and especially on the credit mechanisms available to foreign corporations for taxes paid abroad. A major difficulty is that foreign tax structures and credit mechanisms are far from uniform across countries. Since the Canadian tax system cannot be designed to accommodate each foreign-owned firm individually, the corporate tax system will inevitably be imperfect. Some compromises and some judgment will be involved in advocating both an ideal structure and a direction for reform.

Third, the design of the corporate tax also depends on the other types of withholding taxes, especially a tax at the international level. There are two types of withholding taxes that are relevant to our discussion: (1) the corporate tax itself, which, in principle, withholds equity income from both foreigners and domestic owners, and (2) the nonresident withholding tax, which withholds income specifically from foreigners. Nonresident taxes are currently levied on dividends, capital gains, and interest on short-term assets. Capital gains (except on real estate) paid to nonresidents are currently exempt from Canadian tax (although not from foreign tax) for treaty countries. The nonresident tax is generally 25 per cent for nontreaty and 15 per cent for treaty countries, but most major trading countries and countries that export capital to Canada have treaties with Canada.

The following section of this chapter considers the rationale for taxing corporations in the first place. Our view is that the two main roles for the corporate tax are (1) to act as a withholding device for obtaining tax revenues on capital income at source, and (2) to tax rents. The circumstances under which these roles are appropriate are discussed. Some subsidiary roles are also considered. Next, the design of the corporate tax is considered in view of these roles and also the nature of personal taxation and foreign taxation. Particular emphasis is placed upon the relationship between the personal tax system and the corporate tax system and the need to integrate the two systems. Finally, reform of the existing tax system is discussed in the light of the ideals. Again, the reform concerns the reform of both the corporate tax structure itself *and* the method of integration.

The Rationale for the Corporate Tax

Any taxes are ultimately borne by persons, and tax systems must ultimately be judged by how the burden of taxes is shared among persons as well as by how personal behaviour is affected by the tax system. That being the case, why tax corporations at all? Since any taxes on corporations will ultimately be borne by persons somewhere, why not avoid the complications involved in taxing corporations altogether and simply tax individuals instead?

There are two main reasons for wanting to tax corporations. The first, referred to as the *withholding function*, results from the fact that certain types of income earned by corporations on behalf of their shareholders either can escape taxation altogether at the personal level (as when shareholders are foreigners) or can have taxation deferred at the personal level by reinvestment of the income in the corporation. The second, referred to as the *rent-collecting function*, occurs when corporations earn rents, or pure economic profits, which are regarded as part of the collective property rights of the government acting on behalf of the public. These two roles are discussed in turn.

The Withholding Function of the Corporate Income Tax

The conventional reason for taxing income at the corporate level is that such taxation serves as a withholding device for the personal tax and prevents taxes on capital income from being deferred, levied at preferential rates, transferred to foreign jurisdictions, or escaped altogether.[1] In the

---

[1] This was the main view taken by the Carter Commission; see Canada, *Report of the Royal Commission on Taxation* (Ottawa: Queen's Printer, 1966).

absence of a corporate income tax, personal taxes on the equity income accruing to domestic shareholders could be deferred, perhaps indefinitely, by retaining and reinvesting the income within the firm. In principle, it would be possible to tax reinvested income at the personal level when it accrues to the domestic shareholders of public corporations by fully taxing the resulting capital gains upon accrual. But accrual taxation of capital gains at the personal level is difficult or not feasible, especially on shares of private (closely held) corporations, which are not traded, and on shares held by nonresident households and corporations. Thus, the traditional case for taxing at the level of the corporation is established.

The above argument does not justify corporate taxation of capital income that is distributed as dividends or interest. There do not appear to be any impediments to the personal taxation of distributed dividends or interest by either public or private corporations when those dividends are distributed to resident shareholders. When dividends are distributed to non-resident shareholders, however, there are difficulties at the personal level. These difficulties do not concern the domestic government's ability to with-hold taxes, but rather the eligibility of such personal withholding taxes for foreign tax credits. If the domestic taxes are not creditable abroad, the required return on Canadian equities would have to rise by the amount of the withholding tax in order to compensate nonresidents for the double tax-ation of distributed dividends. In effect, the withholding tax is a tax on the domestically owned portion of the capital stock only; the tax revenues col-lected from foreign owners of the domestic capital stock are exactly offset by an increase in interest or dividend payments made to foreigners. The United States allows Canadian withholding taxes against dividends and interest at a relatively low rate,[2] but corporate taxes are essentially fully creditable up to the U.S. corporate tax rate.[3] Consequently, the Canadian, or domestic, corporate tax allows the domestic economy to tax fully equity income accruing to nonresidents at source whereas withholding taxes do not.

To summarize the above argument, the usual rationale for levying a tax on equity income accruing at the corporate level is to avoid the difficulties of taxing capital gains upon accrual and to secure taxation by the source country of income accruing to nonresidents in a way that permits a full tax credit abroad. In the more detailed discussion of these withholding arguments below, it is useful to consider withholding against foreigners and against domestic residents in that order.

Withholding Against Foreigners

The general principle is that withholding against foreigners should be done against all tax liabilities credited abroad. Such withholding will represent a

---

[2]Under the new tax treaty with the United States, the withholding rates are 10 per cent on branch profit and dividends paid by a subsidiary that is at least 10 per cent controlled by the foreign parent. The tax is 15 per cent on interest paid to the parent.

[3]We ignore a number of foreign tax credit limitations in this discussion.

pure revenue gain for Canada without affecting investment decisions or other types of decisions taken by the firm. Withholding less than that would simply mean forgoing tax revenues that could otherwise be diverted from foreign treasuries. Withholding any more would cause a reduction of foreign investment in Canada, which could be inefficient in the economic sense. Applying withholding against foreigners could, however, invite retaliatory action by other countries—this limits the application of withholding to the extent it does not violate any international laws or treaties such as those related to discrimination between foreign and domestic investment.

Corporations generate both labour income and capital income. There is no need to use the corporate tax for withholding from labour income, since withholding can be done against wage and salary earners at source using the personal income tax. Thus, corporate tax withholding will be restricted to various forms of capital income generated by corporations. As mentioned, withholding is desired only for capital income sources that generate tax liabilities that can be credited against foreign corporate income taxes paid in the foreign country. Of course, pure nonresident withholding taxes on capital income earned by foreigners could be used instead of the corporate tax if full crediting abroad were allowed and other governments did not object to it. In practice, however, the amount of withholding taxes that can be credited is much smaller than the corporate tax liabilities that one might like to withhold and that foreign corporate tax systems allow to be credited. Thus, in the absence of revision of withholding tax rates, we must assume that the corporate tax will remain a main vehicle by which taxes on capital income are withheld from foreigners.

One does not want to withhold against all forms of capital income generated by corporations—only against those forms that give rise to credits abroad. Generally, withholding under the corporate tax does not include interest income. If it did, the corporate tax base could be much larger than the foreign tax base used to calculate the credit since nominal interest is normally deductible from the foreign tax base—a situation that could lead to Canadian corporate taxes being in excess of foreign taxes payable. This is, perhaps, unfortunate for a net debtor nation like Canada. If withholding could be done at the corporate level against interest income, there would be an additional net transfer of corporate tax revenues from creditor nation treasuries to those of debtors. Canada would gain tax revenues at the expense of the rest of the world. Unfortunately, international tax crediting arrangements do not allow that. Thus, the most likely form of withholding that can be achieved under the corporate tax is against equity income alone.

In practice, one may want to treat the two main uses of equity income (dividends and retained earnings) differently for withholding purposes as well. This would be the case where foreign tax credit systems treat dividends differently from retained income. For example, the United States allows subsidiary corporate income taxes to be credited only when dividends are repatriated. This means that crediting is deferred on earnings retained by U.S. subsidiaries abroad. In this case, one might want to treat equity income that is paid out as dividends differently from equity income that is retained. One way to do this, which is further discussed later in this chapter (in "Design of the Corporate Income Tax"), is to allow the deduction of retained earnings from the corporate tax base as well as interest. The difficulty with this as a general policy is that not all foreign firms are treated as U.S. subsidiaries are treated. Even U.S. branch plant operations can get full credit for foreign taxes paid at the time that they are paid rather than when earnings are repatriated. To make retained earnings deductible for them would amount to forgoing or deferring potential tax revenues at the expense of the foreign treasury. Thus, the most commonly advocated corporate tax base for withholding against foreigners is equity income, broadly defined.

Even if foreign treasuries gave no credit on corporate taxes paid abroad, there might still be a withholding role for the Canadian corporate tax. Say that foreigners were to adopt consumption tax systems, or they were going to substitute a value-added tax system for their corporate taxes. In the corporate case, even though we might not want to withhold against all equity income generated by the corporation, we might still want to withhold against that capital income, generated by foreign corporations, that represents pure rents or economic profits. Such withholding, even if not credited abroad, would still be nondistortionary in the sense that it would not affect the investment decisions of foreign firms, since a tax on rents is by definition nondistortionary. One could also argue that this is justified because such rents are legitimately considered as part of the property rights of Canadians. The example of resource rents naturally comes to mind. This argument for taxing the rents from foreigners is closely related to the second general rationale for taxing corporations, and we return to it below.

There is one final argument for withholding that is not contingent upon arrangements for crediting foreign tax. We may want to withhold taxes against foreign corporations on benefit taxation principles to reflect the fact that the tax revenues may be used to provide public services that are of benefit to these corporations (for example, roads, infrastructure, or manpower training).[4] To the extent that this is the case, the corporate tax will also be nondistorting. The difficulty with implementing this rationale for corporate taxation, as with any argument for benefit taxation, is that the benefits of public expenditures as they accrue to corporations are virtually impossible to measure.

Withholding Against Domestic Residents

The requirement to withhold against the capital income of residents that is generated at the corporate level is intimately related to the nature of the Canadian personal tax system. As mentioned earlier, the conventional argu-

---

[4]Some specialists have also applied this argument to the benefits received by corporations from limited liability. See The Institute for Fiscal Studies, *The Structure and Reform of Direct Taxation, Report of a Committee Chaired by Professor James E. Meade* (London: Allen & Unwin, 1978) (herein called "the Meade Report").

ment for withholding at the corporate level against the income of residents, (espoused, for example, by the Carter Commission), arises when the personal tax base is income. In this case, one would ideally like to include in the tax base of individuals all capital income earned on an accrual basis. However, since this is generally regarded to be administratively difficult in the case of capital gains income, most personal tax systems actually tax capital gains on realization. This provides a tax incentive for shareholders to defer tax liabilities by retaining and reinvesting equity income in the corporation to accumulate capital gains rather than paying it out as taxable dividends. To reduce this incentive, the corporate tax is levied on corporate income at source.

If the only purpose of the corporate tax were to prevent the tax-free accrual of capital gains within the corporation, the corporate tax base would need to include only retained earnings. That is, dividend payouts would be exempt. When one combines the withholding role against residents with that against foreigners, however, the entire equity income of the corporation must be included in the base, since it would not be feasible in practice to distinguish equity income generated for residents from that generated for foreign shareholders.

The requirement to withhold against the corporate income retained on behalf of residents in order to prevent the deferment of capital gains tax liabilities no longer applies when the personal tax system is based on consumption. In this case, capital income is effectively untaxed, consequently there is no longer any need to worry about deferment. Income in the form of capital gains that is spent need enter the tax base only on realization and not on accrual. It seems that the general argument for withholding would then apply only against nonresidents, although withholding against foreigners and domestic owners may be practical for administrative and legal reasons.

There is one exception to this rule that withholding would not be required against domestic residents when the domestic personal tax base is consumption. Recall from our discussion in Chapter 4 that under a personal consumption base, tax liabilities on assets that are treated on a tax-prepaid or nondesignated basis are not equivalent in present-value terms to tax liabilities for designated assets if part of the return to the asset consists of economic rents. The acquisition and holding of assets treated on a nondesignated basis have no tax consequence at all. Their acquisition costs are not deductible, and the income earned on them is not taxable. When rents exist, to put nondesignated and designated assets on an equal tax footing requires adding to the tax base that part of the return on nondesignated assets that reflects pure rents. This is virtually impossible to do. As discussed below, however, rents can, in principle, be readily taxed at the corporate level. To the extent that equity assets are held in the nondesignated form, one may want to use the corporate tax to tax at the corporate level rents that would otherwise go untaxed at the personal level.

There is a difficulty with using the corporate tax to withhold against rents accruing to nondesignated equity assets. It is not possible to distinguish at the corporate level between rents accruing to equity held in the form of designated assets and those accruing to equity held in the form of nondesignated assets. If one withholds rents using the appropriate corporate tax, one cannot avoid withholding them against both designated and nondesignated asset holders despite the fact that such rents are already being taxed at the personal level. To avoid this double taxation, one would have to have a system of integration between the corporate and personal taxes, an unavoidable issue to which we now turn.

The use of the corporate tax for withholding inevitably involves some integration of the corporate income tax system with the personal tax system regardless of the form the latter takes. It is this requirement for integration that inevitably leads to a tax system that is administratively complex. Anything that can be done to simplify the system of integration—and still ensure that it fulfils its required functions—will be welcome. As we shall see in this chapter, another of the administrative advantages of basing personal taxation on consumption rather than income is that it opens the possibility for some simplification of the corporate tax for withholding purposes. The appropriate methods used for integration are dealt with more fully below in our discussion of corporate tax design. Here we are interested only in general principles.

Basically, any withholding done against capital income at the corporate level should be fully integrated with personal tax liabilities for domestic residents, with one exception. That exception is rents collected on equity income earned on nondesignated assets which would otherwise escape full taxation altogether at the personal level. This latter exemption may be complex enough administratively to suggest that equity assets should all be held in the designated form.

By full integration we mean that full credit be given to residents for taxes that have been withheld at the corporate level on equity income generated there. This crediting would be justified whether the withholding is motivated by a desire to tax foreigners or by a desire to withhold against the retained earnings of residents. Of course, this latter motive for withholding would disappear under a consumption-based personal tax system. Full integration would ensure that the corporate tax system does not distort capital investment decisions of firms in Canada.

There are various approaches to integrating corporate and personal tax systems. One is to credit the shareholders with taxes paid on their behalf in the same tax year in which the taxes are paid by the corporation. An alternative method is to give credit for corporate taxes paid when equity income is received by the shareholder, including tax-exempt shareholders. This latter method is the one used, for example, in the case of the Canadian dividend tax credit, although the credit is not available to certain tax-exempt entities such as pension plans.

If this latter method of integration, based on crediting shareholders for corporate taxes paid when equity income is received by shareholders, is used, there are some difficult conceptual design problems, which are further discussed in the next section. One way to proceed would be to provide a credit only when funds are taken out of the corporation, whether by dividends or repurchase of shares, or winding down. This method has the advantage of administrative simplicity, because crediting need not occur on capital gains accrued or on capital gains realized on the sale of shares from one taxpayer to another. Neither of these involves funds being taken out of the corporation. The disadvantage of this method is that the crediting may occur long after the corporate tax liabilities have been incurred; as a result, there will be forgone interest on the corporate tax credits which ought to be included in the crediting arrangement, but this is obviously difficult to implement. An alternative that at least partly avoids this problem is to provide tax crediting not only on dividends but also on realized capital gains. This system is bound to be more complex, especially since capital losses must also be integrated as well as gains. Furthermore, a system that integrated realized capital gains would still be imperfect if the motive for the corporate tax is to withhold against foreigners. In this case, the credit should actually be given to domestic shareholders when the capital gains (and losses) accrue. This is obviously very difficult to do. Thus, on administrative grounds, one may be left with doing the crediting when dividends or their equivalent are taken out of the corporation.

Note that in principle the crediting of corporate taxes when dividends are distributed can be done either to the firm doing the distributing or to the recipient domestic shareholders. These alternatives are discussed below in the following section, where it is argued that the former is not feasible when a substantial proportion of shareholders are foreign.

As mentioned earlier, the other general approach to integration is to do the crediting when the corporation actually incurs its tax liabilities. This type of system, which was recommended by the Carter Report, also poses problems. It requires the firm to identify shareholders and to attribute its tax liabilities among them each year. Although this system ensures that crediting is done only on the basis of corporate taxes actually paid, it has the disadvantage of being administratively complex in a world in which shares are changing hands frequently over the tax year and in which some shareholders are foreign. Foreign shareholders are not entitled to a credit on corporate taxes paid.

Unfortunately, any system of integration, necessary as it is, is bound to be complex. The desire to relate the amount of corporate taxes credited to the amount actually paid seems to preclude simple systems that apply a common formula to all domestic shareholders. We shall return to these design problems soon.

The Rent-Collecting Function of the Corporate Tax

A second major rationale for the corporate income tax, one that has been stressed in the technical economic literature, is the desirability of a tax on pure profits, or economic rents. Economic rents are defined to be the revenues that firms receive over and above the full opportunity costs of all the inputs that go into the production of revenues. They include, for example,

• the value of natural resources net of all costs of exploration, extraction, and processing;

• the value of any special advantages that a firm has that cannot be transferred elsewhere (such as location);

• the value of any scarce factor that is fixed in supply (such as prime agricultural land); and

• profits attributable to monopoly power and to government regulation limiting competition.

Economic rents are most prevalent in the primary or resource sector, and there are a number of existing taxes and royalties whose primary justification is to capture some part of the resource rents for the public sector.

Under the personal tax system, rents will be taxed either as a component of capital income under an income tax system or as a source of consumption under a consumption tax system. The use of the corporate tax as a tax on rents would represent an additional discriminatory tax on rents over and above that under the personal tax. The possible desirability of levying a special tax on rents has long been recognized by economists and policy-makers alike. The idea is often popularly associated with Henry George, who advocated financing government expenditures entirely by a tax on land more than 70 years ago.[5] In recent years, more emphasis has been placed on using the tax system to tax rents in the resource industries.[6] The traditional argument in favour of taxing rents has been an efficiency argument. Since rents do not represent the returns required for the supply of any economic inputs, levying a tax on rents will not affect decision-making. That is, it will raise revenue in a purely nondistorting way. Furthermore, on equity grounds, the taxation of rents can be justified if one views the rents (or the assets generating them) as being part of the common property rights of the nation. Thus, in the case of resources, if one thinks of the resource endowment of a nation as being the common property of the nation, it is legitimate for the public sector to exercise its property rights by some form of taxation. In Canada, the argument obviously can be applied to provinces in the case of resources as well as to the nation.

The argument against imposing an additional tax on economic rents is also essentially one of equity, primarily horizontal equity. As Ballentine has argued,[7] imposing a corporate tax on rents subjects that form of capital

---

[5]Henry George, *Progress and Poverty* (New York: Doubleday, 1914).

[6]See Robin Boadway and Neil Bruce, "Theoretical Issues in Tax Reform," in David Laidler, Research Coordinator, *Approaches to Economic Well-Being*, Collected Research Studies of the Royal Commission on the Economic Union and Development Prospects for Canada, Vol. 26 (Toronto: University of Toronto Press, 1985), 137-93.

[7]J. Gregory Ballentine, "Comment," in Wayne R. Thirsk and John Whalley, eds., *Tax Policy Options in the 1980s*, Canadian Tax Paper no. 66 (Toronto: Canadian Tax Foundation, 1982), 211-13.

income to discriminatory taxation, so that persons who own rent-generating assets are treated unfairly by the tax system in relation to persons who do not. This objection is equivalent to saying that the rents are part of the property rights of the asset owner rather than of the state. Obviously a value judgment is involved, and that value judgment may vary from asset to asset. For example, one may judge that the property rights to rents on natural resources rightfully belong to the state, but on some other asset they do not. This judgment may be substantiated by the fact that resource industries have often been singled out in tax systems as industries whose rents are legitimate objectives for taxation schemes. Indeed, some resources are explicitly owned by the state and rent collection from them takes the form of royalties. As we have argued elsewhere, the types of royalty schemes actually in effect represent a particularly inefficient way of capturing resource rents. [8]

Even when it is judged that the rents ought to be viewed as the rightful property of the state, and that involves a value judgment, it might still be the case that implementing such a tax violates the norms of horizontal equity. The persons who own rent-generating assets will presumably have acquired them at a cost that includes the capitalized value of future rents. If the government introduces a tax on rents and does not exempt old assets, persons will suffer a windfall loss represented by a fall in the value of their asset wealth. In judging the efficacy of introducing a rent tax, this transitional effect on owners of existing wealth must be considered, since it has redistributive effects as well as possibly deterring further investment if investors believe that government will freely tax capital once the investment decision has been made. This must be weighed against the longer run gains of having an efficient source of revenues in the future. Again, a value judgment is involved.

Our judgment is that the horizontal equity problem and the transitional problem are not particularly severe, at least in the case of resource revenues. Governments have a tradition of viewing resource rents as fair game for taxation and that will be incorporated into the existing value of the assets. Of course, in reforming the way in which the rents are captured, there are bound to be some windfall gains and losses to asset owners. But that is the case with any tax reform, and there is no reason to believe that it would be particularly severe in the case of this sort of reform. Our inclination is therefore to argue that the use of the corporate tax as a tax on economic rents, over and above its use as a withholding device, might be particularly appropriate for the resource industries at least at the outset. Not only can the rents in these industries be viewed at least in part as the property right of the public, but also rents or economic profits might be expected to be relatively significant in this sector.

The reason for suggesting that the corporate tax can be viewed as a useful device for collecting rents is that one can define the taxable income of firms

---

[8]Robin W. Boadway, Neil Bruce, and Jack M. Mintz, "Corporate Taxation in Canada: Toward an Efficient System," in Thirsk and Whalley, *supra* footnote 7, at 171-211.

to be equivalent to rents. As outlined in more detail in the design section, if one were to define the tax base to include all accrued revenues less all true economic costs on an accrual basis, one would have economic rents as the tax base. In practice, such a tax base would be impossible to implement in that ideal form because it would require one to deduct certain types of imputed economic costs which are not measurable. These include the opportunity cost of equity financing, the true rate of economic depreciation, and the replacement cost of inventory use. Fortunately, these measurement difficulties can be overcome by defining a tax base that has the same present value as economic rents, but whose components are all measurable because they involve market transactions. Such a base is the so-called *cash-flow* tax base. Its composition is discussed in the next section, where we also discuss some alternatives to the cash flow base that have similar properties.

It is important to recognize that a corporate tax designed for rent collecting will generally differ in design from one intended for withholding, unless the only withholding one wants to do is against economic rents. A corporate tax system that combined these two functions would be more complicated than each one taken independently. It is also important to recognize that, unlike the withholding component of the corporate tax, the component of the corporate tax used to capture pure rents must not be integrated with the personal tax system. To give credit to resident households for the taxes collected on rents under this second rationale would be equivalent to undoing the whole purpose of the tax, which is to collect a tax on rents over and above those that are already collected at the personal level.

These differences in design and the fact that one may want to restrict the rent-collecting function to a specific part of the economy, such as the resource sector, would suggest that one may want to view the rent-collecting tax as being a completely separate tax from the corporate income tax used for withholding. Another argument for doing this is that one may not want to restrict the rent tax to corporations. In principle, unincorporated businesses in the resource sector can also earn rents that should be taxed. Extending the rent tax to all firms, whether incorporated or not, would avoid introducing an incentive into the tax system for firms to choose to remain unincorporated.

The withholding function and the rent-collecting function represent the two main rationales for taxing corporations. If corporate taxation were implemented in an ideal way to accomplish these functions, and if the appropriate integrating measures were in effect, the corporate tax would be nondistortionary. Marginal effective tax rates due to the corporate tax, such as those measured in Chapter 3, would be zero. Any distortions on capital market transactions would result from the personal tax, and these would be zero as well if consumption or its equivalent were used as the base.

Other Incidental Arguments for the Corporate Tax

Although withholding and rent collection are the two primary roles for the corporate income tax in our view, there are other reasons why governments in fact use corporate taxation. There are also other reasons that have been adduced by economists for the corporate tax. Here we outline three such arguments, usually referred to as the control argument, the risk-sharing argument, and the vertical equity argument.

The Control Argument for the Corporate Tax

The corporation income tax can be used by the government to alter resource allocation within the private sector by altering the marginal profitability conditions facing the firm. Such a purpose could not be usefully served by either the pure profit or withholding type of corporate tax. The pure profit tax leaves the marginal profitability conditions unchanged while the withholding tax affects the marginal profitability conditions in a general, non-firm-specific manner. If the marginal source of the funds to the firm is from domestic savers, the fully integrated corporate tax affects the marginal profitability conditions only to the extent such conditions are affected by the domestic personal tax system. If the marginal source of funds is foreign, the corporate tax affects the marginal profitability conditions as determined by the foreign corporate tax it is assumed to duplicate.

The corporate tax is levied on the firm; consequently, it is a useful tax for the purpose of altering the marginal profitability of different production activities if that is desired. This can be accomplished by legislating industry- or even firm-specific tax provisions. Such a role, however, will conflict with the perfect integration of the corporation income tax with both the domestic personal tax and the foreign corporation tax. Assuming that the marginal source of finance is domestic, the government can offer more or less favourable tax treatment of certain economic activities, but this will involve, at the margin, over- or under-integrating the corporate tax respectively.

If the marginal source of finance is not domestic saving, however, over- and under-integration of the tax may not affect the decisions of the firm but rather affect only the savings decisions of resident households. When the marginal source of funds comes from abroad, the ability of the domestic government to alter the marginal profitability conditions depends on the way in which the foreign tax credit abroad is determined. For example, if the foreign tax credit in the foreign country applies on accrual (rather than when the earnings are repatriated) and the credit available is limited to the taxes owing under the foreign corporate tax base and rate structure, the domestic corporate tax can do little but duplicate its foreign counterpart. Any attempts to lower the tax rate on corporate income through domestic base and rate adjustments will simply transfer revenues to the foreign taxation authority and leave the tax on the marginal investor unchanged. With full crediting, the domestic corporate tax cannot be used to affect the marginal profitability conditions.

It is probable that the Canadian tax authority can use the corporate tax in practice to affect the marginal profitability conditions (at least to some extent) whether it wishes to improve economic efficiency (discussed below) or to favour or disfavour certain productive activities. For some firms, especially small Canadian-owned private corporations, the marginal source of equity finance is domestic saving, because access to international capital markets is limited. In this case, economic control objectives can be accomplished by over- or under-integrating the corporate tax applying to those firms. Some slack is provided by the foreign tax credit provisions abroad for large international firms whose marginal source of finance is undoubtedly the foreign capital market. The United States, for example, which is of primary importance, taxes foreign investment income from subsidiary corporations with at least 10 per cent ownership by the parent only as it is repatriated. Profits that are reinvested in Canada allow U.S. subsidiaries to defer payment of U.S. corporate taxes to a later time. The value of the deferment depends on the net of corporate tax rate of return on the subsidiary's investment. This means that on equity income accruing to nonresidents from foreign subsidiaries that is reinvested in Canada, the difference between the U.S. tax rate and the Canadian tax rate must be paid whether earnings are retained or distributed.[9] Consequently, the Canadian corporate tax rate, not the U.S., is the relevant rate for firms whose marginal source of funds is reinvested foreign equity income. Also, the flexibility afforded the firm in terms of the timing of its repatriations and the allocation of income and expenses between the source and residence countries allows it to alter its domestic taxable income so as to lower the effective marginal corporate tax rate in Canada and thereby alter the marginal profitability conditions.

The upshot of this discussion is that even if the government wanted to influence specific investment decisions, the use of the corporate tax system to do so is problematic in an open economy such as Canada's. In addition, it is certain to complicate what is already bound to be a fairly complex tax system. One could argue both on grounds of simplicity and on the basis of maintaining tax revenues that if the government insists on interfering with the price mechanism, it might do so in a more direct or targeted way rather than by compromising the general corporate tax system. For example, the use of specific grants may be called for. On the other hand, the ability to use specific grants could be viewed as inviting governments to use their discretion, which may be quite arbitrary, in interfering selectively with the price mechanism. This latter argument can apply equally, however, to the use of specific tax relief measures as seen with the Cape Breton investment tax credit and taxation of resource "megaprojects." Ultimately, the question to be answered in assessing the control argument for the corporate tax is whether or not the government should interfere with the determination of investment decisions via the price mechanism. The investigation of such a question, important though it might be, would take us rather far afield from the issue of this study.

9Assuming U.S. rates are expected to remain constant. For a full discussion of this, see Donald J. S. Brean, *International Issues in Taxation: The Canadian Perspective*, Canadian Tax Paper no. 75 (Toronto: Canadian Tax Foundation, 1984), Chapter 7.

The Risk-Sharing Role of the Corporate Tax

The corporate tax can have an effect on the decision by firms to invest in risky ventures, and this can be viewed as a desirable, albeit to some extent unavoidable, effect of the corporate tax. The economic analysis of the effects of corporate taxation on risk-taking is by nature very complex technically and we can do little more here than point to the type of results that one obtains.[10]

The basic argument is as follows. When a decision-maker has to make choices in an environment in which the outcomes of the choices are uncertain, the actual choices taken depend not only upon the expected value of the outcomes, but also upon the possible variability of the outcomes. If the government were to impose a tax on the outcome, and if the tax were to treat all outcomes symmetrically whether they were positive or negative (that is, if the tax had full loss-offsetting built in), the effect of the tax would be to reduce both the expected return and the variability of the possible outcomes in the same proportion. In these circumstances, the tax would reduce the "price" of taking risk, and the decision-maker may well respond by taking more risk. Thus, the government has influenced the decision to take a risk by the private sector. In turn, the government acquires future corporate tax revenues which themselves are variable. The government is effectively sharing in both the risk and the return of the decision-maker. It is as if the government becomes a nonvoting equity partner in the firm, if the decision-maker is a firm. If the government is better able to pool or spread the risk than the private sector decision-maker it is taxing, then the assumption of part of the risk of the firm's decisions by the government will improve the allocation of resources in the economy. If the government is not able to pool the risk any better than the decision-maker, the allocation of resources will not be improved. Indeed, depending on the structure of the tax on the risky outcomes, resource allocation may be worse.

Thus, a key issue is whether or not the government is better able to pool risk than decision-makers in the private sector. In the case of firms, if capital markets are perfectly competitive and well functioning, and if the government has the same information about the future that is generally available to the market, firms with access to capital markets will be able to pool risks as effectively as the government. That is one of the main functions of capital markets—to facilitate the trading and pooling of risks. In this case, the government would not want taxation to interfere with the risk-pooling function of capital markets. An important result that has been obtained in the analysis of taxation and risk is that a tax on economic profits (or its present-value equivalent, a cash flow tax) that allows full loss

---

[10]For further reference, see Roger H. Gordon, "Taxation of Corporate Capital Income: Tax Revenues Versus Tax Distortions" (February 1985), C *The Quarterly Journal of Economics* 1-27; Jeremy I. Bulow and Lawrence H. Summers, "The Taxation of Risky Assets" (February 1984), 92 *Journal of Political Economy* 20-39.

offsetting will not distort the decision to take risk by the firm.[11] This implies that the corporate tax bases we are advocating for withholding and rent collection will not distort the decision to take risk, since the tax bases are neutral or nondistorting. It must be emphasized that this assumes that full loss offsetting is allowed.

In some cases, firms may not have full access to capital markets to pool their risks. For example, small firms with few owners may find access difficult. Economies of scale in transacting on equity markets may be one reason for this. Another may be that creditors view the information about the future to be inherently less reliable in small firms than in larger ones. Whatever the reason, if access to equity markets is limited so that they have to rely more on the equity funds of a few owners, and if those owners cannot pool risks effectively, there may be a role for the government in facilitating the ability to take risk by small firms. This will automatically occur under a tax system that allows firms to write off the costs of investment up front and taxes them on the returns later on, which is precisely what a cash flow system of taxation allows. To be effective, the system must allow full loss offsetting. In this case, the government is combining a risk-sharing role with the provision of a source of outside finance up front, thereby assisting the small firm both in its cash flow and in its ability to take risk. Those tax systems that allow write-offs up front will also assist the cash flow of the firms. Thus, there is really no contradiction between the withholding and rent-collecting functions on the one hand, and the risk-sharing one on the other. What the consideration of risk adds to the analysis is a rationale for ensuring that the corporate tax system includes full loss offsetting provisions in its design.

Vertical Equity as an Argument for the Corporate Tax

One of the arguments often heard in public discussion is that the corporate tax is an equitable form of taxation because it is implicitly progressive. This argument is based upon the premise that shareholders in corporations tend to have relatively higher incomes than the population at large. Even if one believes strongly in the use of the tax system for redistribution and also accepts the premise that corporate shareholders have relatively high incomes, it is not obvious that the corporate tax should be viewed as an appropriate instrument for redistribution. For one thing, the redistributive effect of the corporate tax depends on how the corporate tax is shifted. For example, the corporate tax may not ultimately be borne by corporate shareholders, it may well be shifted onto labour in terms of lower wages or onto consumers in terms of higher prices. Such theory and evidence as exists suggests that in a small open economy like Canada, where product prices and the cost of capital are determined by international markets, the corporate taxes are shifted onto a fixed factor such as land and to a lesser extent,

[11] Jack M. Mintz, " 'Neutral' Profit Taxation, Risk Taking and Optimal Profit Taxation" (June 1982), 48 *Recherches Economiques de Louvain* 107-32.

labour. In addition, as we have argued in Chapter 4, it is not clear that capital income (corporate or otherwise) is an appropriate base for redistribution taxation. On equity grounds, it seems to us that consumption would represent a close approximation to economic well-being.

Finally, the corporate tax is a very clumsy and imprecise vehicle for redistribution. It is unlikely to be horizontally equitable, since it treats different types of capital income differently (for example, debt versus equity). Though it may be progressive with respect to income in some general sense, it is only imperfectly so. Some low income earners, such as pensioners, will obtain some of their income from owning corporate shares. It is preferable to view the personal tax as the main tax instrument for pursuing vertical equity and leave the corporate tax to those tasks for which it has a comparative advantage—withholding and rent collection. In the following sections, therefore, we concentrate on the design and reform of corporate income taxation mainly with those two objectives in mind.

Design of the Corporate Income Tax

Given the two rationales for a corporate income tax in Canada—namely, to serve as a withholding device or as a rent tax—this section will discuss the methods that may be adopted to implement a corporate tax designed to serve each of these functions. We do not view these two rationales as necessarily opposing each other; one could design a corporate tax that captures rents and withholds income at the same time. Whether one or both of the functions are being addressed will have important implications for how the corporate tax is integrated with the personal tax. This possible dual function of the corporate tax distinguishes it from the personal tax, whose consumption and comprehensive income bases, as we saw in Chapter 4, can be argued for with respect to very different principles and are essentially mutually exclusive. As suggested earlier in this chapter, the rationale for withholding income either against foreigners or against the retained earnings of resident shareholders can be viewed as independent from the role of the tax as a collector of rents. This is especially true when one judges that rents should accrue to the public sector as the rightful owner of property that generates the rent. In this case, a rent tax should be imposed in addition to any withholding tax.

Even though our view is that a corporate tax can consistently serve both these roles, this section will discuss the design of each of these tax bases separately. This allows us to concentrate on the design issues that underlie each function of the corporate tax. Only later will we discuss how the two bases could be combined to withhold income and tax rents at the same time where appropriate.

The Corporate Tax as a Withholding Tax

The corporate tax is a tax levied on capital income at source. It cannot distinguish between income earned on behalf of foreign shareholders and that earned on behalf of resident shareholders. Any withholding of corporate income must be done against both domestic and foreign owners of the corporation. Indeed it cannot be otherwise, since international treaties do not allow countries to discriminate between foreign and domestic residents and limit the ability to withhold against foreigners. Thus, residents must be reimbursed appropriately by integration, again subject to limitations of international treaties.

In designing the ideal withholding tax, we assume that we would like to tax personal income on a consumption tax basis. Indeed, since much of the current personal tax is on a consumption tax basis, we cannot avoid discussion within this framework. The implication of this assumption is that our integration scheme is largely driven by a desire to withhold against foreigners and should be designed as such to the extent it does not violate international treaty arrangements. The other withholding role of the corporate tax—that is, against capital income earned in the form of accrued capital gains—would be appropriate if the personal tax were based on comprehensive income. Our withholding scheme would then also be required with respect to the retention of corporate profits for investment that generate capital gain income for share owners. Although we will not explicitly consider comprehensive income taxation of capital gains accruing to residents in Canada, much of our discussion below will involve analyzing integration with respect to this source of income, since such income accrues to foreigners anyway. [12]

With respect to the withholding role of the corporate tax on foreign income, the most fundamental problem is to ensure that corporate taxes in Canada are credited against foreign tax liabilities. Different governments have different corporate tax systems but our tax based on corporate income at the source cannot easily distinguish equity income accruing to one national from another. Variations in withholding are done only through nonresident withholding taxes, which are 15 per cent for treaty and 25 per cent for nontreaty countries. Thus, our scheme cannot be perfect, since international tax harmonization does not exist and is not simple to achieve; nevertheless, we will want to make our system as neutral as possible. A specific aspect of foreign government tax crediting that is of special importance to Canada is that the U.S. corporate tax system credits taxes paid by subsidiaries abroad only on the repatriation of dividends but credits foreign corporate taxes paid by branch plants immediately. Moreover, other countries have different systems. To be ideal, our system would have to be country-specific, but it cannot be. Thus, our recommendations with regard to the reform of the corporate tax are much more circumspect than in the case of the personal tax.

With this in mind, we first discuss the design of the withholding tax base and then turn to integration under the withholding tax.

---

[12]Where appropriate, we highlight any important differences that arise if personal taxes are levied on a comprehensive income rather than on a consumption tax basis. In this manner, we can be clear as to which feature of the withholding base is dependent on the form of personal taxation that we particularly recommend.

The Withholding Tax Base

If the purpose of the corporate tax is to withhold against foreign tax liabilities, then the appropriate domestic base is one that closely matches the base used in the foreign country for calculating the foreign tax credit to be allowed. In principle, one could withhold against all forms of capital income: dividends, retained profits, interest, rents, royalty payments, etc. If Canada defines its tax base too widely, however, corporate taxes in Canada may not be fully credited unless the rate of tax is chosen sufficiently low to allow for such crediting. This rate of tax could well be close to zero if the tax base in Canada is too general.

Let us first consider the most general corporate tax base applicable in the case in which Canada wishes to withhold against all forms of income. Under this principle, the base would be the following:

Withholding tax base = accrued revenues − accrued current costs
− true economic depreciation − replacement
cost of inventories.

True economic depreciation would involve the valuation of depreciable assets at replacement cost rather than at historical cost with the depreciation (CCA) rate based on actual rates of physical wear and tear less real capital gains. If the above tax base values depreciation and inventories properly, it would be equivalent to all capital income generated in the corporation and used for dividends, retained earnings, and interest that is distributed to capital owners.

This all-inclusive base will not generally correspond to the base used by other countries in crediting foreign tax liabilities against their own corporate taxes. For example, corporate taxes of a Canadian branch plant owned by a U.S. corporation would be credited against U.S. corporate taxes but be limited to the following amount: the U.S. tax rate times qualifying foreign-sourced corporate income earned in Canada (as defined by U.S. law), subject to a pooling of income over time, beginning in 1987.[13] The U.S. definition of foreign-sourced corporate income is accrual revenues net of accrual costs, historical depreciation,[14] first in, first out or last in, first out cost valuation of inventories, and nominal interest payments (under the new interest allocation rules of the U.S. foreign tax credit, interest incurred by the payment may be allocated to a subsidiary using the distribution of assets held by related companies). The all-inclusive base as defined above would

---

[13]Note that in this example we ignore, for the moment, the issues related to income repatriated from U.S. foreign subsidiaries. We also leave aside the distinction between global and specific country tax credits. The U.S. tax credit is a global one based on worldwide income; consequently, Canadian taxes are added to other foreign tax liabilities to calculate the total tax credit. U.S. corporations investing in several countries can average high and low taxed foreign-sourced income to ensure that all foreign tax liabilities are credited.

[14]U.S. tax law defines depreciation for foreign-sourced income based on pre-1981 depreciation schedules rather than the accelerated cost recovery system (ACRS) used by domestic U.S. corporations. This makes the base used to calculate foreign-sourced income substantially larger than the base used to calculate domestic-sourced income in the United States. Thus the ACRS in the United States has had little impact on the amount of Canadian tax that has been credited.

be very different from and much larger than the one against which Canadian taxes are credited in the United States. It would also be larger than the base used by other foreign countries besides the United States. In this case, we would want to narrow or broaden the base to correspond more closely with the ones used by other foreign countries. There are four important issues to consider:

1) Most countries permit corporations to deduct interest, so that it is likely that Canada would wish to do the same. Any corporate taxes withheld on interest would not be credited.[15] If Canada allowed interest payments to be deducted from the all-inclusive base described above, then the corporate tax would withhold taxes on equity income, which is operating income net of interest payments to debt owners. Canada follows the principle except with regard to "thin capitalization" rules, which prevent foreign corporations from deducting interest on debt that is more than 75 per cent of assets.

2) Most foreign corporate tax systems are not indexed for inflation. The cost of depreciation and inventories is generally based on the original, rather than the replacement, cost of acquiring the assets, and companies are allowed to deduct nominal rather than real interest payments. If Canada adopted a corporate tax indexed for inflation, then the base would no longer correspond to that used by other countries. Canadian corporate taxes might not be fully credited for some companies while for others, Canadian corporate tax revenues would be less than the maximum that could be withheld.[16] Nonetheless, indexation may be desirable for other reasons. As discussed further below, indexation is appropriate when Canadian corporate taxes are not credited against foreign tax liabilities and when authorities attempt to integrate corporate and personal taxes.

3) The United States generally taxes its corporations on the income repatriated from their foreign subsidiaries (a minimum of 10 per cent ownership by the parent), thus allowing U.S. taxes owing to be deferred on profits reinvested in subsidiaries. To correspond with this case, the corporate tax in Canada could allow retentions to be deducted. This would be equivalent to taxing corporations on their dividends only, and doing so would preclude the requirement to measure economic depreciation and the replacement value of inventories. The rate would have to be sufficiently high to correspond to tax liabilities creditable at home. This is a particularly attractive tax system in terms of its simplicity. Not only is the dividend base easy to measure and administer, it also makes integration with the personal tax easier, as discussed later. There are, however, two disadvantages with

---

[15] Indeed, Canada has eliminated the 25 per cent withholding tax on interest (15 per cent for treaty countries) payable on bonds issued by nonprofit institutions, governments, Crown corporations, banks, and on long-term bonds upon which a corporation does not pay back more than 25 per cent of the principal within five years.

[16] Indexation in Canada would likely give an incentive to foreign corporations operating in Canada to shift debt financing from Canada to the parent firms, since only real rather than nominal interest costs would be deducted in Canada. This could, however, increase Canadian corporate taxes that are credited against foreign liabilities, since corporations operating in Canada would become more equity-financed.

using dividends as the corporate tax base for withholding purposes. First, not all crediting arrangements are like those of U.S. subsidiaries. Some operations, including U.S. branch plants and other foreign subsidiaries, have all their Canadian tax liabilities immediately credited. In other systems (like the Canadian one) foreign subsidiaries neither pay domestic taxes nor receive credit for taxes paid on dividends repatriated. If we allowed retentions to be deducted, or equivalently taxed dividend distributions, we would be deferring tax credits that could otherwise be obtained from foreign treasuries. Second, if the personal tax base were based on income rather than consumption, then the difficulty of taxing capital gains on an accrued basis would make it desirable to impose the withholding tax on retained earnings and to integrate it with capital gains taxes assessed on a realized basis. It is obvious that this second problem disappears under a consumption base for personal tax purposes. Indeed, as will be explained below, withholding on only dividend income would make integration under a consumption tax much simpler.

4) If other countries moved to a system in which there was no crediting of corporate tax revenues or if they abolished their corporate taxes altogether (for example, by replacing them with commodity taxes), we would no longer wish to withhold on equity income, since the corporate tax would raise the required return on investment leading to a reduction of national income. A source-based tax on foreign capital can be justified only if Canada were to increase income by exploiting monopoly power in some markets. For a small economy like Canada, this is less possible. It would, however, be appropriate to continue to withhold against the rents earned by foreign-owned corporations for the reasons discussed in the previous section. Such a tax would give a nondistortionary source of tax revenue. How such a rent tax can be implemented is the main subject of the next section, so we shall postpone discussion of its base until then. The main issue involved with imposing a tax on rents for withholding purposes is with regard to integration of the rent tax with personal taxes if such integration is desirable. The mechanism for this integration will be discussed below.

To summarize to this point, the design of the corporate tax base for withholding depends very much on what foreign governments will credit. Two likely candidates are a corporate tax on equity income or a corporate tax on the distribution of profits as dividends. In either case, integration with the personal tax would be desirable regardless of the form of the tax base used at the personal level (that is, the consumption or income base). Unfortunately, no single base is unambiguously the best, because different countries have different crediting mechanisms and different tax bases on which crediting is calculated. Thus, the system is bound to be imperfect, and some judgment is inevitably involved.

As argued above, a withholding tax on equity income would be the one most closely related to corporate tax systems of other countries in the sense that most foreign corporate tax bases correspond with equity income. This raises the issue as to whether one wishes to define the tax base as close as possible to true equity income or as close as possible to the bases adopted by other countries. If the former, two measurement problems are encountered: (1) the need to measure true economic depreciation, which is difficult to do for the large number of capital goods involved, and (2) the need to measure income, indexed for inflation, which requires the valuation of assets based on replacement cost and the adjustment of interest deductions for inflation. Such a tax base will differ from the tax bases used in most countries, which differ significantly from true equity income. For example, most are not indexed and most measure depreciation in a relatively arbitrary way. If one wanted Canada's tax base to mirror the tax bases of foreign countries according to which the foreign firms' tax crediting is actually calculated, one may prefer to opt for a base that corresponds with foreign tax bases.

There are, however, several reasons why it might be advantageous to design our tax base to conform more closely with true equity income. One is that Canadian corporate taxes are not always credited against foreign tax liabilities. This arises when Canadian-controlled corporations issue shares to foreigners but the foreign investor has less than 10 per cent ownership of the company. In this case, the Canadian corporate tax can reduce invest-ment if it is marginally financed by nonresident investors. If equity income is mismeasured, the corporate tax will be more distortionary when effective tax rates vary considerably, as we saw in Chapter 3. The same principle applies to investment financed by retentions of U.S. subsidiaries. Because U.S. taxes are deferred by retaining profits, the value of deferment depends on the level of Canadian taxes. In other words, the Canadian corporate tax will influence investment decisions of foreign-owned subsidiaries when capital is financed marginally by retentions. Under both of the above cir-cumstances, the argument to have our tax base mirror the U.S. counterpart vanishes. If a tax has to be levied on equity income, it might be preferable to define the base as closely as possible to true equity income, since, as dis-cussed next, such a base is easier to integrate and will be less distortionary.

A second reason for defining the withholding tax base to be as close to real equity income as possible is to make easier the full integration of corpo-rate and personal taxes. This is discussed later in more detail, but for now we will just say that, roughly speaking, corporate equity income will be reflected in the dividends and capital gain income accruing to the share-owners of the firm. To the extent that equity income is measured incorrectly under the withholding tax, it becomes more difficult to integrate the withholding tax with personal taxes. Tax credits at the personal level are set to offset corporate withholding taxes, and if the underlying capital income obtained by shareholders varies from its withholding tax base, an adjust-ment should be made to achieve perfect integration.

The use of distributed profits (dividends) as a base for corporate withholding taxes avoids these difficulties of mismeasurement. The distributed profit tax base can, however, also create certain difficulties if this withholding tax is not fully credited against foreign taxes or at the per-sonal level. The most serious is the possible incentive provided to reinvest profits rather than issue new equities. Also, shareowners may attempt to convert dividend into capital gain income so that the noncredited withholding tax can be avoided.[17] This is why integration plays an important role in judging whether one withholding base is superior to another.

Integration

Integration involves, in principle, giving a credit for taxes paid at the corporate level when the after-tax corporate income is distributed to the owner. In order to withhold against foreigners, the tax credit is restricted to domestic residents and applies to all taxes withheld with an important exception: when personal taxes are levied on a consumption base only the normal return to savings need be exempt. As discussed in Chapter 4, a personal tax on designated assets will fall on rents or above normal returns accruing to assets of the firm. Rents accruing to nondesignated savings will escape taxation, however, encouraging savers to hold assets in the nondesignated form.

Two solutions can be adopted to avoid this problem. The first is to withhold rents at the corporate level and integrate the rent tax with the personal tax on rent accruing to the designated assets only. Thus, the rent tax is used to withhold taxes on rents accruing to nondesignated assets, since otherwise these rents would be exempt. This solution, however, is administratively costly, because it is difficult to integrate the corporate tax on rents with the tax on designated assets alone—it is nearly impossible to measure the rent separately from the normal return paid to designated savings. The second solution is to require all equity assets to be designated. Rents generally accrue to the owners of equity in the assets generating the rent; consequently, this form of income will be taxed if all equity is held in the designated form. This approach avoids the need to impose a rent tax at the corporate level for the purpose of withholding against rent income under the consumption base. Its only drawback is that all equity shares must be recorded including foreign securities.[18]

If the personal tax is levied on an income rather than a consumption base, all taxes withheld at the corporate level should be integrated with personal taxes. Any special rent tax at the corporate level would be difficult to integrate with personal income taxes because of the administrative problem of measuring rents accruing to savers.

In principle, there are two alternative stages at which crediting for corporate taxes paid can occur. The credit can be given to the corporation when it issues dividends, or it can be given to the shareholder on receipt of dividends and capital gains. The advantage of integrating at the corporate level is that it is easier to ensure that the credit is given only for corporate

---

[17]An important example of this is the case of equity income accruing to nonresident minority owners of Canadian corporations. Unless a sufficiently high tax is levied on capital gains realized by nonresidents, these equity owners will prefer Canadian corporations to retain income rather than distribute profits.

[18]With respect to risk-taking, it is likely that savers will designate their equity assets, since the government will implicitly share any capital gains or losses realized on the purchase and sale of these assets. With equity held in the nondesignated form, more risk is borne by the investor unless the government uses a rent tax at the corporate level to withhold income.

taxes that have been paid. Administration involves creating a pool of corporate taxes out of which the credit can be paid when income is distributed to the shareholders. There is, however, a major disadvantage with such an approach. If the object of the corporate tax is to withhold income accruing to foreigners, then tax credits should not be available on corporate income paid to nonresidents. Integrating at the corporate level would make this difficult, since it is impossible to identify the ultimate recipient of the distributed income, especially where income flows through other corporations. Another problem is that such outright discrimination between resident and nonresident shareowners might invite reprisal from foreign countries.

The other method, where a credit is granted to domestic shareholders, directly enables integration to be roughly achieved. This is the gross-up and credit method by which corporate income distributed to the owner is grossed up by a factor that reflects the underlying corporate tax paid. This grossed-up amount is added to the personal tax base and a credit is calculated to match corporate taxes paid. The exact formula is to gross up income by the factor $1/(1-t)$, where t is the appropriate corporate tax rate. The credit would be equal to this rate t multiplied by the grossed-up value of income. If personal taxes are levied on a comprehensive income basis, the integration scheme is straightforward. Grossed-up income of $1/(1-t)$ times corporate-source income received is added to the tax base. Personal taxes payable are calculated, and a tax credit of $t/(1-t)$ times corporate-source income is granted at the same time. Matters are slightly more complicated under a personal consumption base. If equity income is all designated, the receipt of corporate-source income is grossed up by $1/(1-t)$ and added to the base of the designated asset. When the asset is eventually undesignated, the entire amount of grossed-up accumulated income becomes taxable. The credit, however, should be available to the shareholder as soon as the income is generated by the corporation, regardless of whether the income remains designated. The whole idea is to replicate the situation that would exist in the absence of corporate taxation altogether.

This gross-up and credit method of integration has been adopted in Canada with respect to dividend income, although (as discussed in Chapter 4) it applies only to dividend income received in taxable form, not to sheltered dividend income (such as pension fund income). It has been accepted so far by other foreign countries even though the credit is available to Canadian residents only. The current dividend tax credit has another feature that, in principle, contradicts the integration feature of credit. This credit is available only for dividends paid by Canadian corporations, not foreign ones. In this sense, the dividend tax credit provides an incentive for Canadian ownership of Canadian securities. Even if, in the interest of neutrality, the tax credit became available for foreign securities, it would be difficult to administer it properly. Since corporate tax systems vary widely across the world, the amount of the gross-up and tax credit would need to vary by country. This would be difficult to do, since it is impossible to attribute corporate income to various jurisdictions for multinational corporations.

The ideal gross-up and credit system for Canadian securities is difficult to administer for a variety of reasons. The tax rate that should be used to gross up income is the *average tax rate* paid by corporations, not the statutory tax rate. The average tax rate equals corporate taxes paid in a year divided by a measure of the income upon which corporate taxes are held (dividends and/or capital gains). This average rate will vary from firm to firm so long as the withholding tax at the corporate level either mismeasures income or provides explicit tax preferences or statutory rate reductions for certain corporations. Corporations with taxable losses should, in principle, be receiving corporate tax credits (equal to the corporate tax rate multiplied by corporate taxable losses). If the corporate tax system allows a full loss offset, the rate of tax used for the gross-up and credit should be negative for the shareholders of loss corporations.

There are other administrative problems with ideal integration. If the withholding tax at the corporate level is on equity income, then capital gains and losses should be integrated with reinvested profits. This is difficult to do no matter whether personal taxes are levied on a consumption or income basis. On a consumption tax basis, integration will be necessary for equities held in a designated form. To do so, however, the accrued capital gains need to be calculated each year. If these gains are positive, a credit is granted, and if negative, a tax equal to the corporate tax refund is assessed. The same calculation of credits applies to personal taxes levied on an income basis. Regardless of which tax base is used, such integration is difficult to do. Some shares, such as private corporate stocks, are not traded from year to year. Moreover, share values change not only as a result of the reinvestment of profits but also because of a change in expectations about the profitability of existing assets. Some capital gains and losses are simply windfall gains or losses that should not be integrated, since no corporate tax has yet been paid on them.

These difficulties with integrating capital gains income suggest an alternative method of integration of equity income. That is, to grant tax credits on dividends only but to tax equally all realized capital gains and dividends at the personal level. But using only the dividend tax credit to achieve integration of equity income has its difficulties too. Since corporate taxes on retentions are paid earlier than the time when the dividends arising from retentions are eventually paid out, a credit should incorporate an interest rate factor to ensure that the value of the tax credit is equivalent to the value of the underlying corporate taxes paid on retentions. One possible method to achieve integration of this form is to calculate a special credit on corporate taxes levied on retentions which would be equal to the interest cost of paying corporate taxes early relative to the time that the dividend is paid out. Otherwise, the credit will be insufficient, and there will be an incentive to pass out income in the form of capital gains. If no credit is available (and if capital gains were not taxed equivalently on an accrual basis at the personal level) then the government will have to introduce complex rules to prevent "surplus stripping," repurchase of equity, etc., to ensure full integration via a dividend tax credit method.

These problems associated with integration of retentions and capital gains arise when the withholding tax falls on equity income. If it falls only on dividend distributions, only dividend income need be integrated. The simplicity of the dividend withholding base is quite attractive, although some withholding on retentions is lost with respect to such income accruing to foreigners. If such a base were implemented, it would be important to adopt rules ensuring that capital gain income accruing to nonresident corporations on equities held in subsidiaries is taxed by a sufficiently high nonresident withholding tax, which is currently levied at a rate of 25 per cent (15 per cent under the U.S.-Canada treaty).

Another special integration problem is with respect to nonfinancial corporate income flowing through intermediaries to the household. In this case, integration can be achieved in two ways. The first is to allow income withheld at one level and received by corporations at secondary and tertiary levels to flow tax-free. This is similar to the current treatment of intercorporate dividends, which are untaxed in the hand of the recipient corporation. The problem with this method of integration is that the tax credit given to noncorporate shareholders should be based on the average tax rate imposed on the corporation from which taxes are withheld. When corporate income flows through intermediaries, however, it is impossible to attribute the underlying corporate taxes paid by the corporation, since the intermediary can own many corporate equity securities. Only if average tax rates are the same across all firms will this method of integration work properly. Thus, only if the withholding tax is levied on all corporations at the same statutory rate on equity income correctly measured will exempting intercorporate equity income be desirable and will proper crediting be administratively feasible.

The other method of integration is to grant a tax credit to the intermediary on grossed-up intercorporate income and then impose another tax as the income is paid out. The gross-up and credit received by the intermediary are based on the average tax rate imposed on the income generated by the primary corporation. The one problem associated with this system is that credits and taxes will need to be calculated for every security. Another is the potential loss of some withholding tax revenues levied on corporate income flowing through intermediaries that is eventually paid out to nonresidents in nonwithheld forms of income (for example, interest). Nonresidents, however, will not necessarily minimize their own tax liabilities if reduced Canadian taxes are offset by greater foreign taxes under the international crediting arrangements.

Our discussion of integration suggests several possible systems of withholding and integration. The first is a withholding tax on true equity income indexed for inflation. If all corporate equity income is correctly measured and taxed at the same rate, then the distribution of the income can flow tax-free through intermediaries and the tax credit can be granted to the ultimate noncorporate shareholder upon receipt of capital income. The most serious problem with this system is the difficulty of measuring corporate equity income correctly for withholding tax purposes and providing tax credits for reinvested profits.

A second possibility is a variant of this first proposal. Rather than defining equity income correctly, integration can be achieved by a gross-up and credit method that is based on actual corporate taxes that are paid. This system can only work if the gross-up and credit system also applies to financial intermediaries rather than permitting the income to flow tax-free through the intermediaries. The treatment of retention of profits for integration remains problematical.

The third method is to impose a dividend distribution tax as a corporate withholding tax. If the tax rate is the same for all firms, dividends can flow tax-free through intermediaries and be grossed up and credited at the personal level. Since no withholding tax is imposed on retentions, the problem of integration with respect to this source of income is avoided. The most serious issue, however, is that withholding tax liabilities on retentions of foreign corporations are deferred until dividends are distributed to parents.

The Corporate Tax as a Rent Tax

A corporate tax on rents is designed to capture a portion of any above-normal return paid to factors of production, including that arising from fixity of supply, location, or other special advantages. As argued earlier, one compelling view for a rent tax is that rents generated in an economy should accrue to the government in recognition of the public ownership of the source of such rents. This is clearly the case for resource rents (since provinces "own" the resources) and perhaps for rents created by regulations that are adopted for whatever normative or political objectives to protect businesses from competition. To the extent that this view is accepted, a tax on rents would be called for over and above any tax applied for withholding purposes.

Under the withholding base, any tax applied on rents should be integrated with the personal taxes of residents. We saw in the previous subsection how that might be achieved. To the extent that taxing rents is in itself socially desirable, however, no integration with personal taxes is called for. Although a rent tax can serve as a withholding tax for nondesignated assets under a consumption tax and be integrated with personal taxes levied on designated assets, we have already argued that this is unnecessary if all equity is held in the designated form. For these reasons, we ignore integration of the rent tax with personal taxes in this section.

The main issue discussed in this section concerns the design of the rent tax base. Three tax bases will be considered: (1) a pure profits tax base; (2) a cash flow tax (including a "modified" cash flow base) that applies to real assets; and (3) a cash flow tax applying to a base comprising both real and financial assets. Each will be discussed below.

The Pure Profit Base

The economic rent earned by a business is equal to accrued revenues less the full imputed costs of labour, capital, and other inputs. Revenues less current expenditures (wages, salaries, materials) as they accrue are included in the base. This is a fairly straightforward calculation; the valuation of imputed capital costs is more difficult. The imputed costs of using physical capital include the following:

1) true economic depreciation, defined to be the replacement cost due to the physical wear and tear of an asset less real capital gains;

2) replacement cost of inventories less real capital gains on holding inventories; and

3) the real cost of debt and equity financing (that is, nominal interest and equity costs less the reduction in the real value of liabilities due to inflation).

In contrast to the withholding base on equity income discussed in the section entitled "The Withholding Tax Base," a pure profit here would allow for the deduction of the real cost of equity financing in addition to debt financing. This makes the pure profit base much smaller compared with an equity income base (and more difficult to measure).

The real cost of equity financing is the minimum return that must be paid to attract savings from equity investors. In a competitive capital market, this return on equity would be equal to an interest rate that would be earned on a riskless asset (that is, treasury bill rate less inflation) plus a premium that would compensate the investor for risk arising from the variability in income accruing to the equity owner. With the pure profit tax, no such risk premium need be deducted from the tax base so long as the government provides a full loss offset if tax liabilities are negative. That is, if pure profits are negative, the government grants the firm a refundable tax credit, offsetting the loss to the equity owner. This tax credit would be equal to the tax rate multiplied by the value of taxable loss. In this manner, the government shares equally the profits and losses in pure profits, so that risk faced by the investor is reduced proportionately by the tax rate. If no loss offset were payable, a cost of risk associated with equity financing would need to be deducted. This would be nearly impossible to measure. On the other hand, since a full loss offset is administratively feasible and obviates the need to deduct a risk premium as part of the cost of equity financing, full loss offsetting is desirable.

Several design problems are encountered when attempting to measure the pure profit tax base, and some were dealt with in our discussion of a withholding tax on equity. They include: (1) the difficulty of measuring economic depreciation for most assets, (2) the need for indexation of capital cost allowances and FIFO inventory deductions when inflation exists, and (3) the deductibility of the real cost of debt finance. In addition to the above, a pure profit tax base requires the real cost of equity financing to be deductible as well. Also, the real income accruing to financed assets held by the corporation should be included. This requires accrued capital gains on equities held in other businesses to be included, since capital gains might reflect rents as well. Other assets impose similar problems with regard to measuring rents. Depletable assets that have been extracted generate capital gain income arising from the increase in the real price of such assets. Real capital gains on the holding of land should also be included in the pure profit rent base.

As with the withholding tax on equity income, it is unlikely that the tax authorities could ever develop a neutral pure profits tax, since it would be so difficult to measure pure profits correctly. This suggests that, on administrative grounds, other bases would be more appropriate to use to tax rents. The "cash flow" tax is one such base.

The Cash Flow Tax on Real Transactions

The cash flow tax has long been advocated as a means of taxing rents. [19] In its simplest form, the cash flow or R base is as follows:

> cash flow base (R) = realized revenues from the sale of goods and services − current costs − capital expenditures on physical assets (net of disposals),

where all accounting is done on a cash rather than on an accrual basis, and where capital expenditures include the purchase of inventories. No inflation accounting of the base is needed. With the cash flow base, the present value of taxes payable is equal to the tax collected under the pure profit base. That is, the expensing of capital is of the same value to the firm as the deductibility of economic depreciation and financing costs. [20] Under our current corporate tax, this requires the government to give a firm a 100 per cent capital cost allowance for all assets (including inventories) with no deduction for interest expenses (and no investment tax credit). Any disposal of assets is added to the base and hence taxed.

It is clear that the simplicity of a cash flow tax makes it very attractive. Economic depreciation and the real cost of finance do not need to be measured. All assets are taxed the same and marginal investment decisions are unaffected by the tax. This approach would simplify the Canadian tax law in a very significant way, if the objective were to tax rents only.

---

[19]The idea has been part of the conventional wisdom for some time. In modern times, it is often associated with the names Cary Brown and Vernon Smith. See E. Cary Brown, "Business-Income Taxation and Investment Incentives," in Lloyd A. Metzler et al., eds., *Income, Employment and Public Policy: Essays in Honor of Alvin H. Hansen* (New York: W. W. Norton, 1948), 300-316; and Vernon L. Smith, "Tax Depreciation Policy and Investment Theory" (January 1963), 4 *International Economic Review* 80-91. The arguments are summarized in Robin W. Boadway, Neil Bruce, and Jack M. Mintz, supra footnote 8.

[20]This can be shown as follows. Let δ = depreciation rate, q = price of capital, and r = interest rate. Under the assumption that the firm maintains the same capital stock every period, the deduction for depreciation is equal to δq every period. The present value of deductions for a unit of capital is:

$$V = \sum_{t=0}^{\infty} \frac{\delta}{(1+r)^t}\, q + \sum_{t=0}^{\infty} \frac{rq}{(1+r)^t}$$

$$V = \frac{\delta q}{\delta + r} + \frac{rq}{\delta + r} = q.$$

Under a cash flow tax, the value of the deduction is also q.

Attractive as the base might seem, one feature that can make the cash flow tax less desirable to the government is the unevenness in the tax liabilities over the life of the firm. A business that is starting up will earn little revenue so that its contribution to the tax base initially will be highly negative. To make the cash flow tax neutral, a refundable tax credit would have to be granted when there are taxable losses. While refundability (or loss offsetting) is required so that the investment decision is unaffected, it does mean that the government may need to "finance" capital expenditures by the refundable cash flow tax. This loss in tax revenues to the government will be recovered in later years, but a government concerned about its current deficit will discount heavily taxes payable in the future.

As a way of smoothing out tax payments over time (and reducing the need for refundability), Boadway and Bruce[21] have proposed a "modified" cash flow tax base. This base allows any capital cost allowance to be chosen so long as the amount of financing costs that can be deducted is limited by the undepreciated capital cost allowance base.[22] An example of a "modified" cash flow tax is one that allows the undepreciated capital cost allowance to be indexed by the nominal interest rate. The capital cost allowance (CCA) then is equal to the CCA rate applied to the indexed value of the CCA base. If the firm is wound up, a refundable tax credit would be paid if the value of the CCA base is more than the scrap value of the assets. A tax would be levied if the converse were true.

The "modified" cash flow can allow firms to choose their own CCA rate of less than 100 per cent in each year, including a negative one. If no refundable tax credit is granted (except when the firm is wound up), then firms can manipulate their deductions so that they incur no taxable losses in each year. In this sense, the "modified" cash flow tax allows considerable flexibility.

Compared with a cash flow tax, there are two limitations associated with the "modified" base. The first is the need to determine the appropriate interest rate as a basis for measuring the cost of financing. This would be the riskless rate (government bond rate) if refundable tax credits for tax losses are paid when the firm is wound up. The second is that firms facing difficulty in acquiring financing from the market are better off under the cash flow tax, since refundable tax credits are granted to the firms during

---

[21]Robin Boadway and Neil Bruce, "A General Proposition on the Design of a Neutral Business Tax" (July 1984), 24 *Journal of Public Economics* 231-39.

[22]Suppose d is the CCA rate, r the nominal rate of interest, and q the price of capital. The present value of capital deductions would be equal to the following under a "modified" cash flow tax (where $(1 - d)^t$ is the undepreciated CCA base of time t):

$$V = \sum_{t=0}^{\infty} \frac{d(1 - d)^t}{(1 + r)^t} q + \sum_{t=0}^{\infty} \frac{r(1 - d)^t}{(1 + r)^t} q$$

$$V = \frac{d}{r + d} q + \frac{r}{r + d} q = q.$$

This value is the same as allowing for immediate expensing under the cash flow tax.

their early years of growth. This may be particularly appropriate for small firms. The tax credit received from the government is added to cash flow and can be used to finance the business's investment plan. Of course, a government concerned about its own financial situation would prefer the "modified" cash flow base. Thus, if the government's discount rate is more than the firm's, it would be preferable to use the "modified" cash flow rather than cash flow tax and vice versa.

Both the cash flow and "modified" cash flow taxes encounter several design problems. The first is that deductible costs such as wage costs and leasing payments could be overstated on purpose so that the rent base is dissipated. This would occur if the rents passed on through deductible costs are not taxable in the hands of individuals or corporations that receive them. There would be unavoidable administrative costs involved in trying to ensure that firms do not try to have rents masquerade as wages and salaries, etc.

A second design problem concerns multinational corporations operating in Canada. Overhead, marketing, and other costs of an international nature could be allocated to Canada, reducing the amount of rents earned in Canada. This would require some rule limiting the amount of overhead costs that can be attributed to Canada.[23]

A third problem is with respect to the treatment of financial assets. Because these assets are not included in a cash flow tax as described so far, there will be an incentive for businesses to convert sales revenue (which is taxable) into financial income (which is nontaxable) as a means of avoiding the rent tax. This situation is more likely to occur when the seller of goods and services also provides credit to the customer. This suggests that a broadening of the tax base to include financial transactions would be appropriate to capture rents accruing to financial intermediary services. We turn to this now.

A Cash Flow Base for Real and Financial Transactions

The inclusion of financial transactions in the cash flow base could be accomplished via two methods. The first is what we denote as the R + A base whereby financial assets would be treated on the same basis as real assets. Under the R + A base, the cash flow base would be as follows:

> Cash flow (R + A) = revenues from sales of goods and services − current costs − capital expenditures on physical assets (net of disposals) + financial income (dividends and interest) − purchases of financial assets (net of sales of financial assets).

With the R + A base, financial income is fully included and purchases of assets (net of sales) are deductible. Capital gain income is implicitly taxed,

---

[23]The Saskatchewan uranium tax (a form of a cash flow tax) includes an allowance for overhead and marketing costs that can be attributed to Saskatchewan. This allowance is based on sales or production costs. It is not clear, however, that this is the best method to allocate overhead costs, since these costs are unrelated to sales or production.

since the sale of an asset is included in, and its purchase is deductible from, the tax base.

The R + A base is attractive for several reasons. First, the base generally captures the present-value equivalent of pure profits or rents associated with financial intermediation. To do so on a pure profit basis would be difficult because of measurement problems, since it would need to include accrued capital gains. Therefore, the cash flow equivalent is attractive. Second, firms are not able to convert real sales into financial income to escape the rent tax. And third, the base remains relatively simple to administer even though all financial assets must be recorded.

As with the R base cash flow tax discussed above, a few problems arise with an R + A base. The first is that the degree of loss offsetting may be larger since financial assets in addition to real capital purchases are now deductible from the base. Second, businesses, especially financial intermediaries, are able to avoid paying any taxes on rents accruing to transactions on the liability side (such as the servicing of depositors of a bank).

A second base that could capture all rents is the R + F base, which includes all financial transactions both with respect to financial assets and financial liabilities. The R + F base includes all flows and is defined as follows:

> Cash flow (R + F) = revenues from the sale of goods and services − current costs − capital expenditures on physical assets (net of disposals) + financial income (dividends and interest) − purchase of financial asset (net of sales) + selling of debt and equity issue − interest and dividends paid to bond and equity owners − repurchase of debt and equity liabilities.

The R + F base includes all financial transactions on the liability side in addition to asset transactions that are included under the R + A base.[24] Although the R + F seems more complicated, it has two distinct advantages over the R + A base. First, it will capture any rents associated with financial intermediation on the liability side. This is especially important for financial institutions. Second, the financial base, once calculated, is much smaller. Only net financial income is included (interest received less interest paid out). Only net asset transactions (net asset purchases less net issues of debt and equity) are deductible. Indeed, net financial transactions are equal to retentions (the reinvestment of profits). The R + F base would likely vary less over time compared with both the R base and R + A base. Loss offsetting would thus be less costly in forgone tax revenues to the government.

---

[24]This definition of the R + F base is not the same as the Meade Report's R + F base. In particular, we include *all* financial transactions (both equity and bonds) while the Meade Report excluded equity from the base. However, rents arising from equity financed transactions would not be captured with the Meade Report's R + F base. See the Meade Report, supra footnote 4, and Robin Boadway, Neil Bruce, and Jack Mintz, "On the Neutrality of Flow-of-funds Corporate Taxation" (February 1983), 50 *Economica* 49-61.

The R + F base, despite these advantages, is still subject to some problems discussed earlier with respect to R base and R + A base. Costs can be overestimated so that firms can pass rents on to other firms not included in the rent tax base. Special treatment of international companies is required for the treatment of overhead costs.

Special Design Problems

As we have said before, the design of the corporate tax ultimately depends on the function of the tax base: to withhold income or to tax rents. In principle, one can design the corporate tax to accomplish both functions—all that is required is to integrate the withholding portion of the tax by providing credits at the shareholder level. If the withholding tax is a tax on the distribution of profits, then integration can be easily accomplished. The corporate tax can be a cash flow tax but with a special tax imposed on dividends. The credit at the shareholder level will be equal to the withholding tax on distributed profits.

If the withholding tax is on equity income, then integration can be achieved in two ways. First, the withholding tax can be assessed separately from the rent tax but only the former will be integrated. This is essentially the system we currently have in Canada with respect to resource industries, where the corporate tax is integrated and the mining and oil taxes are not. The second is to combine withholding and rent tax bases and administer a single tax. One possibility is to tax the base revenues less current costs at a combined withholding and rent tax rate, grant a credit to the firm equal to gross investment at the combined tax rate, and grant another credit to the firm equal to economic depreciation plus real borrowing costs at the withholding tax rate.[25] The shareholder receives a credit for dividends and capital gains at the withholding tax rate. Other versions of this combined tax system can be used so long as total tax collections are the same. However, economic depreciation and real interest expense incurred with debt financing must still be measured.

Under both the withholding and rent tax systems, several design problems emerge that have not yet been discussed in detail. These are as follows:

1) *Full loss offsetting.* As we argued earlier, a refundable tax credit or its equivalent should be granted to firms when they incur tax losses. This

---

[25]This can be seen as follows. Under a withholding tax, the total tax collection is:

$T_w = t(R - C - D - B)$,

where R = revenues
C = current costs
D = economic depreciation
B = borrowing costs.

The rent tax base under a cash flow tax is:

$T_R = u(R - C - I)$.

Combining the two tax bases yields:

$T_R + T_W = (u + t)(R - C) - uI - t(D + B)$.

would be required for the rent and also for the withholding tax depending on how integration is administered. When there are tax losses associated with the equity income withholding tax base, a credit could be given to the firm, but, for integration purposes, a tax (such as negative dividend tax credit) should be imposed on the income received by the individual.

Loss offsetting can be accomplished by various means. One method is for government to provide a tax credit equal to the value of the tax write-off of losses. This is an administratively simple way of providing financing to the firm, since the credit can be paid once it is confirmed that expenditures have been made (thus avoiding some of the problems that arose with the scientific research tax credit). A second method is to allow the firm to carry forward tax losses at the nominal rate of interest. So long as tax rates remain the same over time, this will be equivalent to the refundable tax credit in present value terms. If the firm is wound up, the tax losses can be applied against the sale of assets. Full loss offsetting requires, however, that when tax losses are more than the wind-up value of the firm, a tax credit be granted for the value of the difference. The advantage of the carryforward system is that it allows the government to postpone the granting of tax credits, although for businesses needing cash flow, the refundable tax credit is better. The third method for loss offsetting is to flow through tax losses directly to investors. As long as the tax rate of the investor is the same as that of the business, it does not matter who receives the tax write-off. With a progressive tax schedule on the personal side, this is unlikely to happen— rarely would the personal and corporate tax rates be the same, thus the value of the tax loss write-off could be more or less than the corporate tax rate. This problem could be avoided by letting the tax credit rather than the loss or deduction flow through.

2) *Incorporation.* If the rent tax is applied only to corporate income and is not integrated, there will be a disincentive for businesses to incorporate. In this manner, an additional tax at the corporate level will not be neutral with respect to the organization of firms. As a means of escaping the rent tax, firms may choose not to incorporate. This problem can be avoided if the rent tax is applied to unincorporated businesses as well. For the withholding tax, no disincentive will be incurred with respect to integration so long as corporate and personal taxes are fully integrated. Otherwise, incorporation will be affected.

3) *The treatment of small businesses.* It is often alleged that small businesses require special tax concessions, since it is more difficult for them to acquire capital on the same basis as large firms. The appropriate remedy, however, is not to lower corporate tax rates (as is currently done) but to assist cash flow. For this reason, full refundability of tax losses would provide the financial assistance required by small businesses.

4) *Treatment of exploration and research and development.* Risky activities such as mineral exploration and research and development have often been viewed as deserving special tax concessions. It is alleged that these firms are unable fully to diversify their risks on capital markets. This may or may not be the case. With well-functioning capital markets, risks of this

sort ought to be diversifiable by shareholders through their portfolio selection or by firms through agglomeration. Even if such diversification is not possible, no special tax measures are needed. Under a rent tax in the form of a cash flow tax, no special concession is needed since tax losses can be made fully refundable. From the point of view of risk taking, the government through the rent tax will share the risk with private investors, effectively making the government a silent partner in the firm. If exploration and research and development are viewed to be insufficient for other reasons (such as investors being unable to appropriate all the returns), then a subsidy may be desirable. A grant is preferable to a tax concession, since it is selective and the government can control better the standards that may be used to determine eligibility.

5) *Tax competition.* It is often alleged that Canada must impose a tax system similar to its international competitors, so that the tax system will be "competitive." The argument suggests that tax concessions may be necessary as a means of drawing capital from abroad.

It is by no means clear that the tax system in Canada should be the same as in other countries—for example, the U.S. system. One argument in favour of uniformity concerns the withholding role of the corporate tax. The more similar the Canadian tax system is to the foreign tax systems, the more likely that Canadian corporate taxes will be credited against foreign taxes. There is, however, scope for some divergence. Canada's tax system can diverge from other tax systems to the extent that corporations can manipulate income and deductions to ensure that all Canadian taxes are fully deductible against foreign taxes. For example, foreign subsidiaries can decide not to claim all earned CCA deductions and investment tax credits in years in which income is repatriated, so that they can minimize future Canadian corporate payments when reinvesting profits by claiming both past and current deductions and credits. This increases the value of deferring taxes owing to foreign governments on income earned in Canada since retentions of subsidiaries are exempt from taxation by other jurisdictions in which the parent resides. It would be difficult, however, for Canada to adopt a very different tax system from those of other countries if the aim is to maximize the total amount of tax credited against foreign corporate taxes.

Tax competition will especially arise when one country tries to maintain its competitive advantage in export markets. Often tax concessions are provided to create employment or to pursue other such political objectives. It is unclear, however, that the tax concessions in favour of capital should be used for these means—for example, employment can be encouraged by the subsidization of labour, without complicating the tax code. In the absence of these political or economic objectives, it is not apparent why one country has to compete with another by providing tax concessions to some industries. Such concessions may assist one industry but make others worse off, since they would have more difficulty in attracting labour and capital resources. Rather than following corporate tax systems adopted by other countries, it may be better for Canada to choose the most efficient corporate tax in its own interest. One can, however, argue that tax competition will be appropriate if Canada can exploit its monopoly position in world markets by reacting to tax concessions provided by foreign countries to their own industries. Because these "beggar-thy-neighbour" policies make all countries worse off, international cooperation is a superior means of achieving increased national income.

6) *Provincial tax harmonization.* Cooperation between federal and provincial governments has led to considerable harmonization of corporate taxes in Canada. In general, provincial corporate tax bases vary little from the federal one even for those provinces (Quebec, Ontario, and Alberta) who have not entered into a tax agreement to allow the federal government to collect taxes on their behalf. Even though there is little difference between federal and provincial corporate tax bases, the opposite is true for provincial resource taxes. Provincial mining, oil, gas, and coal taxes currently vary substantially across provinces and type of mineral and project. They complicate tax law and induce variations in effective tax rates on resource investments.[26] If, however, a common rent tax base were adopted in this sector, more harmonization of these taxes would be achieved. There is a tendency for provinces to compete with each other by subsidizing certain activities especially with respect to the processing of minerals. Such competition for processing projects is more beneficial in terms of generating higher after-tax returns for resource producers than it is to provinces in terms of promoting investment. Harmonization of tax bases would contribute to a reduction in tax competition that would possibly make all provinces better off. With a cash flow tax as a common rent tax, considerable simplification would be achieved as well.

Reforming the Existing Corporate Tax

The previous section described how a withholding tax and a rent tax could be designed as ideal tax bases for the purpose of taxing corporate income. In this section, we present our own proposals for reform of corporate and resource taxes in Canada. Below, we first describe our principles for tax reform in this area and then detail specific proposals with respect to the withholding and rent tax bases.

Principles Underlying Corporate Tax Reform

There are three general principles we advocate to guide the reform of the corporate tax:

1) The personal tax should be applied on a consumption base, or its present value equivalent. Rents accruing to individuals should enter the tax base if and when consumed.

2) The corporate tax as generally applied should be a withholding system, primarily on income accruing to foreigners. Integration should be achieved by providing tax credits at the individual level.

---

[26]For a discussion of mining taxation in Canada, see R. W. Boadway and J. M. Mintz, "Marginal Effective Tax Rates in the Canadian Mining Industry," in M. J. Wojcieckowski, ed., *Canadian Mining Taxation*, Conference Proceedings no. 17 (Kingston, Ont.: Centre for Resource Studies, Queen's University, November 7, 1984), 76-90.

3) An additional system of rent taxation should be adopted in those industries where significant rents are likely to accrue and where the property rights with respect to the ownership of rent are taken to be the state's. The resource industry would appear to be the most important candidate for this form of taxation, although other industries may also qualify (such as in the case of utilities, transportation, and communication, where the government allows firms to be protected from entry for regulatory reasons).

With these overriding aims, the personal tax should be designed as outlined in Chapter 4. The corporate tax should basically withhold against equity income or dividends, but not against interest income. Whether equity income or dividends is the appropriate base for withholding depends on whether it is preferable to use a wider base for raising taxes or to achieve a more administratively simple system. It is the reform of the corporate tax for withholding purposes to which we turn first.

The Corporate Tax as a Withholding Tax

It is our view that the consumption-based personal tax ensures that all equity assets are treated as designated assets. Thus, the only role of withholding is against foreigners. One possibility is to replace the corporate tax entirely with nonresident withholding taxes on equity income in the form of dividends and capital gains. The difficulty is that this requires the renegotiation of treaties, since the current withholding rate is only 15 per cent with treaty countries, and the possible revision of tax-sharing agreements.

Since withholding by a simple withholding tax is not feasible, one is left with the corporate tax as a withholding device at source. Ideally, the amount withheld should equal the corporate tax credit available abroad. As discussed in a previous section, this is difficult to ensure because countries have different rates, bases, and methods of crediting. Thus, any system will necessarily be imperfect. The two alternative tax bases that could be adopted for withholding are the following:

1) *Equity income base.* If this base were to be adopted, the corporate or income tax base should be made as close to equity income as possible. If so, it would be easier to integrate at the personal level, since the base corresponds to the equity income that shareholders receive. It is also less distorting on investment made by Canadian-controlled firms and by foreign-controlled firms that use reinvested profits to finance investment. Integration can be achieved by using a single rate of credit, thus avoiding the necessity of measuring "average" tax rates that are based on the underlying real equity income earned by the corporation. Also, financial intermediaries are exempt in the sense that intercorporate dividends and capital gains are untaxed.

To implement an equity income base requires that capital cost deductions include economic depreciation, the replacement cost of inventories, and real interest (that is, an indexed system). It involves eliminating (1) accelerated depreciation, (2) the inventory allowance, (3) the investment tax credit, (4) the earned depletion allowance, and (5) differential statutory corporate tax rates.

The effect of these reforms would be to reduce differential marginal tax rates. Industries and capital goods would be taxed on a similar basis, although effective corporate tax rates could be higher unless the statutory tax rate is reduced. This is shown in Table 5.1, which compares effective tax rates on capital for the aggregate of all industries for various reforms if adopted in the 1972-1981 period. It also assumes that Canadian corporate taxes are not credited against foreign tax liabilities. These results show that the effective corporate tax rate on inventories would have been reduced, but for other assets increased, if the tax base were indexed and economic depreciation used. The increase in effective tax rates would result from two sources: (1) the elimination of fast write-offs; and (2) the loss in nominal interest deductions, which offsets the gain to businesses of indexing their depreciation and inventory allowances. Thus, adoption of indexation and economic depreciation for tax purposes would remove tax differentials but not necessarily increase investment in the aggregate, since the tax base would be broadened.

Table 5.1   Effective Corporate Tax Rates and the Required Rate of Return on Capital Under Various Alternative Policies Based on the Tax System of the 1972-1981 Period

	Current	Economic depreciation[a]	Indexation of current write-offs[b]	Cash flow tax
		per cent		
Required marginal return to capital gross of taxes (net of depreciation)				
Land	4.1	7.3	7.3	4.8
Buildings	5.5	7.3	6.9	4.8
Machinery.....................	5.4	7.3	5.7	4.8
Inventories	9.1	7.3	7.3	4.8
Average.......................	6.3	7.3	6.3	4.8
Effective corporate tax rates				
Land	−15.7	35.0	35.0	0
Buildings	12.5	35.0	30.6	0
Machinery.....................	11.0	35.0	16.6	0
Inventories	47.2	35.0	35.0	0
Average.......................	23.4	35.0	24.5	0

Note: See Table 3.1 for values taken from various parameters as described below.

[a]Under this proposal, CCA is equal to economic depreciation and no inventory allowance and investment tax credit is allowed. The marginal return to equity is $r_g = r/(1 - u)$, where $r = \beta(i - \pi)(1 - u) + (1 - \beta)(\rho - \pi)$, u = corporate tax rate, π = inflation rate, i = nominal interest rate, ρ = nominal opportunity cost of equity, and β = debt-asset ratio. The effective tax rate is $(r_g - r_o)/r_g$, where $r_o = \beta + (1 - \beta)\rho - \pi$.

[b]Includes current rates of depreciation and the investment tax credit. Indexation in this case allows for indexed capital cost allowances, indexed FIFO inventory valuation, and the deductibility of real interest. No inventory allowance is included in this case. The marginal return to capital is $r_g = R_g - \delta$, where R_g = user cost of capital and δ = economic depreciation rate. The formula for the user cost is $R_g = \frac{(r_f + \delta)}{(1 - u)}[1 - uZ](1 - \phi)$, where δ = economic depreciation, ϕ = investment tax credit, Z is the present value of CCA deduction on indexed base and equal to $d/(d + r)$ where d is CCA rate on declining balance basis. All other parameters are the same as footnote a. Note that if $d = \delta$, then $R_g - \delta$ is equal to $r_f/(1 - u)$. The effective tax rate is the same as above.

As we pointed out earlier in this chapter, a withholding tax on equity income has several disadvantages. If the domestic tax base is very different from that of other countries, the Canadian corporate tax will not be fully credited or will be insufficient in raising tax revenues. The result will depend on how Canada's average tax rate on equity compares with that of other countries.

Another problem is that integration of the corporate and personal tax bases is bound to be imperfect, especially in regard to capital gains on sheltered savings and for firms in a loss position.

A third problem with basing the corporate withholding tax on equity income is that it is impossible for authorities to measure accurately economic depreciation and the replacement cost of inventories. Some assets such as research and development, goodwill, and advertising are extremely difficult to assess with respect to the physical wear and tear of the asset. For many assets, it would not be administratively feasible to calculate real capital gains, since market prices are not observable for them. Thus, a withholding tax on equity income would necessarily be imperfect and cause some distortions.

Another reform possibility is to be less concerned about choosing the perfect base for equity income (for example, ignore the problem of indexing or measuring depreciation correctly) but integrate the imperfect base with the personal tax based on the average tax rate faced by the firm. This would require that the gross-up and tax credit system apply to intercorporate dividends and capital gains received by financial firms as well as by individuals. The advantage of this system is that Canada's withholding tax can match more closely existing tax systems in other countries, which tend not to be based on true equity income properly defined. It still, however, relies on correct measurement of capital income and institution of integration for capital gain income.

These administrative issues make the withholding tax on equity income rather unappealing. For this reason, we propose an alternative for consideration that is simpler to administer and that achieves many of the objectives we have set forth in this chapter.

2) *Dividend base.* An alternative corporate tax system that is particularly attractive on administrative grounds is to tax corporations on dividend distributions. This base is equivalent to letting firms deduct retained earnings from an equity income base except that the base can be calculated directly as dividends. The distributed profits base is desirable only if personal taxation is on a consumption basis, because under that tax there is no need to withhold against retained earnings.

The advantages of a withholding tax at the level of the corporation on dividends distributed are several. First, dividends are directly observable, so the base can be easily measured. Second, domestic integration is simple. Statutory rates can be used for grossing up dividends and calculating the dividend tax credit since the base for determining the credit is the same as the base on which distribution tax has been paid. Intercorporate dividends do not have to be included in the base. Capital gains need not be integrated. Similarly, loss offsetting is not a problem. The financial decisions of firms will be unaltered so long as tax is fully credited at the personal level or against other foreign taxes. Finally, the tax is very simple compared with the alternatives.

As suggested earlier, there are three disadvantages to a dividend distribution tax. The most important is that foreign corporations are not taxed in their home country on the basis of dividends paid out, thus the tax paid in Canada would be calculated on a different basis from that used for determining the foreign tax credit. One must be careful in setting the rate to generate roughly the same amount of revenue that firms would get credit for at home. A second problem is that corporate tax revenues on branch plants that finance investment by reinvesting their earnings will be deferred. A third problem is that when the dividend distribution tax is not credited at the domestic shareholder level or against foreign tax liabilities, there will be an incentive for firms to convert dividends into capital gain income if the latter is taxed less.

These problems with the dividend withholding tax can be avoided by combining a tax on equity income with the dividend distribution tax. Even if the corporate tax on equity income is imperfect because of mismeasurement, it will have no effect on a firm's decision if it is fully credited against the dividend distribution tax. Only the dividend distribution tax will be credited at the share-owner level. One can also impose a tax on equity income as an advanced tax on distributions which will be fully credited against the dividend tax, with the excess carried forward at the nominal interest rate. If the equity income is converted into capital gains, the domestic shareholders will not earn their dividend tax credit, so firms owned by them will have an incentive to pay out dividends. Eventually corporate equity income accruing to foreigners will, in most cases, be paid out as dividends. The other advantage of this system is that retentions of branch plants operating in Canada will also be taxed earlier than under a pure dividend tax.

We find the dividend distribution tax very attractive as a withholding tax. The addition of a second withholding tax on equity income would permit tax revenues to be collected earlier although with some loss in simplicity. This second withholding tax could, however, make transition simpler in moving from the current tax system to the new system of corporate taxation.

The Rent Tax

The strongest case for a tax on rents is in those industries in which substantial rents are likely to accrue. This suggests that the rent tax be initially instituted for resource firms only. These firms are already paying a variety of special taxes purportedly intended to capture a share of rents for the public sector. Ideally, provincial mining, oil, and gas taxes should be converted into a cash flow tax that follows the R base—revenues less costs and the expensing of investment expenditures. Loss offsetting would be accomplished either by a refundable tax credit or by the carryforward of credits at a rate of interest. If governments wished to increase tax liabilities up front, a "modified" cash flow tax could be used that applies a depreciation rate to a capital cost allowance base that is indexed by the nominal government bond rate.

The potential abuse of the rent tax by firms overstating costs and passing on rents to untaxed industries would require restrictions by tax authorities with respect to costs that are not easily observable. Once authorities and the public understand how a rent tax can operate, we recommend the institution of a general rent tax along the form of the R + F base on all businesses in Canada. This requires the inclusion of both financial and real transactions in the rent tax base. This wider base would reduce the ability of firms to escape a rent tax.

Implementation of Corporate Tax Reform and Conclusions

The current corporate tax is essentially a withholding tax on equity income, but it includes various tax incentives for investment, both intended and unintended. The Minister of Finance, in May 1985, proposed a widening of the corporate tax base, abolishing a large number of fast write-offs, such as accelerated depreciation or investment tax credits. Generally, we agree with this direction for reform although we would add, as additional reforms, the removal of earned depletion, the nondeductibility of exploration and development expenses from the resource allowance base, and the lower corporate tax rate for small businesses and manufacturing. A lower corporate tax for manufacturing firms is not desirable, since the U.S. foreign tax credit is based on a fairly wide definition of corporate income. Only when Canadian corporate taxes in a particular sector are not credited would Canada desire to provide a specific tax preference for an industry.

The indexation of the corporate tax base for inflation is desirable if Canada relies on a withholding tax on equity income. To the extent that we move to a tax on distributions, indexation is needed only to reduce tax differentials on investment income that is passed on in the form of capital gains.

Our proposal is eventually to change the corporate tax from a withholding tax on equity income to one on dividend distributions with a credit given for the distribution tax against personal taxes levied on dividends received by residents. This could be accomplished by retaining the corporate income tax as a tax on equity income but allowing this tax to be credited against the new dividend distribution tax. Any excess credits would have to be carried forward with interest at the prevailing nominal interest rate. Essentially, this reform involves the reinstitution and extension of the distribution tax levied on small corporations to all companies and the use of a higher rate of tax (for example, a 50 per cent distribution tax would imply a 33⅓ per cent underlying tax rate on distributed profits). The current corporate tax on equity income could be reduced by lowering statutory rates in favour of the dividend distribution tax. The dividend tax credit would be imposed so that it fully integrates the distribution tax at the corporate level.

Transition would be relatively simple to accomplish as well. Even if the tax on equity income maintained certain "incentives," these tax concessions would be eroded in value to the extent they were offset by the dividend distribution tax.

The implementation of a rent tax would also be simple to accomplish in the resource industries. Mining tax bases currently do not allow interest to be deducted. All that is required is to increase depreciation rates so that capital expenditures net of disposals should be expensed, rather than depreciated. Processing allowances should be abolished once provinces agree to harmonize their tax bases. Tax losses should be fully refundable through carryforward or refundable tax credits. Flow-through provisions should, however, be eliminated. To recoup tax revenues, statutory mining tax rates should be increased substantially.

For oil and gas, reform would be more substantial. All costs should be deductible and capital expenditures net of disposals should be expensed. The provinces should abolish royalty schemes that are complicated by the attempt to reduce taxation of less productive wells. After all, total rent taxes collected under a cash flow tax would be sensitive to productivity since less productive wells earn fewer rents.

All these reforms would be coupled with reform of the personal tax in the direction of a consumption tax base as discussed in Chapter 4. Our recommendation for reform of the corporate tax could be carried out if personal taxes were levied on an income basis as well. The only requirement is that the capital gains tax rate be adjusted to ensure that companies have an incentive to pass out income in the form of dividends.